SUPPORT FOR LEARNING DIFFERENCES IN HIGHER EDUCATION
THE ESSENTIAL PRACTITIONERS' MANUAL

SUPPORT FOR LEARNING DIFFERENCES IN HIGHER EDUCATION
THE ESSENTIAL PRACTITIONERS' MANUAL

Geraldine Price and Janet Skinner

Trentham Books

Stoke on Trent, UK and Sterling, USA

Trentham Books
Westview House   22883 Quicksilver Drive
734 London Road   Sterling
Oakhill   VA 20166-2012
Stoke on Trent   USA
Staffordshire
England St4 5NP

First published 2007

British Catalogue-in- Publication Data
A catalogue for this book is available from the British Library

ISBN: 978 1 85856 411 1

Designed and typeset by Trentham Print design Ltd, Chester and printed in Great Britain by Hobbs the Printers Ltd, Hampshire.

Contents

Introduction

Over the last decade, changes in the learning environment in Higher Education have been introduced to reflect new educational paradigms as well as technological advances. The impact of widening participation, a commitment to life-long learning, modularisation of curriculum design and semesterisation have all played their part in changing the context of learning. A significant change has been the number of dyslexic students who now participate in Higher Education. Although many dyslexic students are now identified in the school system, there are still many who arrive at university having had no identification of dyslexia. This changing landscape means that those involved with the support of dyslexic students are faced with new and complex challenges.

The need to identify students' needs is essential and requires expertise and knowledge. Specialist Dyslexia Tutors (SDTs) have emerged as the professionals who take on the role of assessor, academic skills tutor and student advocate. The multiplicity of the role requires a depth of knowledge of the causes of dyslexia and other specific learning difficulties, an understanding of the pedagogy of support and a sensitivity to the needs of individuals.

This handbook provides background information about dyslexia awareness, and the impact of dyslexia on learning in the Higher Education context (Chapters 1 and 2). The role of the SDT is explored within a framework of initial and continuing professional development (Chapter 3). The identification and assessment processes are examined in detail, grounding theory firmly in practice (Chapters 4, 5, 6, 7 and 8). Issues relating to support are scrutinised both in terms of the development of skills for learning and the impact of dyslexia upon specific disciplines (Chapters 9, 10, 11 and 12). Finally, ways forward for dyslexia support services are discussed (Chapter 13).

How to use the handbook

The emphasis is upon the *practicalities* of the role of the Specialist Dyslexia Tutor. We are aware that SDTs are busy professionals, and with this in mind each chapter gives an outline of the learning outcomes at the beginning and '*Using the Chapter*' enables the reader to navigate the sections of the chapter efficiently, locating areas of interest and need quickly. You will find some suggestions for *further reading* which are related to the themes at the end of each chapter.

We decided to use the generic term 'she' when referring to SDTs and dyslexic students. This does not mean that the male population is excluded! The term 'Specialist Dyslexia Tutor' (SDT) has been used throughout to encompass both the role of assessor and tutor.

Our thanks

All books are the result of experience, discussion and collaboration. We would like to thank the staff at the Learning Differences Centre for allowing us to adapt some of the materials; Allene Tuck and Jane Warren who were consulted about the support of Fine Arts and Music students; and Mike Valerio who took many photographs for the front cover. Last, but in no means least, Tony Price for his meticulous proof reading of our manuscript.

Geraldine A. Price
Janet Skinner
July, 2007

1

Definitions and Research

This chapter provides a brief overview of the current debates and controversies linked to definitions and research. It emphasises the need for Specialist Dyslexia Tutors to clarify their own conceptualisation of dyslexia from informed research evidence.

Using this chapter

This chapter will enable you to:

1. Understand the need for clear definitions

    1.1 Why bother with definitions?

    1.2 Types of definition

2. Explore a causal theoretical framework for dyslexia and frameworks for diversity

3. Overview the research landscape

    3.1 Phonological deficit theory

    3.2 Sensory Theories of Dyslexia

    3.3 Working Memory Theory

4. Consider what neuroscience can offer the SDT

1. Defining dyslexia: myth, illusion and reality

Listening to those in academic settings talking about dyslexia demonstrates the illusionary nature of this highly controversial subject. There are those who will state categorically that it is a figment of the imagination, a convenient label for those who cannot accept the realities of academic life. Others will passionately defend the subject.

To answer the question 'What is dyslexia?' would seem a simple task. Trying to define the term dyslexia/specific learning difficulties has been the subject of acrimonious and, some would say, futile debate for decades. The difficulties in defining the terminology reflect divergent opinions about causes and remediation and reflect trends in approaches. It has been the subject of research for neuro-psychologists, cognitive psychologists, geneticists, neurologists, educational psychologists and, of course, educationalists, each with their own terminology and theoretical constructs. To try to develop a definition which would be acceptable in all these areas would be impossible. There has been no agreement after over 100 years on the definition of the disorder or syndrome, variable or otherwise, of dyslexia or specific learning difficulties. Research literature demonstrates no agreement internationally on a definition of terminology. But there is agreement about the seriousness and intractability of the learning problems encountered. Many of the definitions reflect the current research issues, the need to develop a taxonomy for dyslexia and models of identification.

The populist perception of the 1970s and 1980s that dyslexia was a middle-class syndrome, a euphemism for slow learners, and that it was a myth, did little to enhance pedagogy and is a legacy which will take time to disperse. However, an enduring correlation and a pivotal element in most of the research of this time were the links between dyslexia and reading difficulties. It is a moot point whether this is relevant to the adult population and in relation to the Higher Education (HE) context and the compensated adult, dyslexic learner.

1.1 Why bother with definitions?
The professional working in the field of dyslexia needs to have a clear concept of dyslexia and has to be able to express the way she defines dyslexia, for numerous reasons. Primarily, the definition is required to provide a kind of short-hand between professionals so that everyone is speaking about the same thing. Secondly, and most importantly, a clear definition is needed to enable the Specialist Dyslexia Tutor (SDT) to identify whether or not a person is dyslexic. Lastly, this definition is sometimes indispensable when SDAs are discussing their assessment findings with other professionals, such as chartered and educational psychologists and to establish clear identification for the purposes of student funding. To some extent, the definition encompasses the SDA's and SDT's beliefs and conceptions. Definitions of dyslexia grow out of personal experiences and knowledge.

1.2 Types of definition

The term dyslexia is itself controversial. There are some who prefer to use the term 'specific learning difficulties' because it more accurately describes the problems which are experienced by this group of people. However, there are others who consider the term dyslexia less offensive than a label which focuses on a person's difficulties, particularly in relation to adults. Nicolson cited in Fawcett (2001) suggests that the term dyslexia is neutral and, therefore, could be less threatening to the dyslexic person.

> The advantage of the label 'dyslexia' is that it has no intrinsic meaning – it says nothing about the underlying cause, and is neutral as to whether the cause is visual, phonological, motor or some combination. (Nicolson, cited in Fawcett, 2001:5)

There are many definitions of dyslexia. Definitions are often reflections of their times and the stage of thinking and research reached. One of the earliest definitions to gain credence came out of a world conference which recognised the need to have a clear definition:

> ... A disorder manifested by difficulty in learning to read, despite conventional instruction, *adequate intelligence* and *socio-cultural opportunity*. It is dependent upon fundamental cognitive disabilities which are constitutional in origin. (Authors' emphasis) (World Federation of Neurology, 1968, cited in Critchley, 1970:11)

Many of the early definitions adhered to a medical model of dyslexia, and the terminology reflected this by using terms such as disorder, syndrome and deficits. Such definitions are offensive to some who feel that the strengths of the dyslexic person are minimised and the weaknesses and problems are accentuated.

A discrepancy definition is one which is used by many professionals in the educational and psychological spheres. It has come under attack mainly because the discrepancy underlying this definition has historically been between high intelligence levels and low literacy levels. This would suggest that one could only be dyslexic if one was intelligent and could barely read or write! It is highly controversial but is used frequently by local authorities in policy statements, and, as such, has implications for Disabled Students' Allowance (DSA) funding.

> Developmental dyslexia is a learning disability which initially shows itself by difficulty in learning to read, and later by erratic spelling and lack of facility in manipulating written as opposed to spoken words. The condition is cognitive in essence, and usually genetically determined. It is not due to intellectual inadequacy, or to lack or socio-cultural opportunity, or to emotional factors, or to any known structural brain defect. (Critchely and Critchley, 1978:1)

A looser definition of discrepancy is now adhered to and covers discrepancies between reading and listening comprehension, and verbal and non-verbal performance. The notion of *difference* is perhaps more appropriate. Thus, it is possible to explore differences in performance levels in a variety of areas. Whichever definition is adopted, it will provide the SDA and SDT with the means to explore mismatches and differences which occur in psychometric assessment and the functional, everyday performance of an individual.

Operational and cognitive definitions have grown out of the increase in the body of knowledge about dyslexia, derived mainly from research. Such definitions provide explicit information about the underlying cognitive features of dyslexia, and the behaviour or performance factors which can be observed by professionals. Such definitions include: skills relating to reasoning, problem-solving, processing; phonological abilities; observable behaviours and differences in performance.

The British Dyslexia Association's (BDA) current definition is often preferred because it is a compromise and can be applied to a dyslexic person regardless of age:

> Dyslexia is a combination of abilities and difficulties which affect the learning process in one or more of reading, spelling and writing. Accompanying weaknesses may also be seen in speed of processing, short term memory, sequencing, auditory and/or visual perception, spoken language and motor skills. (BDA, 2006)

However, the International Dyslexia Association's definition may appeal to others in that it brings the notion of differences into the equation:

> Dyslexia is a learning difficulty characterised by problems in expressive or receptive, oral or written language. Problems may emerge in reading, spelling, writing, speaking or listening. Dyslexia is not a disease; it has no cure. Dyslexia describes a different kind of mind, often gifted and productive, that learns differently. (The International Dyslexia Association, 2000)

In the HE environment Frith (1997) reminds us that dyslexia is not a phenomenon of school: it is for life. 'Dyslexia is not a disease which comes with school and goes away with adulthood.' Thus, McLoughlin *et al*'s definition might have more appeal because it has relevance to the adult dyslexic person:

> Developmental dyslexia is a genetically inherited and neurologically determined inefficiency in working memory, the information-processing system fundamental to learning and performance in conventional educational and work settings. It has a particular impact on verbal and written communication as well as on organisation, planning and adaptation to change.(McLoughlin *et al*, 2002:19)

The synergy between this operational definition and the assessment and identification processes will not be missed by experienced SDAs and SDTs.

2. Theoretical perspectives: Frameworks and diversity

Research into the causes of dyslexia has exploded in the last two decades and provides the practitioner with a wealth of information which can inform practice. However, each research field explores the problem of finding the cause from a different viewpoint with diverse research questions.

> The definitions of 'dyslexia' seem to be variations on a physiological theme, each variation being composed by a different specialist. (Ravenette, 1968 in Young and Tyre, 1983:18)

Early causal theory explored the hypothesis that dyslexia was a reading difficulty. Much of the early research, therefore, concentrated upon dyslexic children. Whilst it provides an insight into the reading process for normal readers, it is not always the sole and primary cause of dyslexia in adults (McLoughlin *et al*, 2002). Numerous deficit models of dyslexia have been posited: phonological, visual, sensory, double deficit and neurological.

Frith's theoretical model was a watershed in the development of thinking about dyslexia: she wove into a theoretical framework many of the threads which were an integral part of current research (Frith, 1985, 1995). She

Figure 1: Frith's Causal Model

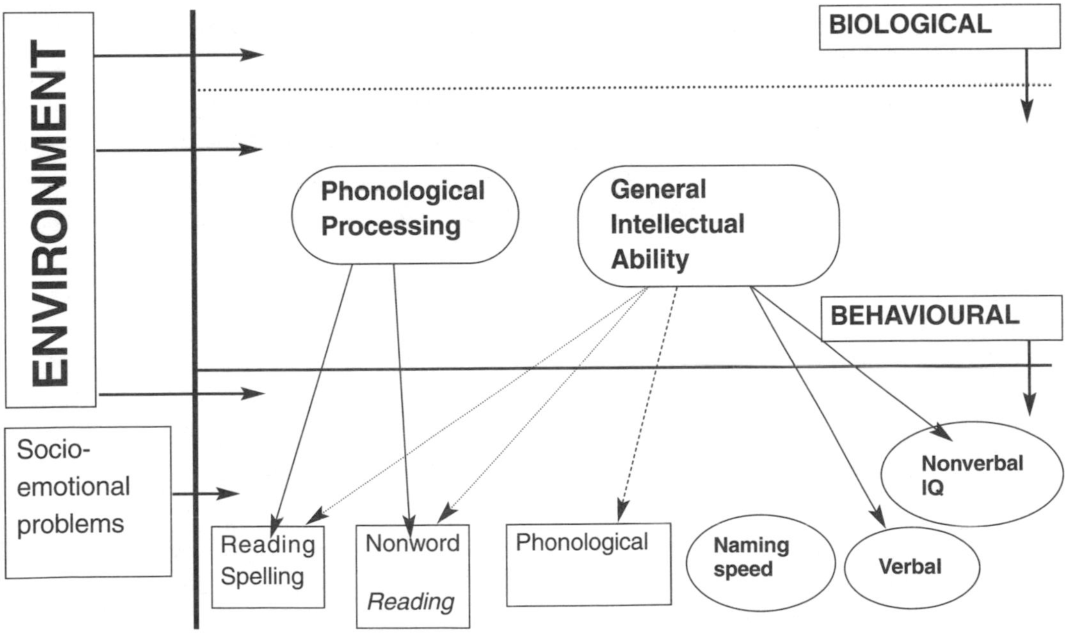

developed a causal model of dyslexia which embraced observable behaviour, the classroom context; cognitive deficits, the identification and diagnostic process; and the biological factors which included genetic and neuro-anatomical features, information to which teachers had no access but which could be examined from observable behaviour. The over-arching aspect in her model was the environmental influence which could affect any or all of the three causal levels.

In figure 1 above, the arrows show the causal links in the three-stage model. It provides a framework which draws together research in different fields and lends itself to the demonstration of causal links with other specific learning difficulties such as dyspraxia and attention deficit (hyperactivity) disorder. Thus, it is suggested that physiological problems emanating in the brain, such as hemispheric size differences found in post-mortem studies of dyslexic brains (Galaburda, 1989) or different chromosomal structures (Cardon *et al*, 1994), may have an effect upon the cognitive processing functions. These may result in different neural circuitry for processing phonological information, for example. This, in turn, could be one of the reasons why a person has experienced difficulties with spelling and reading which result in 'persistent difficulties' (DfES, 2005). Tracing the causal links is reversed for the SDT whose starting point will be the behaviour and performance of the student.

This social-interactive theoretical framework is attractive to practitioners in HE because it brings together research and practice which has application with adult dyslexic students. Not only does it explore the reasons why dyslexic people come across difficulties in their studies, but it also helps to explain the influence of the individual's environment and previous educational experiences upon learning. These prior occurrences help to explain the individual's starting point in HE. It provides a learning differences approach to both assessment and support.

3. Overview of the research landscape

The research landscape is like a large jigsaw puzzle which can be constructed in a variety of ways, depending upon where the links are forged. Studies of the dyslexic brain make compelling reading. They provide answers to why dyslexic learners act the way they do and can help the SDT understand why these students experience difficulties and score poorly on intelligence tests. Brain researchers and geneticists have now joined the quest to answer the question of the underlying problem which causes dyslexia. Could it be that the anatomical structure of a dyslexic brain is different from that of a non-dyslexic, so

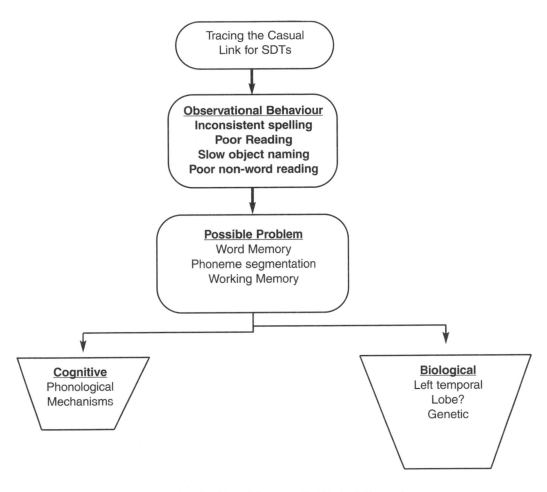

Figure 2: Application for Practitioners of a Worked Example

that reading, spelling and language processing are affected? However, there are still many areas where there is disagreement. Finding evidence at the biological level to account for cognitive anomalies is still in its infancy. For example, gene markers have been found on chromosomes 6 and 15 but as yet there is insufficient evidence to develop a genetic theory of dyslexia (DeFries and Alarcon, 1996). The main research areas which relate most to the dyslexic student in HE are:

- Phonological Deficit Theory
- Sensory Theory
- Working Memory Theory

3.1 Phonological deficit theory is the most dominant theory, and it has many supporters. Research evidence demonstrates that dyslexic people, by and large, have difficulties processing sounds. At the cognitive and behavioural levels, they will have problems manipulating sound patterns in speech (auditory perception); isolating sounds within words (particularly at the phoneme level which is the smallest unit of sound); and storing and retrieving sound information. These cognitive functions will have an impact upon reading and spelling. There is evidence from neuroscience that the perisylvian area (the region which deals with phonological processing) of the left hemisphere of the dyslexic brain shows inconsistencies which would explain phonological deficits (Frith, 1997). The perisylvian region contains:

Broca's area which plays a part in speech articulation and production;

Wernicke's area which is involved in speech comprehension;

Insular Cortex which acts as a bridge to send many messages to different parts of the brain;

Inferior Parietal Lobe which deals with spatial elements.

All these aspects of the brain work in concert to enable a person to process phonological information effectively and effortlessly. Damage or deficits in any one of these areas will affect the overall working. Of course, many dyslexic adults learn to bypass their inherent phonological difficulties. They no longer rely totally on the identification, manipulation and processing of sounds to support spelling and reading but rather use morphological and contextual clues to enable them to read and spell. The reasons why there are those who find this theory unconvincing are two-fold: firstly not all dyslexic students have phonological deficits; and secondly, some adult dyslexic people seem to function adequately in literacy tasks which require phonological skills, which suggests that this deficit may not be the sole cause of dyslexia. However, a closer look at the cognitive profile and everyday performance of these dyslexic adults might reveal that the phonological deficits persist but that the adult dyslexic student compensates adequately. This has led discussions to explore the notion of sub-groups of dyslexia.

3.2 Sensory theories of dyslexia

Research into whether dyslexia is the result of visual or auditory difficulties has see-sawed over the last thirty years. As new evidence became available, prior, convincing research discussions were toppled in favour of the latest research. It is encouraging that there is a move to synthesise the disparate findings to try to explain how the results inform knowledge and understanding of how a dyslexic person operates. Hinshelwood's (1917) observations of young Percy initiated the **visual deficit hypotheses** which suggested that dyslexia was the result of deficits in the visual processing systems. Visual processing is reliant upon many complex systems, and various theories have been posited to explain dyslexic difficulties in visual processing: binocular instability (Pavlidis, 1981) and the development of a dominant eye (Stein and Fowler, 1982); and difficulties in the transient, Magnocellular System (Stein, 1997, 2001). It is recognised that visual processing plays a part in the reading and writing processes, and, therefore, any deficits or dysfunctions will result in difficulties.

It is suggested that dyslexic people are unable to process fast, visual, in-coming information. Stein *et al* (1997, 2001) have posited that impairments in the Magnocellular System result in processing difficulties. This system passes visual information to the brain for processing. It consists of mago and parvo cells which are responsible for processing different types of information. The mago-ganglion system deals with timing and motion while the parvo-ganglion system works on colour and fine detail. These two systems help the brain to take in spaces between words (mago) and shapes of letters (parvo). Hence they have a direct impact upon reading, and problems in these systems could mean that the brain tries to sort out this sort of information:

Thew ord sare n otsp aced cor rect ly.

This shows lack of spatial location of letters.

Difficulties in the parvo system may result in reversals of letters such as 'b' and 'd'.

The work of Irlen (1991), Evans (2001) and Wilkins (1995) suggests that some people experience distortions of the print when reading. However, not all dyslexic people have these problems and diagnoses of non-dyslexic readers have also shown symptoms which have been attributed to visual stress difficulties.

Stein's work on magno-cellular theory has initiated much discussion, and it would appear that parallel work which explored auditory processing (Tallal, 1984, 1997) could be amalgamated within the umbrella of temporal, sensory difficulties. Thus, it is suggested that problems in the brain circuitry which deals with the timing of auditory and/or visual information are prevalent in many dyslexic people. This means that they are not able to process information which comes in at speed.

3.3 Working memory theory

Working memory, automaticity and double deficit hypotheses can be seen to provide further insight into the causes of dyslexic performance. Working memory could be described as the power-house of the memory which controls many functions. It enables people to multi-task: the ability to conduct more that one operation simultaneously. It also ensures the flow of information between short-term memory (likened to information on a computer screen) and long-term memory (information stored on the hard disk of a computer). Pickering and Gathercole's work (2004) shows that dyslexic people have problems in various aspects of working memory which affect speed of processing or automaticity. The notion of automaticity was explored by Nicolson and Fawcett (2001) who define this as:

> The process by which, after long practice, skills become so fluent that they no longer need conscious control. (Nicolson and Fawcett, 2001:508)

This has given rise to two closely-related theoretical perspectives: the Cerebellar Impairment Deficit Hypothesis and the Dyslexia Automatisation Deficit (DAD) Hypothesis. This will affect all types of tasks and not those limited to literacy and numeracy.

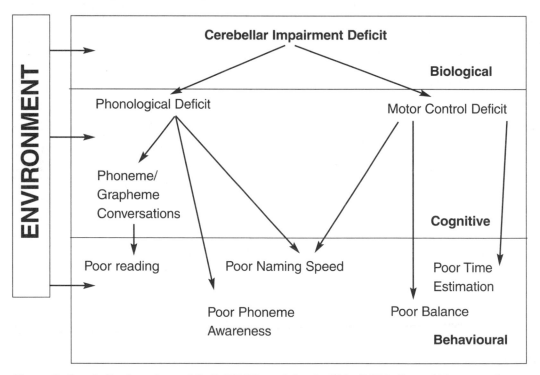

Figure 3: Cerebellar Impairment Deficit/DAD explained within Frith's Causal Framework

Another hypothesis, the Double Deficit Hypothesis, suggests that dyslexic people display combined difficulties in phonological weaknesses and working memory capacity deficits. Thus, these affect the speed at which they can process language information (Wolf and O'Brien, 2001)

The theoretical considerations illustrated in this chapter are a taster of current thinking and research. Appendix One provides a summary overview with references for further exploration.

4. What can neuroscience offer the SDT?
Neuro myths abound, and a note of caution is sounded regarding the increase of neuro-babble which is available in the Media and on websites. What is important is that the SDT evaluates the information in the light of strong evidence. There is a move to unite two strong research fields: education and cognitive science. At last the two fields are talking to each other to find out if and how the respective research can be related to what amount to two very different approaches. However, information about the functions of the various parts or regions of the brain will inform the SDT's understanding of the complex subject that is dyslexia.

Learning how the brain is wired up and the circuitry involved in academic tasks is enhanced by current clinical research. For example, knowledge of synaptic connections and how they develop demonstrates that there are critical developmental periods for learning specific skills which is of significance for teachers in terms of brain receptiveness (Berninger and Richards, 2002).

In conclusion...
This chapter provides the backdrop to the elements of assessment and explores the underlying theoretical causes of dyslexia which should be borne in mind during all aspects of professional practice.

Further Reading:

Blakemore, S and Frith, U (2000) *The implications of recent developments in neuroscience for research on teaching and learning: Discussion document.* London: Institute of Cognitive Neuroscience, University College London

Frith, U (1995) Dyslexia: Can we have a shared theoretical framework? *Journal of Educational Psychology,* 12, 6-17

Goswami, U (2004) Neuroscience, education and special education. *British Journal of Special Education,* 31(4), 175-183

Gregg, N (2003) Diagnostic issues surrounding students with learning disabilities. In Stanovich, K E (1991) Discrepancy definitions of reading disability: Has intelligence led us astray? *Reading Research Quarterly,* 26, 7-29

Reid, A A, Szczerbinski, M, Iskierka-Kasperek, E and Hansen, P (2007) Cognitive profiles of adult developmental dyslexics: theoretical implications. *Dyslexia: An International Journal of Research and Practice,* 13(1), 1-24

Stanovich, K E (1994) Annotation: does dyslexia exist? *Journal of Child Psychology and Psychiatry,* 35, 579-595

Thomson, M (2002) *The Psychology of Dyslexia.* London: Whurr Publishers

Vogel, S, Vogel, G, Sharoni, V, and Dahan, O (eds) (2003) *Learning Disabilities in Higher Education and Beyond: An International Perspective.* Baltimore: York Press

Appendix One: Summary Overview of Theoretical Perspectives

Dyslexia Hypothesis	Underlying Theory Connections	Key Researchers

Double Deficit:
Difficulties associated with a combination of weak phonological ability and speed of processing resulting in poor fluency in various types of tasks.
	■ Rapid naming rates:
	    Rapid Auditory Naming (RAN)/Rapid Auditory Processing) (RAP
	    Rapid Visual Processing – Magnocellular Theory
	■ Automaticity – Dyslexia Automatisation Deficit (DAD) – cerebellum theory
		Wolf and O'Brien
		Stein
		Tallal
		Fawcett and Nicolson

Phonological Deficit: Difficulties processing phonological information. Difficulties associated with storage, retrieval and speed of processing.	■ Perisylvian region of the brain shows inconsistencies ■ Linked to how the cerebellum manages language regions in the brain, which affects the phonological loop within working memory	Bradley and Bryant Snowling Frith and Frith Goswami Paulesu Fawcett and Nicolson
Visual Processing Deficits: Difficulties processing in-coming information at speed; Difficulties with visual perception of print.	■ Magnocellular theory – transient sensitivity ■ Meares-Irlen syndrome ■ Binocular vision ■ Motion sensitivity	Stein Tallal Frith Wilkins Meares-Irlen Evans
Sub-Types: View that there are different types of dyslexia ranging from verbal, visual to phonological (P) and lexical (L)	■ Based on many of the above theories	Boder Coltheart Everatt Denkla Johnson and Myklebust

Dyslexia Hypothesis	Underlying Theory Connections	Key Researchers
Verbal Processing Deficits: Written language problems caused by difficulties in language processing – prone to spoonerisms; problems with segmentation and synthesis of sounds; word finding problems; verbal memory difficulties	■ Magnocellular theory – transient sensitivity	Vellutino Snowling Denkla and Rudel Stein Tallal
Hereditary Factors/Genetic Causal Factors	■ Markers on genes ■ Incidence in families – particularly twin studies	Olson DeFries Cardon Grigorenco
Working Memory Deficit: Problems with memory capacity and sequencing speeds slow down many cognitive functions	■ Working memory structural theory ■ Based on interconnections between central executive, auditory loop (phonological) and visuo-spatial sketchpad	Miller Baddeley Gathercole Pickering
Hemispheric Difference: Dyslexic brains physiologically different in size. Dyslexic brains access different regions from non-dyslexic brains to perform	■ Symmetry of brain – larger right hemisphere ■ Different circuitry ■ Learning Differences – loosely connected with learning style, though very little evidence as yet	Galaburda Hynd Shaywitz Pugh

2

Demands upon learning in the HE context

This chapter explores the factors which make adult learners in HE different from pupils in schools. The needs of the dyslexic, adult student present dilemmas for both the student and the specialist dyslexia tutor. The chapter considers expectations of prior learning and academic skill development from the students' and academic tutors' perspectives

Using this chapter

This chapter will enable you to:

1. Understand students' expectations of study at HE – dispelling myths and expectations of support

    1.1 Expectations and assumptions

    1.2 Academic support from the department

2. Examine pedagogy and professional practice issues for support

3. Understand dynamic collaboration and cognitive education

4. Explore the issues of the timing of support

5. Understand the type of support for dyslexic difficulties

    5.1 Counselling/mentoring

6. Examine the student life-cycle and the implications for dyslexia support

    6.1 Anticipating workload schedules and patterns

    6.2 Departmental structures and key staff

7. Understand the learning environment

8. Be aware of skill analysis matched to academic activity

Learning is a complex process: it pervades the cognitive, cultural and social domains. At the heart of this process is the individual, the human being. The demands placed upon learning should not be reduced, therefore, to an analysis of the underlying skills which are needed for studying both in a generic sense and within a particular subject base. This would be to minimise the learning experience. This chapter examines what it is like to be at university from the student's perspective so that the Specialist Dyslexia Tutor (SDT) can understand how best to respond holistically to the range of learning experiences to which the dyslexic student is exposed. What is proposed in this chapter is an eclectic approach to support with the student at the heart.

Learning takes place within a context and is influenced by that context. More so than ever before, HE institutions are being pushed, willingly or otherwise, to become research-led institutions, and this shifts the focal point of learning. Over the last decade, changes in the learning environment in HE have been introduced to reflect new educational paradigms, socio-political pressures as well as technological advances. The impact of widening participation, a commitment to life-long learning, modularisation of curriculum design and semesterisation have all played their part in changing the context of learning. These, in turn, provide new challenges for dyslexic students entering HE. The notion of student-centredness has been at the heart of educational principles in schools since the early 1980s but has only recently been firmly located within institutional policy and strategic thinking in HE. Many of these modifications have resulted in a greater emphasis upon independent learning which presents students with new and different challenges. Students who enter HE today are expected to be more pro-active in the learning process and to take control of their own learning. The role of the student is in a state of metamorphosis, yet most students come to the learning context with set ideas and expectations.

Adult dyslexic learners should not be regarded simply as dyslexic pupils grown up (McLoughlin *et al*, 2002). Their academic needs are equivalent, and the difficulties they encounter with written expression and background reading are comparable, though at a different level. The emotional needs of an adult learner are also akin to those of the dyslexic pupil in that self esteem and self confidence can be fragile.

1. Dispelling the myths: expectations of support
Students enter HE with a variety of expectations and assumptions of what it will be like to be a student. These are related to external factors such as prior

educational experience, support provision and timing of identification of the specific learning difficulty as well as internal factors such as self esteem, confidence and learner type. Nevertheless, it is important for the SDT to be aware of the different expectations and assumptions so that she can discuss these during initial meetings to ensure that the student does not take things for granted nor have unrealistic hopes.

1.1 Expectations and assumptions

These expectations and assumptions can be seen from two main perspectives:

- Academic support from the department
- Support for dyslexic difficulties

1.2 Academic support from the department

Students often anticipate that their departmental, academic tutors will be available to help them formulate ideas for essays, for reassurance that what they have written meets the requirements of the task, to glance at drafts of written work and provide assistance and guidance in developing academic skills. Many students anticipate that there will be individual tutorials where progress and support is provided. Often students become frustrated when their academic tutors are not on hand to respond to their immediate needs.

There is a widely-held misconception that within academic institutions there is central provision for students who are in need of individual academic study skills support. This provision varies from institution to institution and is an area of expansion and development in many of the traditional universities.

Students' expectations of support on arrival could be negative or positive depending upon their previous experiences. Some students have had regular weekly (and sometimes daily) support from teachers in school or college. This support has often been closely linked to curricular needs and generally teacher-driven. In this type of system, the role of the student is quite passive, with the support tutor leading and organising the sessions. Curriculum support has been enhanced by close liaison between the support tutor and the subject specialists. This has been an achievable educational objective made possible by the size of the establishment.

Students entering HE may expect the provision to be the same or similar and are often unprepared for the shift in responsibilities. They may not be ready for the need to be pro-active and to organise their own support sessions. It is a big step for some students, particularly those who have come through the traditional route of school – college – gap year – university, to adjust to the new role. They have to take responsibility not only for procuring individual and specialised tuition but also for organising the timings of sessions. Individual sessions within HE are student-led, and this can place considerable stress upon some students. The locus of control is situated firmly with the student who is expected to lead and direct the SDT. This shift in power feels uncomfortable for students who lack self confidence and who are anxious about their learning.

2. Pedagogy and professional practice issues for support

> ... it seems to us that if you are to act as tutor to dyslexic students you need to be both a generalist and a specialist counsellor. Generalist in that you need to be a good listener but specialist in that you need to have a knowledge of dyslexia ... your job is both to deal with the anxieties which the students bring up and to know which aspects of their academic work they are likely to find easy and difficult. (Gilroy and Miles, 1995:53)

The success of intervention and support hinges upon sound pedagogy and the skilful expertise of the SDT. Since the mid-1990s teaching models have evolved to respond to the growth in the dyslexic population in HE. The most dominant paradigm which has emerged is the confluence of principles of adult learning, holistic interaction, dynamic collaboration and cognitive education. There are educational and pragmatic reasons why this paradigm has come to the surface.

The introduction of Personal Development Plans (PDPs) formalised a shift in thinking in Higher Education Institutions (HEIs) (QAA, 2000). PDPs require the student to be a pro-active partner in learning by defining personal goals and targets, through reflective evaluation of skills and knowledge. This presupposes that students are reflective learners who are aware of the skills needed for their academic experiences. The synergy between metacognition (or learning to learn) and action planning in the form of PDPs has created a climate for learning and teaching which is ideally suited to Special Educational Needs (SEN).

> The self-managing learner is one who is self-aware, capable of exercising choice in relation to needs, of taking an active self-directing role in furthering his or her own learning and development. (Harrison, 2000:315)

The key to adult learning is relevance. This has implications for teaching approaches. It engenders a top-down model whereby the external curriculum drives the support programme. Thus, the student is expected to bring along to her individual sessions the materials and resources for the SDT to use for teaching. It is a student-led environment which encourages the student to take control of the learning situation.

3. Dynamic Collaboration and Cognitive Education

Knowledge of how students learn, the curricular pressures and subject-specific demands are vital components of successful tutorial support of any dyslexic student.

If SDTs are to provide a rich learning environment which enables the dyslexic student to develop and reach her potential, an understanding of the possible barriers to study is important. This contextualised knowledge will enable the tutor to raise the student's metacognitive awareness. If the student has an understanding of the learning process and can monitor progress throughout, there will be greater efficiency and quality of learning. Metacognitive strategies provide a barometer of success for the student and attempt to change the student from 'passive and anxious' (Brown, 1992) to the student as an active learner.

The problem-solving paradigm as the architecture or structure for cognition is of paramount importance in cognitive psychology (Newell, 1990, Flower and Hayes, 1981). Cognitive models are concerned with the cognitive sub-processes and how these work, and how they are linked. Cognitive education was described by Bruner (1990) as education which is related to 'meaning making'. It offers an alternative for success for the dyslexic student by deflecting weak memory capacity in the learning process and tapping into strengths such as problem-solving (Flower and Hayes, 1981; Palincsar and Brown, 1989; Flower et al, 1992; Bereiter and Scardamalia, 1992; Palincsar et al, 1993). Cognitive education is a collaborative enterprise which stems from cognitive psychology whereby strategic intervention of the expert (SDT) is modelled as part of the process of handing over control. It embodies the apprenticeship models which Flower and Hayes and Bereiter and Scardamalia found to be productive for learners and mirrored a developmental model for understanding and self-awareness in learning. It hinges upon the SDT's sound knowledge of the underpinning skills required for curricular activity yet sits well with a student-led approach to teaching support.

Dynamic collaboration in cognitive education is a method of providing appropriate intervention and support to adult learners which is:

- curriculum based
- personalised
- flexible
- holistic

It includes both educational and mentoring aspects of support which meet the academic and emotional literacy demands. The collaboration between the tutor and the student is constantly changing to respond to novel student experiences and developmental progression. The dynamics of the partnership also fluctuate, and the locus of control ebbs and flows to reflect the gradual empowerment of the student in the learning environment.

4. Timing of support sessions

The timing and pattern of support can cause tensions for both students and SDTs. Much of this is tied up with supply, demand and educational aims and objectives. It is rare that students will be given (or will need) weekly tutorial support sessions. However, a significant minority of students will have weekly sessions for some part of their time at university. Students in receipt of the Disabled Students' Allowance (DSA) are often allocated weekly tutorial/study skills sessions by their Local Authority. It is rare that such a pattern of support provision would be needed throughout the duration of the course if the student is developing metacognitive strategies for working and is gradually taking over control of learning. It would be considered an unrealistic assumption that they will be able to see the SDT on a daily basis. Yet, some students have grown up in a dependency culture and have impracticable expectations of specialist provision in HE.

> I think that it's because I went to a lovely private school where they wrote everything up on the board and you copied it down in your book and I suddenly came to the University and you have to go and find the books yourself. It's a bit of a culture shock! (2nd Year Archaeology Undergraduate)

An explosion of the dyslexic student population in HE has resulted in great pressure upon the services. Consequently, daily or weekly support sessions may be institutionally unrealistic but also may not sit well with active involvement and the development of metacognitive control on the part of the student. Student-centredness is not only about placing the individual's needs at the heart of the system but also about the individual taking responsibility for identifying needs for development and growth. Support must be in the context of an individual's developmental continuum. However, some students think that they have to come for sessions on a very regular basis and feel almost apologetic that this is not what they want. This misplaced obligation needs to be dispelled at the initial meeting when the student draws up her learning support agreement with the SDT. Thus, students may need to adapt to a personalised approach to provision which takes into account dual aspects: the internal – the student's strengths and weaknesses; and the external – the course demands and associated skills.

5. Type of support: Support for dyslexic difficulties

If you are trying to support dyslexic people, you must always find out what it is they want support in. Many adults do not want more literacy support. (Fawcett, 2001:8)

Students' views of the type of support they will receive in their individual sessions with the SDT can be linked to previous experiences. There are some dyslexic students who have coped with the academic pressures of GNVQ, AS and A level examinations because they operated within the limits of their skills and abilities. The educational experiences have not placed undue demands upon them, though many have stated that it took longer to perform tasks than their non-dyslexic peers. The perceptions of support for this group of students is related to the type of support which the school provided for others. These students may have attended schools where some of their peers were withdrawn from classes to attend extra literacy lessons because they had difficulties learning to read. Their judgements about this type of support are not entirely objective and may have been influenced by lack of understanding of the process of matching provision to individual needs. On the other hand, students who have had a negative experience of support in early schooling or in sixth form college are often reluctant to take up their entitlement. Students' life stories have highlighted inappropriate support as the strongest factor in rejecting available provision in HE (Farmer *et al*, 2002, Morgan and Klein, 2000, Hunter-Carsch and Herrington, 2001). Many students comment upon the 'more of the same' syndrome which appeared to drive provision for them in school. This refers to an apparent pre-occupation with individual language development programmes which concentrate upon lower-order skills, such as decoding skills, spelling and handwriting, at the expense of the development of higher-order skill acquisition. Thus, some students think that specialist support sessions at university will consist of having to learn spellings. Whilst it is not the intention of this book to be critical of the good work which is conducted in schools, it is vital that SDTs are mindful of the perceptions of the recipients of this support.

A growing body of mature students who have returned to education provides another dimension to students' perceptions and expectations of support in HE. The timing of the identification of dyslexia, socio-economic background and self-esteem and confidence influence expectations. The impact of identification after compulsory education is multifarious and individual. On the one hand, it has a bearing upon academic performance, while on the other hand, it can affect self-esteem and self-perception (McLoughlin *et al*, 2002, Morgan and Klein, 2000). As McLoughlin pointed out, some dyslexic adults, returning to study at HE level, experience a type of role reversal and revert to a childhood dependency mode. Although these students have often had successful careers, developed compensatory strategies and may have been responsible for supervising others, the way in which they adjust to the return to academic study may be affected by their own negative, childhood experiences at school (McLoughlin *et al*, 2002). These factors have a compound effect on the use made of support services in terms of the frequency and type of support required.

> There are several external factors which undoubtedly influence the individual's perception of the significance of dyslexia on his or her life. Perhaps the most important variables are the stage at which dyslexia was first diagnosed and the type of support, both emotional and academic, that was received. (Morgan and Klein, 2000:49)

Balancing the need to increase functional literacy with the development of academic and personal skills related to a chosen subject discipline is the real challenge for the SDT. Vygotsky's notion (1962) of the student's 'zone of proximal development' emphasises the need to examine the individual's strengths and areas for development within the *current* context of learning. This context is related not simply to the subject demands but also the ebb and flow of the student year.

5.1 Counselling and mentoring

An holistic approach to support must take into account the emotional as well as the academic needs of the adult learner. Indeed, many mature 'returners' who are dyslexic have anxieties and educational baggage which they need to deal with before they can make real progress in their learning. The cognitive, interactionist paradigm which has been explored in this chapter would not be complete without this layer of support.

Acknowledging the emotional needs of the adult dyslexic student contributes to appropriate provision and learner satisfaction. Nevertheless, it should be stressed that SDTs are trained teachers not trained counsellors. Many good specialist training courses include aspects of emotional learning, and there are many techniques which tutors can use which have their origins in counselling.

The SDT has to learn to be a good listener if she is to fulfil her role effectively in a non-judgemental and non-invasive manner. It is often easier to deal with the emotional aspects of learning by focusing on something concrete, such as techniques and strategies for coping with academic situations and tasks as a means of increasing self-esteem and self-confidence. Knowing when to remain silent, when to provide helpful prompts, and setting clear boundaries in the collaborative venture are crucial elements and provide yet another dimension of the dynamic collaboration.

6. The Dynamics of the student life cycle

There is a tradition in schools and colleges of strong liaison between support and subject-specialist staff. Whilst this type of liaison is exemplary, it is neither possible nor appropriate in the HE setting because it could mitigate against the pro-active role of the student. However, this background is vital to the working partnership between SDT and student. SDTs in HE have to take into consideration the natural pressure points which are inherent in the system in order to provide effective, contextualised support and guidance. This underlines the complexity and multidimensionality of the role. An awareness and knowledge of the following is the foundation of provision:

- the student life cycle
- the learning environment
- course demands and skills

HE institutions are not homogeneous places. The way in which the curriculum is organised is departmentally driven but is within a broad, organisational framework. Semesters, student terms, core/compulsory units, electives and end-of-year examinations are some of the terms with which students have to grapple. However, the significance of all these terms is allied to organisational as well as study demands.

Two semesters form the umbrella framework within which terms, taught units and assessment cycles revolve for all year groups, including undergraduate and postgraduate studies. Whilst the length of the student year varies according to different institutions, there are similarities in the structures. The two semesters are split into three university terms: Autumn, Spring and Summer. Terms are usually ten weeks in length, although some university colleges operate an eight-week term. Vocational courses have longer term times. These term times may correspond with professional practice. So, for example, Schools of Education often have eleven or twelve week terms to correspond with the termly cycles of local primary and secondary schools.

Key months during the academic year are October, January, February, April, May and September:

October: Registration and course enrolment; semester one time-table set in specified buildings and rooms on campus.

January: End of first semester and completion of units; first semester examinations (a few departments still adhere to the pre-semesterisation system and only set end of year examinations); advance notice of access arrangements for examinations sent to individual students; choice and enrolment on second semester units.

February: Beginning of semester; new semester two time-table set in specified buildings and rooms with different unit tutors.

April: Projects or dissertations for final year students to be bound and submitted.

May: End of semester two taught unit elements; advance notice of access arrangements for examinations sent to individual students; end of year examinations; consideration of choices for courses and units for following year; submission of proposal for final year project or dissertation for second year students; allocation of project supervisor.

September: Re-sit examinations.

6.1 Anticipating workload schedules and patterns

Whilst assignment deadlines approach with alarming regularity, there are some pressure points which SDTs need to bear in mind. Many departments require assignments for undergraduate studies to be handed in by mid-November and just before the end of year examinations in May or June. It is worth getting the students to discuss with the SDT their semester time-table, units being studied and the assessment deadlines. In most HE institutions nowadays, this information is available electronically on departmental intra-nets so the SDT can check on dates if necessary.

For second year undergraduate students, Easter time is another pressure point. They are expected to grapple with final deadlines for second semester assignments; preparations for revision for end of year examinations (the marks of both count towards the degree); and the formulation of proposals for the third year project which is usually started in the Summer term. The latter is of considerable importance because of the mark weightings for this piece of work. Often departments expect students to carry out some research of their own and produce a polished 10,000 word assignment. A well designed, well researched and well presented project could mean that a student may be able to move up a degree level. Many undergraduate dyslexic students can achieve a first for their dissertation, which will bring up their overall scores for the final degree. Some students have ambitious ideas and would like to go abroad to gather research information and data; others may wish to design and produce a piece of machinery. The creativity of the dyslexic students soars but the organisational aspects of the project have to be kept within a manageable and realistic frame – which can be supported by the SDT.

6.2 Departmental structures and key staff

One of the strengths of the HE environment is the autonomy of the departmental structure. Each department, within the institutional boundaries of quality assurance and academic standards, is able to devise and develop its courses and units; set its own time-tables and write the examination papers. Many departments are organised hierarchically, and it is vital that the SDT is aware of these in order to provide accurate advice to dyslexic students about where and whom to go to for further subject support.

Most departments will have a Head of School or Department who deals with the development, management and strategic progress of the research, teaching and enterprise aspects of activity. These may be remote figures who are only approached if all other lines of communication have failed! Many departments have tutors who are responsible for either undergraduate or postgraduate admissions. In larger departments, a senior academic has responsibility for a specified year group. For example, Dr. Bloggs may be in charge of second year undergraduates. S/he may oversee the progression of students in the year group; deal with academic-related problems encountered by individual students; and be responsible for co-ordinating the various courses offered for that year group. The development of new courses, units structures and academic excellence is usually delegated to other senior, academic staff. Each course has a director or leader who is responsible for the development, structure, academic content, academic standards, assessment modes of the course, and for a team of unit tutors who are lecturers and researchers in their own specified field of expertise. All courses have code names and are divided into coded units. In many institutions, the units are divided into core and electives. With electronic registration, enrolment etc. the codes are essential pieces of information.

Most students soon become acclimatised to this system and only remember the unit code and not its title. This is an admirable defence mechanism on the part of the student with dyslexia: a strategy to ensure that working memory resources are not overloaded. However, the SDT has to be aware of both the unit coding and the unit title in order to provide effective support which is linked to the appropriate academic skills and demands for specified units. Increasingly, academic departments allocate one member of staff who has responsibility for dyslexia or disability within the department. This person often liaises with the Learning and Teaching Co-ordinator who also has a part to play in making the department 'dyslexia aware'.

Who to approach for help within a department is dependent upon the departmental structures. Information about academic study can, therefore, be drawn from a variety of sources.

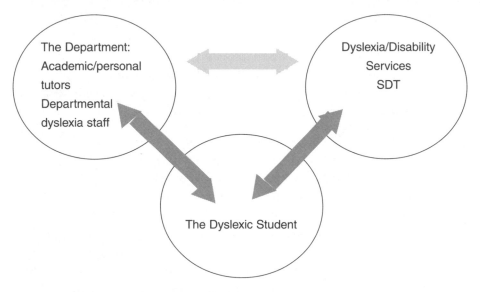

Figure 1: Interconnectivity of Learning Environment

Whilst it is true to say that each institution and each department within that institution is organised differently, the above diagram will provide a framework into which the SDT and the student can locate named academic staff in their own context.

7. The learning environment

Effective study skills tutoring must combine an understanding of study skills techniques (especially those involving memory tasks, organisation and time management) with the ability to work alongside the student in identifying the skills required for a course – whether it be note-taking from lectures or handling particular styles of presentation – and progress to a discussion of the particular difficulties each task presents the individual. The outcome should be the construction of both short-term and long-term strategies. Dyslexic students may not be fully aware of their particular areas of difficulty and the value of multi-sensory techniques for learning. (Singleton, 1999:9)

Awareness of the course demands, matched to an individual learning profile, are key ingredients for successful support for dyslexic students. The student's ability to access learning and the curriculum is multifaceted and relies upon internal and external factors, both of which need to be within the control of the student. The development of learner autonomy requires the student to develop meta-knowledge, of herself as a learner, and also meta-learning, an understanding of the dynamics of the learning environment.

The SDT needs to take into consideration three interlocking dynamics which strongly affect students' experience: the temporal, the physical and the social environments.

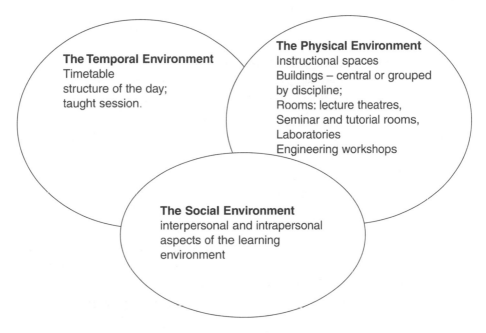

The Temporal Environment
Timetable
structure of the day;
taught session.

The Physical Environment
Instructional spaces
Buildings – central or grouped
by discipline;
Rooms: lecture theatres,
Seminar and tutorial rooms,
Laboratories
Engineering workshops

The Social Environment
interpersonal and intrapersonal
aspects of the learning
environment

Figure 2: Dynamic Environments

Radloff (1998) highlights the complexity of each of the learning environments in figure two by reminding us that concentrating upon one of the elements will not bring about radical changes for the learner. The Social Environment incorporates inter- and intra- personal management. The challenge is to ensure that the student gains an understanding of her individual cognitive and learning style (intra) and the *significance* of these in the learning environment (inter). The student has to learn how to adapt to the differing Physical Environments. Room size and layout, acoustics, external levels of distractibility, individual space (some dyslexic students need to spread out their papers etc. in order to learn), audio-visual technology and comfortable furniture and lighting can play a large part in enhancing the learning environment. The Temporal Environment is the one over which the student has least control and is usually institutionally devised so that joint honours' courses, for example, can be timetabled more effectively without clashes.

The physicality of the time-table can be a challenge for some students. SDTs have to be knowledgeable of the layout of the campus so they can respond to student queries. For some students with severe spatial and perceptual difficulties, such as dyspraxic students, the SDT may need to walk through the routes with students so they can strengthen the visual imprint and gain confidence in locating buildings which are not in their department. If students have difficulty with orientation, they sometimes ask for accommodation close to campus and look to Dyslexia Services to support their claim.

8. Skill analysis matched to academic activity

In order to provide the most useful support, the SDT has to be aware of the student's 'expertise gap' (Heaton and Mitchell, 2001) and the underlying skills which are needed to function in a variety of learning environments. A task analysis approach provides the SDT with a system for scrutinising the range of skills. As part of background preparation for support, SDTs are encouraged to explore electronic, departmental information in order to evaluate the underlying skills students require to succeed on their courses.

In conclusion...

The role of reflection, metacognition and self-regulation has to be developed and nurtured by the SDT to ensure that the student with dyslexia is able to access her curriculum efficiently. In partnership, the SDT can guide the student to be one step ahead of the game in all the learning environments in which she finds herself.

Further Reading

Glynn, T, Wearmouth, J and Berryman, M (2006) *Supporting students with literacy difficulties.* Maidenhead: Open University Press

Hacker, D J, Dunlosky, J and Graesser, A (eds (1998) *Metacognition in educational theory and practice.* Mahwah, NJ: Lawrence Erlbaum Associates

3

Training and the Specialist Dyslexia Tutor

This chapter explores the emerging role of the Specialist Dyslexia Tutor(SDT) and the concomitant factors which contribute to a vibrant and knowledgeable body of professionals.

Using this chapter
This chapter will enable you to:

1. Understand the role of the Specialist Dyslexia Tutor (SDT)

2. Understand current DfES guidelines for SDTs

3. Be aware of the current procedures for the regulation of Practising Certificates

4. Be aware of how to develop you own Continuing Professional Development (CPD) portfolio

    4.1 What are 'training activities'?

    4.2 What are Competence-based Portfolios?

1. The role of the specialist dyslexia tutor

The role of the SDT is of paramount importance, both for the institution in which she works and the individual student. SDTs play a vital role within support services for dyslexic students and are the professionals who have the knowledge and experience to provide an assessment, leading to recommendations for developing individual teaching programmes. There has been considerable controversy in recent years about the role of the SDT and whether or not assessments carried out by specialist teachers are as valid as those carried out by educational psychologists. This was brought to a head when Local Authorities (LA) had to deal with large numbers of applications for the Disabled Students' Allowance (DSA) and were faced with a substantial body of evidence upon which the LA officers were expected to make decisions about releasing funds to students. The time was ripe for an overhaul of practices and procedures so that LA officers, who are not trained SpLD specialists, could administer the process fairly.

The DfES Working Party (2005) into the Assessment of Dyslexia, Dyspraxia, Dyscalculia and Attention Deficit Disorder (ADD) in Higher Education was formed to address the issues and to set forth guidelines for a national structure. Membership of the Working Party consisted of individuals representing organisations with national roles in promoting standards in SpLD assessment, support and teacher training. Members will have relevant experience in SpLD assessment, support and/or teacher training. The aim was to produce guidelines for the assessment and identification process, in the first instance for FE and HE (the sectors involved in DSA applications) which would be cascaded to Secondary and Primary sectors in the future. The final DfES report (2005) outlined procedures, recommended relevant tests and suitable reporting formats for *all* professionals involved in assessment. This will be referred to as the DfES Working Party Guidelines (2005).

This kite-mark for good practice has been embraced by many SDTs and some psychologists working in the HE environment. The intention is that disparities between educationalists and psychologists will be dispelled. The notion of parallel tracks to training and qualifications was introduced: the training routes to assessment would be governed by education and psychology. However, it will take time to embed the practices and to change attitudes. Nevertheless, in the not-too-distant future, teacher assessors' reports will have greater currency. So students will benefit from a more professional service with national standards, sound quality assurance and a Code of Practice and Ethics. With this as a backdrop a welcome change in the training for SDTs has come about, with stringent frameworks for qualifications, the licensing of teacher assessors and structures for continuing professional development (CPD). A rolling programme of guidelines and regulations has been devised for SDTs and training providers:

- New reporting regulations came into effect in 2006

- Practising Certificates will be needed from September 2007 onwards

- Renewal of Practising Certificates every three years, conditional on relevant CPD evidence portfolio.

2. DfES Working Party guidelines for training

The DfES Working Party spawned two Standing Committees: the National Committee for Standards in SpLD Assessment, Training and Practice (SASC) and the National Committee for SpLD Test Evaluation (STEC). These committees regulate practice. Both standing committees publish reports of meetings and guidance which can be accessed through the DfES, Professional Association of Teachers of Students with SpLD (PATOSS), Dyslexia Action (DA – formerly Dyslexia Institute) and British Psychological Service (BPS) websites.

Whilst there is a proliferation of courses for SpLD, only certain of these are recognised and meet the new regulations (See Appendix A). The depth of knowledge required for this specialist field continues to grow as new research and empirical evidence become available. Accredited courses are approved by the British Dyslexia Association (BDA), PATOSS or the BPS (See Appendix B for the practical skill outcomes for such courses). The essential element of training in psychometrics brings teachers' training in line with that of psychologists.

Training for the Practising Certificate in Assessment should provide a minimum of:

- 60 hours of lectures, seminars and guided learning hours plus private study time
- 12 hours of lectures and seminars to be devoted to study of psychometric testing
- training in writing assessment reports
- 3 diagnostic assessments carried out under supervision, one of which is observed

3. Practising certificates

A practising certificate embodies the principles of professional qualifications, professional achievement and a commitment to CPD. For those in FE/HE who write full diagnostic reports for DSA purposes, the holder's practising certificate number is required. This applies to SDTs and Psychologists.

Registers of individuals holding current practising certificates is one essential part of ensuring that standards are maintained in the profession. These registers are held by PATOSS and BPS. The introduction of a national structure for the provision of practising certificates was complicated because it had to provide different routes to reflect the needs of those recently trained and those who gained SpLD qualifications some time ago. Having gained a recognised, post-graduate qualification, the SDT is eligible to apply for a practising certificate. These certificates are issued by BPS, PATOSS and DA. The PATOSS routes are discussed below as an example of procedures and to provide professionals with knowledge of what is required to obtain a practising certificate. There are two routes: route one is the most frequently followed (See PATOSS website for full details of procedures).

Route 1: Applicants holding membership of a relevant professional body
This route is for those with recognised qualifications.

Route 2: Applicants not holding membership of a relevant professional body
This route is for those who do not hold one of the approved qualifications but may be eligible to apply for a Practising Certificate through Accreditation of Prior Learning/Experience (APL/APE).

4. Continuing professional development (CPD) and competence-based portfolios

Obtaining a post-graduate specialist qualification is just the beginning. Life-long learning or continuing professional development has always been recognised as a part of professional life. It ensures that SDTs can keep up with new approaches to testing and teaching. It can be stimulating and provocative. Above all, it ensures that as a professional body we are able to provide quality and up-to-date support for SpLD students. Keeping abreast of innovative and controversial topics can help the professional reflect upon her practice.

The common definition of continuing professional development is:

> the systematic maintenance, improvement and broadening of knowledge, understanding and skills and the development of the personal qualities necessary to undertake your duties throughout your working life. (PATOSS CPD Guidance: www.patoss-dyslexia.org.uk)

Underpinning this practice is the notion that the professional is in control of her own learning and should plan this systematically to meet her individual needs and circumstances. The needs of a senior SDT in charge of a large department will be different from the needs of those who have been practising for three years. A vital component of the competence-based portfolio is that it is a vibrant document which provides evidence not only of attendance and participation or delivery of training activity but also demonstrates reflection and evaluation of how these activities help to inform practice. One approach to planning individual CPD is to conduct a 'SWOT' analysis.

SWOT ANALYSIS

Strengths

What are your professional skills?

What do you do well?

- Technical assessment skills and knowledge

- Teaching approaches and skills

- Clear communication skills – e.g. modelling 'hidden' thinking skills for a student

Weaknesses

Where are your skills/knowledge lacking?

What would you like to improve?

- from your own point of view

- from the point of view of other people

  - colleagues

  - line manager

  - students (from feedback on your sessions)

Opportunities

What are the opportunities facing you?

What are the interesting new trends?

- changes in professional practice

- emerging new specialisms

- developments in technology

- moves towards quality assurance

- assuming a management role

Threats

What obstacles do you face?

Is your professional role changing?

- legislative changes

- limited opportunities for progression

- threat of redundancy

- changes in the infrastructure of your institution

In order to apply for renewal of a Practising Certificate SDTs will be required to produce evidence of CPD. Each awarding body will have its own ideas about what constitutes evidence but a closer look at the PATOSS guidelines covers many of the principles. It is only the procedures which will vary.

PATOSS requires applicants to provide a recent, full diagnostic report. This evidence must demonstrate professional ability to:

i) select appropriate tests

ii) administer, score and interpret cognitive and attainment tests, including standardised tests

iii) make appropriate teaching and support recommendations based on the assessment

iv) write a report on assessment which is appropriate for purpose.

SDTs are expected to keep a self-reflective log of training activities in which they have participated during the three year period. PATOSS requires members to supply evidence of 20 hours of training activities over the period of three years.

4.1 What are 'training activities'?

A variety of training activities are required to cover the broad spectrum of professionals and levels of expertise. It may be appropriate at this stage to define some of the terminology.

Participation includes preparing, delivering and/or attending courses.

Attendance means attendance at the complete course. Part attendance does not count at all.

Course includes

- face-to-face sessions or sessions delivered by distance learning which could be part of a course, conference or seminar. These must result in reflective analysis of how the content may have an impact upon practice

- a course wholly provided by distance learning that involves assessment by dissertation and written examination

- structured coaching sessions, delivered face to face, of one hour or more, which have written aims and objectives and which are documented showing an outcome

- structured mentoring sessions involving professional development, of one hour or more, delivered face to face, which have written aims and objectives, and are documented showing an outcome

This ensures that there is flexibility in demonstrating knowledge and professional development and that each individual can choose activities which are most relevant to her working environment (See Appendix C as a sample of detailed types of activities produced by PATOSS).

4.2 What are competence-based portfolios?

Evidence-based portfolios are not something new to SDTs. In order to obtain the specialist qualification, individuals had to maintain a teaching log and assessment portfolio of evidence to demonstrate skills and competence. The CPD portfolio is an extension of this idea in that each individual will maintain a file of information which she regards as demonstrating her growing expertise. For example, this file may contain details of conferences attended, attendance certificates and a brief reflection of the value (or otherwise!) of the conference to practice. One of the easiest ways of monitoring progression and development is to keep a log which can be cross-referenced to different parts of the portfolio/file. Thus, the log provides a summary of activities (See Appendix D for an example of a log).

In conclusion...

To ensure that the professional body adheres to recognised standards, specialist qualifications have to be achieved according to the DfES Working Party regulations and guidance. However, as this chapter shows, this is but one aspect of training and that keeping up-to-date with current research and practice will ensure that the network of SDTs is highly regarded and respected.

Appendix A: Recognised Accredited Courses

■ All courses leading to AMBDA
  [See SpLD Specialist Teacher Training Courses for list of providers]

■ University College London
  Certificate in the Diagnostic Assessment and Management of Literacy Difficulties [from 2000 to 2004]

■ Certificate of Competence in Educational Testing (Level A) when combined with an ATS-level SpLD qualification
  [See SpLD Specialist Teacher Training Courses for list of ATS training providers]

■ London South Bank University
  LLU+ Postgraduate Diploma in Adult Dyslexia, Diagnosis and Support M Level (7) [from February 2007]

■ Oxford and Cambridge and RSA Examinations
  OCR Level 7 Certificate in Assessing and Teaching Learners with Specific Learning Difficulties (Dyslexia)

■ Dyslexia Action's post graduate diploma entitled Blended Learning

Appendix B: Practical Skill Outcomes of Accredited Courses

- understand the nature of specific learning difficulties and identify learners with SpLD

- demonstrate an understanding of the cognitive and affective issues observed in learners with SpLD

- understand the theory and application of psychometric and educational assessment

- identify appropriate methods and materials both for screening learners and for in-depth assessment of individual needs

- select appropriate methods and materials, based on an understanding of current theory

- administer tests correctly and interpret resulting data accurately

- produce professional reports written in a language easily accessible to non-specialists

- make teaching and learning and assessment recommendations that are directly linked to assessment findings and to the individual's needs

- understand current legal and professional issues, rules and regulations relating to or affecting individuals with SpLD

- complete relevant forms and reports to meet varied individual needs

- understand all aspects of processing documentation and managing special arrangements for learners with SpLD

- effectively communicate findings and implications of any assessments to relevant individuals both orally and in writing as required, with due regard to building a positive framework

Appendix C: PATOSS CPD Activities

Activity	Explanation/comments
1. Participation in courses	■ Preparing, delivering, and/or attending courses that are of particular relevance and benefit to an individual's area of work, and are a minimum of 60 minutes in length ■ Actual time may be claimed
2. Coaching and mentoring sessions of less than one hour [see CPD Supplementary Guidance Notes]	■ Structured coaching sessions and structured mentoring sessions involving professional development, delivered face to face, of between 30 minutes and 60 minutes in length, and which have written aims and objectives and are documented showing an outcome ■ Actual time may be claimed
3. Coaching and mentoring sessions delivered from a distance [see CPD Supplementary Guidance Notes]	■ Structured coaching sessions and structured mentoring sessions involving professional development, delivered from a distance (eg by telephone, e-mail or fax), of 30 minutes or more in length, and which have written aims and objectives and are documented showing an outcome ■ Actual time may be claimed
4. Writing on assessment or practice	■ For example, articles for journals, publications for in-house guidance, newspapers articles and the internet ■ Actual time may be claimed
5. Work shadowing	■ Participation in structured work shadowing schemes with clear aims and objectives and requiring feedback or reflection on the shadowing activity ■ Actual time may be claimed
6. Research	■ Research that relates to SpLD assessment and practice topics or has relevance to the practice/organisation and which results in some form of written document, presentation, questionnaire/survey, etc ■ Actual time may be claimed

7. Reading on SpLD assessment and practice topics [see CPD Supplementary Guidance Notes below]

- Reading on topics which inform practice, e.g. test manuals, books, professional journals, articles from the internet. Reading must result in a reflective analysis of how must result in a reflective analysis of how material may impact on practice

- Actual time may be claimed

8. Listening to/watching audio/visual relevant material

- Must result in a reflective analysis of how material may impact on practice

- Actual time may be claimed

9. Production of a dissertation

- Study for or production of a dissertation counting towards a qualification recognised by PATOSS

- Actual time may be claimed

10. Distance learning courses where there is provision for the answering of enquiries or for discussion [see CPD Supplementary Guidance Notes]

- Distance-learning courses may be delivered by correspondence, dvd, video/audio cassettes, television/radio broadcasts or computer-based learning programmes

- Actual time may be claimed

11. Preparation and delivery of training courses forming part of the process of SpLD assessment qualification or CPD training

- Actual time may be claimed

12. Participating in the development of specialist areas of SpLD assessment and practice by attending meetings of specialist committees and/or working parties of relevant professional or other competent bodies charged with such work

- Actual time may be claimed

13. Study towards professional qualifications

- Evidence of successful completion of course must be provided

- Actual time spent may be claimed

Appendix D: CPD Log

CPD Activity	Reflection of Activity to Professional Skills and Knowledge	Type of Evidence Submitted	Date Completed

4

The identification process

This chapter looks at the reasons why screening is important and considers some of the different tools available to use for a screening assessment. It considers other factors involving students on placement and fieldwork as well as those with English as an Additional Language.

Using this chapter
This chapter will enable you to:

1. Understand the need for screening

    1.1 Increasing demand for screening assessments

    1.2 The importance of screening

2. Examine a variety of screening approaches and tools

    2.1 Dyslexia checklist questionnaires

    2.2 Computerised checklist questionnaires

    2.3 Informal screening interviews

    2.4 Questions to use in an informal interview

    2.5 Placement and fieldwork

    2.6 Additional questions for students on health courses

3. Compare different tools for measuring a student's 'at risk' factors for SpLD

    3.1 Lucid Adult Screening Assessment (LADS)

    3.2 Dyslexia Adult Screening Assessment (DAST)

    3.3 Recording the results of the screening assessment

4. Interpret the results of screening data to come to a decision about the nature and causes of the difficulties

4.1 General or specific difficulties?

4.2 Dyspraxia/developmental co-ordination disorder

4.3 Attention deficit (hyperactivity) disorder

4.4 Asperger's Syndrome

4.5 Overlapping features of AD(H)D and Asperger's syndrome

4.6 Overlapping features of dyslexia/dyspraxia and ADD

4.7 Overlapping features of dyspraxia/AD(H)D

4.8 English as an Additional Language (EAL)

5. Discuss the results with the student

6. Carry out an overlay screening test

Dyslexia screening is not a purely administrative job, but rather a role requiring considerable knowledge as well as a complex range of professional and interpersonal skills. (Singleton, 1999:88)

1. Why screen?

A full assessment is costly in terms of both time and money, and most institutions feel it is necessary to have an initial screening to justify the financial implications of a full assessment. The screening process is a way of eliminating other factors which might be causing study difficulties and to find out whether the student is 'at risk' of dyslexia. The initial screening assessment is only the first stage in the assessment process. Students are often confused by this and think that an initial screening assessment will provide them with a definite diagnosis. This is not the case. At the end of a screening assessment it is possible only to give an opinion about possible factors which might indicate dyslexia. A full assessment will be necessary to confirm this.

1.1 Increasing demand for screening assessments

A growing awareness and acceptance of dyslexia has led to an increasing number of students identifying themselves as dyslexic when they start at university. Whereas several years ago students were often advised not to declare their dyslexia in case it jeopardised their place at their chosen institution, nowadays more and more students are quite happy to tick the dyslexia box on their UCAS application forms. Nevertheless, there are still many students who enter higher education unaware that they are dyslexic and who come forward for screening assessment at some stage during their undergraduate courses and sometimes even during their postgraduate courses.

Academic tutors are similarly referring more of their tutees for initial screening assessments when the students start to under-perform academically or fail an assignment or examination. In some cases students are allowed to stay on the course pending the outcome of the initial screening assessment.

Academic tutors sometimes query why the identification of an SpLD has not occurred prior to entry to HE. Thus, the SDT is often called on to provide some answers and to reassure staff that the needs of these recently identified students are as important as the needs of students who have been aware of their dyslexia for most of their lives. Widening participation has meant that more students have the opportunity to enter university than in the past, many after completing an Access course. Some students have chosen practical and/or scientific 'A' level subjects, not always because they preferred these subjects but because they felt they would not have to write as many essays.

Gilroy and Miles (1995) point out that the move to university can be extremely stressful for dyslexic students. Some may have managed to compensate for any difficulties caused by their dyslexia whilst they were at school, without even realising they had dyslexia. They might have spent hours and hours studying but they were able to cope because they were in a very structured environment. Sometimes these coping strategies begin to break down at HE level when the student is faced with an array of different tasks to cope with such as living away from home and organising domestic and financial matters as well as study. Sometimes the move to self-directed study can be overwhelming. These extra pressures might make it more difficult for students who had always been aware they were struggling but who were reluctant to seek help.

Sadly, there is a substantial minority of students requesting screening assessments at the dissertation stage because they have managed to develop strategies which work well until they are faced with an extensive piece of coursework which involves a great deal of research and organisation as well as writing.

1.2 The importance of screening

Singleton (1999) has described screening as a 'delicate task' (1999:88) and emphasised the importance of using trained dyslexia specialists because it demands a 'complex range of professional and interpersonal skills' (1999:90). According to Singleton, the screener should possess counselling and interview skills, have a good knowledge of dyslexia at HE level, be experienced at working with dyslexic students, be able to distinguish between dyslexia and language difficulties and also have knowledge of the institution's policy and procedures.

1.3 Recognising the emotional needs of students

Sometimes the screening process can be cathartic for some students, but be emotionally draining and upsetting for others. It is not unusual for students to be quite overwhelmed. At times the role of the SDT is very much that of counsellor. Empathic and good listening skills are an essential part of any job description for an SDT. For many students, requesting an initial screening is very difficult. Some students will have taken several weeks or even months to decide to come forward. Some students need reassurance about what the screening procedure will involve. Others who are beginning to fail with their studies, despite working very hard, are reluctant to think that their problems might be due to dyslexia and are only requesting a screening because of the insistence of their academic departments. Such students are often reassured by being allowed a short consultation session with an SDT to discuss their difficulties and to decide whether or not to proceed with screening. It is important for dyslexia departments to be sensitive to this and not to push students into booking a screening until they are ready. Often the SDT can be sufficiently reassuring during this initial chat, and the session will lead to a screening assessment anyway.

It is important to establish at the very beginning of any screening assessment that the student really wishes to proceed and has not been persuaded to attend almost against her better judgement. It is equally important that the SDT puts the student at ease right away by talking about the reasons for booking an assessment or asking questions about the student's course before starting. Similarly, the SDT needs to explain that the initial screening assessment is the first stage in what might be a lengthy assessment procedure.

2. Screening approaches and tools

The Association of Dyslexia Specialists in Higher Education (ADSHE) carried out a survey in 2002 to investigate the screening process within Higher Education institutions. It appeared that there was no standard procedure although most of the twenty eight institutions who responded used an interview as part of the process.

Screening assessments approaches and tools available specifically for adults include:

- identification checklists and questionnaires
- informal screening interviews and questionnaires
- tools for measuring a student's 'at risk' factors for SpLD
- combination of interview and assessment

2.1 Dyslexia checklist questionnaires

Many questionnaires have been published, mainly electronically, which list the characteristics commonly associated with dyslexia. These can be completed by the student without any reference to trained professional guidance. The student is asked to give a yes or no response to a series of questions relating to sequencing, reading, spelling, memory, word retrieval etc., some of which are considered more likely to be indicative of dyslexia than others. At the end of the checklist the number of positive answers are counted and the likelihood established as to whether these are indicators of dyslexia. It is important that the student is able to discuss the findings of such questionnaires with an SDT as soon as possible.

2.2 Computerised checklist questionnaires

Some HE institutions use the **Quick Scan** online questionnaire, which is part of the longer Study Scan assessment (Zdzienski, 1997). The student is to do this independently and is given a printed report which gives details of her strengths and weaknesses with a possible indication that dyslexia might be present. No explanations are provided to justify the conclusions of the results. Some students might be quite worried to be informed that they might be dyslexic, without being given any reason. Again, it is important that a student who has taken a questionnaire on her own is given a follow-up appointment with an SDT as soon as possible.

2.3 Informal screening interviews

To ask an adult to fill out a lengthy questionnaire can be quite intimidating, and the information provided can be of limited value. A more informative and valuable alternative is to use a questionnaire filled out by the SDT as a basis for an interview. Questions can be asked which stimulate a full discussion about the student's particular strengths and weaknesses. The student can be asked questions about all aspects of study, and the SDT adds to the questions as appropriate, encouraging the student to provide details about how she approaches study and what strategies are used. In this way diagnostic observation techniques are employed by the SDT to interpret responses.

McLoughlin *et al* have pointed to the importance of the interview as 'critical to identification' (2002:43). Others have stressed the complexity of assessing adults. Dyslexic adults often approach assessment with additional problems of low self-esteem and lack of self-confidence (Lee, 2000). The SDT needs to be aware of such issues in the initial screening process, and later, of course, in the full assessment, but in the initial stages it is sometimes difficult to make a decision about whether or not it is dyslexia which is at the root of the student's difficulties. This is why it is essential that initial screening assessments are carried out by SDTs and not left to unskilled or untrained personnel.

2.4 Questions to use in an informal interview

When designing questions for use in the interview it worth bearing in mind what lies behind the type of questions which are regularly used in questionnaires. They have their origins in the causal theory of dyslexia. Thus, in order to ascertain if a student's difficulties are caused by dyslexia, the questions need to cover a range of themes which will provide positive and negative indicators of dyslexia. In other words, the questions will provide evidence that dyslexia could be the reason for the student's difficulties or evidence that dyslexia can be eliminated and other reasons for failure and difficulty considered instead. Questions should be related to the causal theories described in chapter one. Thus, the themes to be explored should be: general background and history; education; reading; note-taking; spelling; writing; language and listening; sequencing and memory. The proforma in Appendix 1 gives suggestions about questions that could be asked.

The interview questions at all times are meant as a guide, and the student should be encouraged to give as much detail as possible. Most experienced SDTs will make use of supplementary probing questions as appropriate. The SDT will be looking at how the student approaches her studies – what works as well as what does not work. For example, answers to the question, 'What is the usual way of approaching an essay?' can provide information about the student's learning style, organisational and planning skills as well as writing skills.

Some institutions will use an interview as a basis for the initial screening assessment and will make a judgement about full assessment based on the findings. This is quite valid, and if time is limited it would be preferable to base a judgement on an interview rather than solely on one of the available screening tools.

2.5 Placement and fieldwork

Some students might have placements or fieldwork trips as part of their academic studies. It is, therefore, appropriate to ask additional questions about these aspects of the course in order to gain a fuller picture of the students' profiles. (See Chapter 12: *Supporting students on placement and fieldwork*)

2.6 Additional questions for students on health related courses

Screening interview questions tend to focus on academic study but students on courses such as nursing, medicine and physiotherapy can spend up to half their time on placement. Some dyslexic students will find aspects of placement quite challenging. Additional questions can be asked to ascertain the student's ability for:

- following instructions
- writing patients' or clients' notes
- reading patients' or clients' notes and other documentation
- remembering patients or clients' names
- remembering specialised terminology such as drug names and medical conditions
- recalling procedures
- remembering and recording phone messages accurately
- misreading dates or confusing times
- reading and filling in charts
- filing
- finding the way around the wards or departments
- completing tasks on time
- reacting quickly in a busy environment
- understanding exactly what is required
- multi-tasking

(See also: Chapter 12: *Supporting students on placement and fieldwork*)

3. Tools for measuring a student's 'at risk' factors for SpLD

The informal interview provides rich data upon which to make a decision about the types of difficulties experienced by the student in order to assist in the identification process. Many SDTs favour using a tool which provides some measurement of a positive indication of dyslexia, and a variety of tools are available for use. Some of these are computerised while others provide a paper and pencil approach. The two most frequently used tools are discussed below:

3.1 Lucid Adult Dyslexia Screening Assessment (LADS)
(Singleton *et al*, 2002)

This adaptive computerised test will take about twenty minutes – the number of items varies according to the individual student's performance. It consists of four subtests: reasoning, word recognition, word construction and working memory. It tests indirectly core skills which are generally considered to be weak in the dyslexic individual: phonological processing, lexical access and working memory.

Reasoning
The student sees a 3 x 2 matrix appearing on the screen with 1 empty square. She has to choose 1 of 6 missing patterns from the bottom of the screen to fit in the empty square. This is testing logical reasoning using visual strategies.

Word recognition
Four non words and one real word appear on the screen. The student has to click on the real word. It is a timed test which measures lexical decoding skills.

Word construction
The student hears a three-syllable non-word once only and has to reproduce the word by clicking on the syllables in the correct order. This is testing lexical encoding of non-words from syllables. To answer correctly the student has to have good phonological knowledge and skills.

Working Memory
This is a backwards digit span test. A series of numbers is given once only and the student has to listen and type the numbers in reverse order.

Recording the results
The test is scored electronically, and the results can be viewed on screen or printed immediately. The probability of dyslexia is determined as: low; borderline; moderate or high. The electronic report is produced with space for the assessor's comments. It is useful to record here any relevant information from the interview questions. It will provide information for the full assessment, if appropriate. The test is very pressured because of the timing, which is emphasised throughout both in the instructions and in the format. Some students find this extremely stressful and are unable to perform to the best of their ability. It is heavily reliant on auditory skills as there is no opportunity to hear instructions repeated. Many students find the working

memory reverse digit sub-test easier because they can hear and also visualise the numbers as well as using the pattern on the number key pad. The test is useful because it provides some indication of possible weaknesses which might be due to dyslexia.

3.2 Dyslexia Adult Screening Test (DAST) (Fawcett and Nicolson, 1998)

This test takes about thirty minutes to complete and tests rapid naming ability, non verbal reasoning, phonological skills, memory and literacy skills.

The SDT asks the questions and records the student's responses on the scoring sheet. 11 sub-tests are included:

Rapid naming

The student has to name a page of pictures of everyday objects as quickly as possible. The reasoning behind this test is that dyslexic people are slower than non-dyslexics to name pictures. This test is a quick method of measuring speed of processing, and the candidate's ability to label and retrieve language information.

One-minute reading

This is a test of individual words, measuring fluency and accuracy in decoding.

Postural stability

This is intended to detect any difficulty with balance. The student is blindfolded and the examiner has to push a balance testing instrument 'gently' into the student's lower back. If the postural stability test is used, the student's permission will be required. However, many experienced assessors are uncomfortable with this test. Firstly, it is difficult to achieve an accurate setting of the test instrument. Secondly, there are ethical considerations to be taken into account relating to touching students and the safety aspects of the test: some students who experience severe dyslexia are in danger of falling over and could injure themselves.

Phonemic segmentation

This tests the 'ability to break down a word into its constituent sounds, and to manipulate the sounds' (Fawcett and Nicolson, 1998:9). The authors of the test consider that this assesses both phonological skill and working memory.

Two-minute spelling

The SDT reads out individual words which increase in difficulty. This tests the student's ability to spell unconnected words. It assesses spelling as well as phonological knowledge.

Backwards digit span

This tests working memory. There is a tape where digits are spoken at one second intervals. The student has to repeat numbers in backwards order. This is considered to be an essential component of any assessment and is included in most full assessments by Educational Psychologists as well as SDTs.

Nonsense passage reading

The student has to read a short paragraph containing non-words as well as real words. The SDT notes down any errors. This will provide information about phonological processing difficulties, as it will be far more difficult to read non-words than real words.

Nonverbal reasoning

There are cards with eight questions testing sequencing, analogies and similarities and differences. The way in which these types of tests are designed relies upon visual discrimination and is, therefore, not solely a test of reasoning ability. Thus, a low score may not indicate weak reasoning but may be the result of visual discrimination difficulties. However, a test of nonverbal reasoning is useful in that it can provide a rough estimation of general ability (see Chapter 5 where intelligence and 'g' factors are explained). Low scores may indicate that general low ability is the root cause of any difficulties rather than a specific learning difficulty. Dyspraxic students, however, can often find tests of this kind very difficult because of sequencing and spatial awareness difficulties.

One minute writing

The student is given a short passage to copy which tests copying speed and fine motor skills. A dyspraxic student is likely to find this task quite difficult.

Verbal fluency

The student is given one minute to name as many words beginning with the letter 's' as they can. For those with dyslexia this is a particularly difficult task because it relies upon verbal labelling and retrieval, aspects which are related to causal factors of dyslexia.

Semantic fluency

The student is given a minute to name as many animals as they can. Usually, dyslexic students' scores for these two sub-tests are discrepant with the semantic fluency score being higher than the verbal fluency score. The reason for this is that dyslexic people will perform relatively better on the semantic task because they are able to use visual hooks and memory joggers to retrieve the words. For example, some students think about a visit to the zoo and the animals they saw.

Recording the results

The results are calculated and an 'at risk' quotient (ARQ) is indicated. A graph of the strengths and weaknesses provides a useful visual record for the feedback discussion with the student.

This screening test is fairly time-consuming but provides the SDT with useful information about students' strengths and weaknesses. However, as with the LADS test, it is only a preliminary sketch and cannot provide a diagnosis. One drawback is that it uses the non-verbal reasoning result as an indicator of dyslexia, whilst in the LADS the reasoning sub-test is used as a comparison. Thus, unexpected performance or low scores in other sections may lead to an indication of dyslexia. It might be more useful for the SDT to bear in mind that non-verbal reasoning is not an indicator of dyslexia and to look carefully at any results where the non-verbal reasoning is low to avoid a false positive score.

3.3 Recording the results of screening assessments

Although producing a formal written report of the screening assessment is generally unnecessary, a written record is essential in order to inform a full assessment. Appendix 2 gives an example of a simple proforma which can be used if DAST has been carried out. With LADS the print out sheet is usually sufficient.

A word of caution

Interpretation of the scores is the most important aspect of the process. Expertise and knowledge are the crux of differential diagnosis. At times, novice SDTs can be misled by scores because they have not taken into account the possible causes of low scores. It is worth considering what statisticians mean when they use terminology such as 'false positives' and 'false negatives'. A false positive is a situation whereby a student may be identified as dyslexic (positive identification), yet this is not the case (false). This may be due to a number of factors such as test design and tasks as discussed earlier in the chapter when considering the purity of the results from non-verbal reasoning tasks. In other words, the student may have other underlying difficulties which are causing the low scores. A false negative occurs when the screening test states that dyslexia is not present (negative) when this is later found not to be the case (false).

4. Interpreting the results of the screening process to come to a decision about the nature and causes of the difficulties

It is very important to look at both the results from the LADS or DAST and the student's responses from the interview in order to make a judgement as to whether or not to refer the student for a full assessment. In many cases the answers from the interview are more revealing than the results of the computer assessment. Results from either the DAST or the LADS might indicate that the student is not at risk of dyslexia yet the SDT can be quite convinced that there is a dyslexic type difficulty. In such cases it is advisable to recommend further testing.

4.1 General or specific difficulties?

Responses from the interview questions can help SDTs tease out potential difficulties which could be due to causes other than dyslexia. If there is any doubt about whether or not to refer for full assessment it is usually advisable to recommend a full assessment than not to refer a student who turns out much later on to be dyslexic. In the latter case the student will then have missed out on a considerable amount of support.

Some students have low general ability and struggle in many of the areas of the screening tests such as DAST or LADS. Both literacy skills and memory skills are weak but the reasons are due to low ability rather than dyslexia. A similar profile might be apparent if the students have weak academic skills, perhaps because of poor schooling or because they have been out of education for some time.

If the results of the screening assessment are inconclusive, and there appear to be few indicators of a specific learning difficulty from the interview, it might be worth referring the student for an academic study skills session to see if the difficulties can be resolved through academic support. If the student is still struggling or still worried, she can be referred for a full assessment at a later date. It could be that an injection of support for a specific difficulty – say essay writing – might well solve the problem.

4.2 Dyspraxia/Developmental Co-ordination Disorder

It is generally agreed that dyslexia often co-exists with other specific learning difficulties such as dyspraxia, Attention Deficit (Hyperactivity) Disorder (AD (H)D) and/or speech and language difficulties. Both Grant (2005) and Pollak (2005) have pointed to the considerable overlap between the different specific learning difficulties which Pollak refers to as aspects of neurodiversity.

As Drew (2005) points out, research into dyspraxia/developmental co-ordination disorder is comparatively new. Additionally, much of the research involves work with children rather than adults. There seems to be no consensus on which term to use – *dyspraxia* or *developmental co-ordination disorder*. For the purposes of this book, the older term, *dyspraxia*, is used for two reasons: firstly, many educationists are more familiar with this term and secondly, the co-ordination difficulties associated with the condition are, generally speaking, less apparent with students in HE than the educational difficulties and differences. It is useful to think of a specific learning difficulty as a continuum, with difficulties and differences ranging from severe to mild and considerable overlaps between the different conditions. In particular, many of the students presenting with dyslexia at university also have elements of dyspraxia.

There is a variety of definitions for dyspraxia. The DfES Working Party Guidelines definition of dyspraxia is useful for SDTs:

> A student with dyspraxia/DCD may have an impairment or immaturity in the organisation of movement, often appearing clumsy. Gross motor skills (related to balance and co-ordination) and fine motor skills (relating to manipulation of objects) are hard to learn and difficult to retain and generalise. Writing is particularly laborious and keyboard skills difficult to acquire. Individuals may have difficulty organising ideas and concepts. Pronunciation may also be affected and people with dyspraxia/DCD may be over-under sensitive to noise, light and touch. They may have poor awareness of body position and misread social cues in addition to those shared characteristics common to many SpLDs. (DfES Working Party Guidelines (2005)

Many of the challenges posed by dyspraxia are similar to those of dyslexia. However, the SDT should be aware that dyspraxic students might be somewhat disorganised and struggle with time keeping and managing workload. Some dyspraxic students will find note-taking and handwriting difficult, as well as organising their ideas in written form. Spelling and reading and other verbal skills on the other hand are often areas of strength. Dyspraxic students might find non-verbal reasoning tests such as matrices very difficult because of sequencing weaknesses and poor spatial awareness, which have nothing to do with intelligence. Others might need support with equipment in laboratories. Some students might initially have difficulty finding their way around the campus because of a poor sense of direction. Some students with dyspraxia have speech and/or language difficulties. They may talk continuously with an uncontrolled pitch, volume and rate of speech and repeat themselves. Some have difficulty organising the content and sequence of their speech.

Dyspraxic students might have poor self-esteem, possibly because of past experiences. The SDT needs to be sensitive to any signs of anxiety and stress. Drew (2005) points out that many dyspraxic students have had a poor educational experience prior to entry to university and that they need to arrive at an understanding of their own strengths and abilities in order to make the most of their time in HE. Careful questioning will be able to find this out.

The medical aspect of dyspraxia is outside the remit of the SDT. It is its impact upon the educational setting which is the main consideration of the SDT. Students at HE level might well have some co-ordination and other motor difficulties remaining but have generally been able to deal with these difficulties reasonably well. Whilst the SDT is not expected to carry out a full assessment for dyspraxia, it is useful to ask questions from an appropriate checklist so that the student can be referred on to an appropriate professional for full diagnostic assessment and identification.

Answers to dyspraxia checklists should be interpreted with caution because of the overlap with dyslexia. Some of the questions commonly asked, such as 'Do you find it difficult to telling left from right'? and 'Do you find it hard to remember and follow instructions?' could equally well indicate dyslexia. The SDT should carefully note positive responses to questions such as 'Are you extra sensitive to light and touch?' Answers from such checklists, together with the screening assessment results, will enable the SDT to make a judgement about whether there is an indication of dyspraxia and whether the student should be referred to an appropriate professional.

4.3 Attention Deficit (Hyperactivity) Disorder (AD(H)D)

Currently, AD(H)D and Asperger's Syndrome (AS), which are part of the autism spectrum, are mainly considered to be medical conditions rather than a behavioural learning difficulty. However, this was true of dyslexia at one time, so this way of looking at it might well change in the future. Much of the literature concerns the effects of AS and AD(H)D on children but it is now recognised that AS and AD(H)D can persist into adulthood although the presenting features might vary. It is rare that an adult is diagnosed with AD(H)D in adulthood, but when this does happen it is usually apparent that the symptoms have always been present, but not recognised in childhood. Many adults with either AS or AD(H)D will not make it into university but this is changing and such students can be as successful as any, if given the appropriate support. As is the case with other specific learning difficulties, each individual is unique with his or her own pattern of strengths and weaknesses.

> Attention Deficit Disorder (ADD) exists with or without hyperactivity. In most cases people with this disorder are often 'off task', have particular difficulty commencing and switching tasks, together with a very short attention span and high levels of distractibility. They may fail to make effective use of the feedback they receive and have weak listening skills. Those with hyperactivity may act impulsively and erratically, have difficulty foreseeing outcomes, fail to plan ahead and be noticeably restless and fidgety. Those without the hyperactive trait tend to daydream excessively, lose track of what they are doing and fail to engage in their studies unless they are highly motivated. The behaviour of people with ADD can be inappropriate and unpredictable; this, together with the characteristics common to many SpLDs, can present a further barrier to learning. (DfES, Working Party Guidelines, 2005)

It is generally agreed that people with AD(H)D have difficulties in three main areas: inattentiveness; hyperactivity; impulsivity. Characteristics may include:

- inability to keep focused on tasks or to complete tasks
- lack of organisation and planning
- distractibility
- moving from one unfinished activity to another
- losing property or forgetting equipment
- being restless and fidgety
- talking excessively
- doing several things at once
- excessive impulsivity – interrupting others, blurting out answers before questions have been completed
- difficulty awaiting turn in a group
- making inappropriate comments

Just as an SDT is not qualified to assess for dyspraxia, she is unable to screen for Attention Deficit (Hyperactivity) Disorder. It is not advisable to ask direct questions about AD(H)D, but if the SDT notices any typical signs during the interview, the student can later be referred to a suitably qualified professional if it seems appropriate. This is why some knowledge of AD(H)D is advisable.

4.4 Asperger's syndrome

Most students with Asperger's syndrome (AS) will be aware of the condition before the start of the course, but it is important for the SDT to have some knowledge of what it involves in case she is concerned that the student shows signs of AS.

AS is part of the autism spectrum. Students with AS can be very successful at university as they are very focused on their particular subject. However, they may find some aspects of study such as group work very difficult, as well as social interaction with other students. Students with AS might experience some of the following:

- inappropriate behaviour in social situations
- difficulty interacting with other people or picking up on social cues
- indifference to other people's feelings and lack of empathy

- need for compulsive routines

- non-verbal communication difficulties; limited facial expressions; difficulty maintaining eye contact; inability to understand gestures/ expressions

- ability to concentrate intensely on study but within a narrow, specific range and the tendency to talk at great length about a subject of interest

- good attention to detail

Below is a very simplified look at the different SpLDs. A more detailed examination of the differences and overlap between the different types of neurodiversity can be found in BrainHe. http://brainhe.com/ (See also Appendix 3: Overlapping features of SpLD)

Common, generic indicators experienced by all SpLDs	Autistic spectrum indicators	Dyslexia indicators	Dyspraxia indicators
Difficulty with personal organisation and/or organisation of ideas in written form Difficulty with multi-tasking Left/right confusion Short-term working memory difficulties	Difficulties with social communication Tendency towards obsessive behaviours	Weak spelling Slow reading rate Word retrieval difficulties	Poor muscle tone; difficulty with practical tasks and physical co-ordination; poor spatial awareness; sensitivity to noise/light/touch

Figure 1: Overlap between dyslexia/dyspraxia/Autistic spectrum indicators

4.5 English as an additional language (EAL)

It is often difficult when screening a student with EAL to decide whether her difficulties are due to imperfect English or to dyslexia. So at the screening stage it is important to establish during the interview whether any reported difficulties occur in the student's first language as well as in English. For example, questions can be asked about the reading process, memory, organisation of written work and confusion with numbers. Questions about the difference between English and the student's first language are often helpful. For example if a student is used to writing from right to left she might find

English quite difficult. Questions about the student's familiarity with written and spoken language and how long she has been learning English are relevant. Questions about the education system can also be helpful: some students will have been taught in a formal way and are used to rote learning rather than personal research might struggle initially with the English education system. Sunderland and Klein (1997) discuss in detail the types of questions that can be asked. (See Appendix 4: *Additional questions to ask students with EAL.*)

The SDT might need to be aware of any differences in the cultural attitude towards the concept of dyslexia or any learning difficulty, as it might be considered a stigma in some cultures. Some students might put off requesting a screening assessment even though advised to by their tutors, because of anxiety about their parents' opinions.

McLoughlin and Beard (2000) found that the DAST screening worked well with students with EAL, although they caution that there is a risk of a false positive result because of language difficulties particularly in verbal fluency and semantic fluency tests. They found that language did not affect many of the sub-tests, as long as instructions were explicit. For example, the student should be quite clear that the **Rapid Naming** test is testing the speed of response and not knowledge of English. This test can also be carried out in the student's first language if at all possible and the results compared.

5. Discussing the results with the student

Some students automatically assume that an 'at risk' result means that they are dyslexic. It might be necessary to explain to the student that a screening assessment is not as accurate as a full assessment and that it is not possible to tell for sure whether or not dyslexia is present. The SDT can explain what indicators of dyslexia are present and why a recommendation is made for a full assessment. The student then will be able to make an informed decision about further assessment.

6. Coloured overlay tests

It will sometimes be apparent from the initial screening interview that some students experience reading difficulties which might be caused by visual stress. This is sometimes referred to as visual perceptual difficulty or Meares-Irlen syndrome but it is best to avoid giving a student another label if possible. They might report that they frequently lose their place in the text, that they omit words or lines, or read lines more than once. They might dislike reading print on white or glossy paper and report frequent headaches or blurring of text. Students can be affected by glare from the page as well as being sensitive to the contrast between the black print and the white background. Reading in sunlight and under fluorescent lighting can cause print to become distorted or blurred. Letters sometimes appear to move or even disappear from the edge of the page. Questions might have indicated that they experience eye strain or excessive tiredness or even headaches when reading for a sustained period of time. Some students might report that they cannot concentrate for more than a short time when reading or working on a computer screen.

There seems to be a little confusion about the connection between a visual perceptual difficulty and dyslexia. Some people will experience difficulties with visual stress but have no other indicators of dyslexia or other specific learning difficulties. It is not, however, the remit of this book to enter into a discussion as to whether visual perceptual difficulty should be considered a disability in its own right and eligible for support from the Disabled Students' Allowances (DSA).

The use of coloured overlays and sometimes coloured lenses can aid the reading process for many students. Coloured overlays reduce some print distortions by changing the contrast on the page when reading, and this can lead to an improvement in reading speed, accuracy and comprehension.

A screening test can be carried out either at the initial screening assessment (depending on time available), during the full assessment if the student is not too fatigued, or as a stand alone assessment. Some Access Centres recommend that the student receive a screening overlay test, and some funding bodies are often willing to pay for this as part of the student's DSA.

6.1 Carrying out an overlay test

It might be that reading difficulties are caused by weak sight or other health conditions such as migraine. The student should be encouraged to have an eye test to rule out this possibility.

It is not enough simply to show the student a few different coloured overlays. The process needs to be more structured. It is a good idea to start by asking detailed questions about the reading process (unless this has already been established in the initial screening).

- Does reading make you tired or restless?
- Do you find it difficult to concentrate and remain focused on the text?
- How long can you read before you have to take a break?

- Do you feel tired or drowsy when reading?

- Do you have difficulty remembering or understanding the text?

- Does reading give you headaches?

- Do you dislike reading under fluorescent lighting?

- Is it more difficult to read pages which are very white or glossy?

- Is it easier to read text on a coloured background?

- Do words blur or move around on the page?

- Do you skip lines or sentences and lose your place?

- Do you misread words?

- Do you dislike reading aloud?

The student can then be presented with a short piece of text with the different overlays to establish whether one particular colour or combination of colours eases the reading process. The overlay testing kits produced by ioo (www. ioo sales.co.uk) or by Cerium (www.ceriumvistech.co.uk) suggest a careful order to avoid different shades of one colour following each other. The Wilkins' Rate of Reading Test (Wilkins, 1996) can be carried out to test the effectiveness of the chosen overlay on the reading process. This consists of four sheets of individual simple words which are read for one minute with and without an overlay. One of the authors of this book experimented with a non-standardised test using more adult words than the Wilkins' test, but this did not prove to have any advantage. Using the simple words of the test, the student does not need to concern herself with decoding. If appropriate this can be followed by a short reading test using the overlay of choice or simply presenting the student with an academic text which she can read with and without the overlay. Sometimes the student will find that two colours are equally comfortable. However, if the student completes the Wilkins' Rate of Reading Test (or other reading test) with each overlay, it is often apparent that one of the colours makes reading easier.

It is a good idea to end the session by talking about changing the background colour on a computer screen and using coloured paper for printing. University student union shops usually sell coloured paper nearly as cheaply as white. Not many university departments as yet will accept essays printed on coloured paper, but perhaps in the future this will be more acceptable.

In conclusion ...

This chapter has discussed the importance of the initial screening assessment as the first stage in what could be a lengthy process to a full diagnostic
assessment. It has proposed a model of an interview based on questions
related to study, followed by a short screening assessment. The interview provides the SDT with information about the student's perception of her difficulties; the screening assessment is the first stage in gathering evidence and
finding out the nature and reason for these difficulties which is useful in
supplementing the information gained from the interview. Responses from
the interview together with the results of the assessment will determine
whether or not the student should be offered a full assessment. The SDT will
need to look at various factors including the possibility of other SpLDs and
also need to take into account that having English as an additional language
might influence the student's performance on screening assessments.

Further reading

Colley, M (2000) *Living with Dyspraxia*. Chippenham: Dyspraxia Foundation Adult Support Group

Harpur, J, Lawlor, M and Fitzgerald, M, (2004) *Succeeding in College with Asperger Syndrome*. London and New York: Jessica Kingsley Publishing

McLoughlin, D, Fitzgibbon, G, and Young, V, (1994) *Adult Dyslexia: Assessment, Counselling and Training*. London: Whurr Publishers

Reid, G and Kirk, J (2001) *Dyslexia in Adults, Education and Employment*. West Sussex: John Wiley and Sons

Singleton, C (1999) *Dyslexia in H.E: policy, provision and practice*, Report of the National Working Party, University of Hull

Wilkins, A J (2003) *Reading through Colour*. Wiley: Chichester

Useful websites

Examples of dyslexia adult screening questionnaires can be found at:

www.bdadyslexia.org.uk/adultchecklist.html

www.futurenet.co.uk/charity/ado/adomenu-

An example of a dyspraxia checklist can be found at:
www.dyspraxiafoundation.org.uk/services/ad_symptoms

Appendix 1: A Screening Interview Proforma

General Background / History
- Do you have any health conditions which might affect your studies? (vision/hearing/speech therapy)
- Does anyone else in your family have an SpLD?
- When you were at school, did you have any difficulty plotting graphs/drawing shapes or using a compass or protractor?
- When you were at school, did you experience any difficulty with coordination or sport? For example, catching a ball?
- Do you play a musical instrument? How easy was this to learn? Do you have any difficulty reading music?
- Have you ever had difficulty telling left from right?
- Do you struggle with map-reading or finding your way to an unfamiliar place?
- Do you ever mix up dates and times and turn up at the wrong time for appointments?
- Do you have any difficulty filling out forms?

Education
- Did you miss any schooling?
- Did you receive special examination arrangements/support at school/college?
- Did you have any difficulties with study at school? Did you have difficulties learning to read/write/spell?
- What type of examinations did you take? What grades were achieved?

Reading
- Do you take a long time to read a page from an academic text-book?
- Do you have to read a page more than once in order to understand it?
- Do you accidentally skip lines or sentences and lose your place?
- Do you read for pleasure?
- Do you dislike reading white or glossy pages? Do the words get blurry or move? Do you get headaches when reading?
- Do you dislike reading aloud?

Note-taking
- Do you have difficulties keeping up with notes in lectures?
- Do you tend to write down everything the lecturer says?
- Can you make sense of your notes after the lecture?
- Do you find it difficult to make your own notes from research reading?

Spelling
- Do you think your spelling is poor? Can you give examples? Are there some words that you find particularly difficult? Is there any pattern?

Writing

- Do you think your handwriting is difficult to read?
- Do you find it difficult to plan essays well?
- Do you have difficulty getting your ideas into a good order when writing assignments or essays?
- What is your usual procedure for approaching written assignments?
- Does writing essays or reports take a long time to complete? On your current course? In previous courses?
- Do you have problems with grammar/sentence structure/punctuation?
- How do your coursework marks compare with exam marks?
- Do you run out of time in exams? On your current course? On previous courses?

Language/Listening

- Is English your first language?
- Do you sometimes have difficulty finding the right word?
- When you have to say a long word, do you sometimes find it difficult to get all the sounds in the right order? (e.g. preliminary, anemone, phenomenon, specificity etc)
- Where do you study best? Are you easily distracted when studying in the library?
- Does background noise in lectures affect your concentration?

Sequencing/Memory

- Do you find it difficult looking up information in the library? (If yes, do you know why?)
- Do you find it difficult to do calculations in your head?
- When you were at school, did you have any difficulty learning multiplication tables?
- Do you have any difficulty with common sequences such as months of the year or the alphabet?
- Do you mix up numbers, particularly when copying them down?
- Do you find it difficult to remember telephone messages?
- Do you find it difficult to learn information for exams?
- What techniques do you use for revision?

Appendix 2: Screening Assessment Record Sheet

Student Name: Course:

Assessor: Date:

Previously assessed: Yes/No   Previous report: Yes/No

Reason for screening assessment:

DAST ARQ:

Rapid naming	One Minute Reading
Phonemic segment	Two minute spelling
Backwards span	Nonsense passage
Non verbal reasoning	One minute writing
Verbal fluency	Semantic fluency

Dyslexia indicators

Dyspraxia indicators (from checklist)

Main difficulties:

Full assessment recommended yes/no

Reasons

Appendix 3: overlapping features of SpLDs

Overlapping features of AD(H)D and Asperger's Syndrome

- Inappropriate social skills (more pronounced with Asperger's syndrome)
- Impulsive behaviour or speaking impulsively, interrupting others or speaking out of turn (more pronounced with Asperger's syndrome)
- Difficulty with following rules
- Being very impatient and easily frustrated
- Being emotionally sensitive
- Can find personal relationships quite difficult

Overlapping presenting features of dyslexia/dyspraxia and ADD

- Poor personal organisation
- Weak organisation and time management when studying
- Poor note taking and writing skills
- Poor concentration; easily distracted or tends to daydream
- Difficulty with reading comprehension
- Difficulty with expressing thoughts in speech or in writing
- Feelings of frustration and poor self-esteem

Overlapping features of dyspraxia and ADD

- Losing or misplacing objects
- Poor organisation skills
- Difficulty in estimating how much time is needed to complete a task

Appendix 4: Additional questions to ask students for whom English Is an additional language

Education

- How long have you been learning English? Did you learn English at home or at school? Did you learn to speak English before you learnt to read and write?

- Do you consider that your oral English is of a higher standard than your written English?

- What teaching methods were used?

- Did you have difficulties learning to read/write/spell in your first language?

- Were the problems experienced when learning English similar or different?

- Did you receive special examination arrangements/support at school/college?

- What was your experience of school compared with your experience on the present course? (*Looking for whether much of education was rote learning; whether she was expected to answer questions/give opinions etc*)

- What type of assessments/examinations did you take? (*Looking for whether they were formal exams/coursework/multiple choice/essays/short answers*)

- How different is the assessment method on your previous course?

- Is English your principle medium of spoken or written English now?

Reading

- Do you take a long time to read a page of text in your first language?

- Does it take you a long time to read in English? Same? Longer? (Is the alphabet the same? Does this affect your understanding of English?)

- Do you have to read some pages more than once for full understanding? Does this happen when reading in your first language too or only when reading English text?

- Do you accidentally skip lines or sentences in your first language? In English?

- Do you find it difficult to remember the sense of what you have read?

- What type of reading tasks were you expected to undertake in your first language?

Note-taking

- Do you have difficulties keeping up with notes in lectures?

- Did you have to take notes/dictation in your first language? What difficulties did you have?

- Do you tend to write down everything the lecturer says?

- Can you make sense of your notes after the lecture? Does this happen with your first language? With English?

- Do you find it difficult to make your own notes from research reading? Does this happen when reading in your first language?

Spelling
- Do you think your spelling in English is poor? In your first language?
- (How would you describe your spelling?)

Writing
- Do you think your handwriting is difficult to read? Is English script different from that of your first language? (Are there are any letters not recognised in first language? Different symbols? Left to right?) Is it more difficult to write neatly in English?
- Do you find it difficult to plan essays well? Did you write many essays in your first language?
- Is there a difference when writing for your current course and when writing in your first language?
- What is your usual procedure for approaching written assignments?
- Do you have difficulty getting your ideas into good order when writing assignments or essays? In your first language? On your current course?
- Does writing essays or reports take a long time to complete? On your current course? On previous courses?
- Do you have problems with grammar/sentence structure/punctuation? Does this happen when writing with English or writing in your first language? (Is there any difference between punctuation/grammar structures of English and your first language?)
- How do your coursework marks compare with exam marks? How does this compare with previous experience in your first language?
- Do you run out of time in exams? On your current course? On previous courses?

Language and Listening

Ask the same questions for both languages.

- Do you sometimes have difficulty finding the right word?
- When you have to say a long word, do you sometimes find it difficult to get all the sounds in the right order? (e.g. preliminary, anemone, phenomenon, specificity etc)
- Where do you study best?
- Are you easily distracted when studying in the library?
- Does background noise in lectures affect your concentration?

Sequencing and Memory
- Do you find it difficult to learn information for exams? Is there a difference between the methods you adopt for your present course and the methods you used in your first language at school or other course ?
- What techniques do you use for revision? Is it easier to learn information in your first language?

5

Elements of assessment

Assessment which leads to an identification is a complex process. This chapter provides an overview of assessment. It looks at the purposes of assessment, different types of assessment and psychometrics. The knotty problem of intelligence is explored.

Using this chapter

This chapter will enable you to:

1. Understand the purposes of assessment

    1.1 Assessment Cycle

2. Understand assessment approaches

3. Understand the term 'differential diagnosis'

4. Examine why is measurement helpful

5. Understand the features of psychometric assessment

6. Explore the issues relating to defining intelligence

7. Explore the value of IQ tests: uneven cognitive profile

8. Consider how tests are standardised

    8.1 How to evaluate standardised tests?

9. Be aware of the different types of tests

    9.1 Standardised or Norm-referenced tests

    9.2 Criterion-referenced tests

    9.3 Informal/diagnostic tests and assessment

1. Why assess? The purposes of assessment

Assessment is a process, not a one-off event in the student's life. There are those who oppose assessment, seeing it as a negative experience. Yet in the hands of an experienced and sensitive professional, the assessment process can be positive and even life-enhancing for the student. It has a dual purpose: a means of empowering the student; and a vehicle for deciding upon teaching provision. It is also a means to provide additional funding in the form of the Disabled Students' Allowance (DSA). For both student and assessor, the assessment process will lead to:

- clarity and an overview of the current levels of attainment and performance

- identification and understanding of strengths and weaknesses – providing an individual profile

- information for teaching and learning, to ensure that intervention and support are not haphazard or random.

1.1 Assessment Cycle

Identification of a specific learning difficulty is but one aspect of the assessment process for the educational assessor. Thus, for the SDT, assessment is a cyclical process because it is on-going and integrated with teaching support,

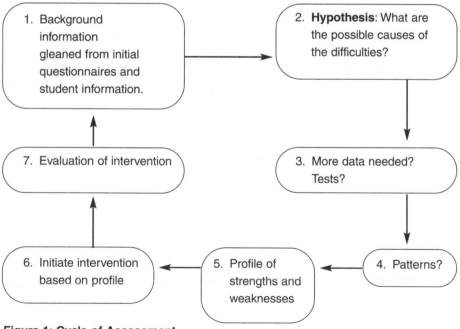

Figure 1: Cycle of Assessment

identification (or otherwise) being but one feature of this holistic experience. The adoption of an hypothesis-testing approach to gathering information ensures that the assessor is able to keep an open mind and, hopefully, does not make assumptions about background information and test data. For the experienced professional, assessment does not constitute a checklist of tests which are used in a rigid sequence. Rather it is a dynamic process. It is akin to being a juggler, keeping many ideas in the air at the same time. The experienced assessor looks for patterns in performance which would enable her to make an *accurate* diagnosis and identification. As information emerges the profile and hypotheses change. The SDT has to make informed spontaneous decisions about which tools to use to find out reasons for particular performances and to gather as much relevant information as possible to inform her identification (see Figure 1).

Let us examine a worked example of this process with a hypothetical student.

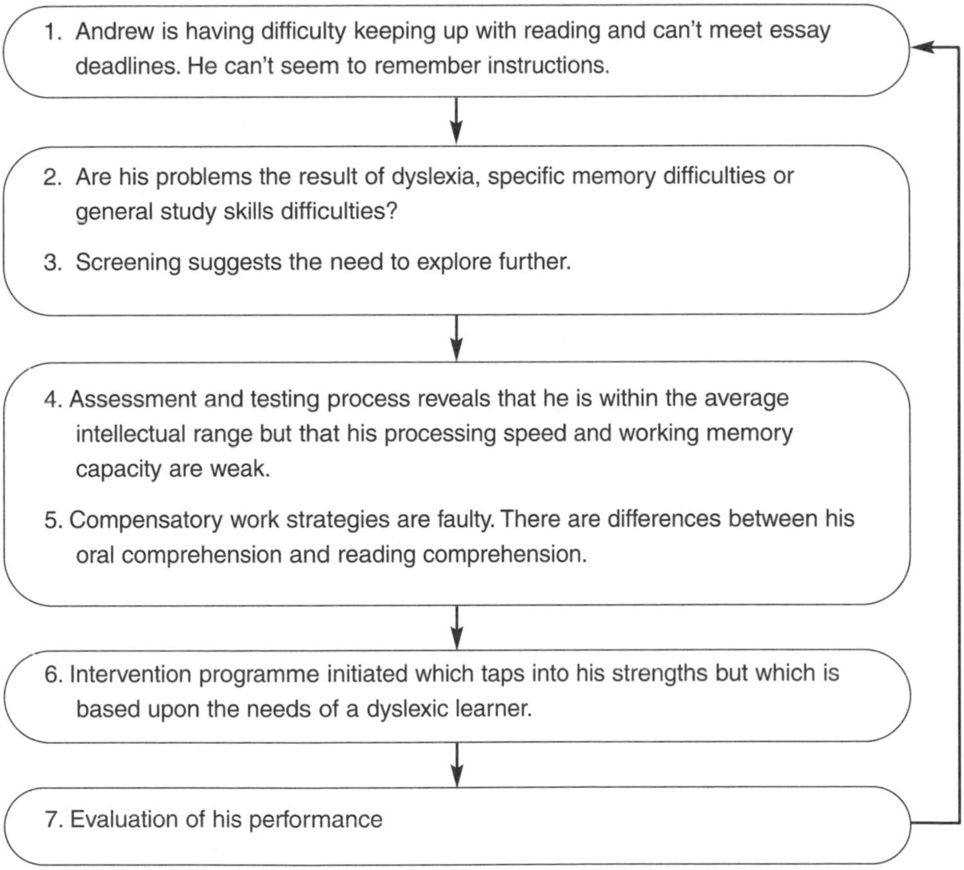

1. Andrew is having difficulty keeping up with reading and can't meet essay deadlines. He can't seem to remember instructions.

2. Are his problems the result of dyslexia, specific memory difficulties or general study skills difficulties?

3. Screening suggests the need to explore further.

4. Assessment and testing process reveals that he is within the average intellectual range but that his processing speed and working memory capacity are weak.

5. Compensatory work strategies are faulty. There are differences between his oral comprehension and reading comprehension.

6. Intervention programme initiated which taps into his strengths but which is based upon the needs of a dyslexic learner.

7. Evaluation of his performance

Figure 2: Hypothetical Student

The assessment process is made up of layers of information – how many will depend upon the complexity of the identification. After the initial screening and individual questionnaire interview, it may be necessary to proceed to a full diagnostic assessment, which will be divided into two strands: the attainment performance and the cognitive performance. If there are still unanswered questions, the SDT will need to explore some of the aspects of performance in more detail.

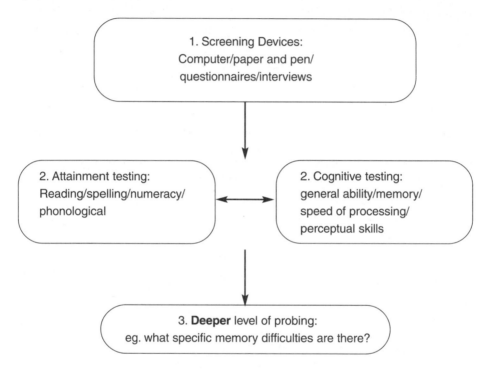

Figure 3: Layers of the assessment process

2. Assessment approaches

It is crucial that the SDT is clear about the stance she is taking when assessing and testing a student. This will drive the types of questions and the specific tests she will use. In fact, it will determine the way she goes about the whole process. There are two over-riding approaches which are often adopted: Cognitive and Behavioural.

The cognitive approach takes a 'with-in' student view. Hence the questions might pertain to finding out what the cognitive strengths and weaknesses of the individual are. Feedback and reporting will contain recommendations relating to teaching methods which are based upon the individual's cognitive profile. This type of approach will place emphasis upon the student's visual and auditory cognitive skills, speed of processing and working memory capacity, for example. It will relate this profile to the learning environment.

A behaviourist approach suggests that any difficulties the individual experiences are the result of external forces within the environment. This relates to a social inclusion model. Reporting will demonstrate the problems within the environment, and what needs to be changed to enable the individual to function adequately.

Within the wider umbrella, there are a number of methods of assessment which can be adopted:

- Cognitive -
  - values measurement of performance and adopts psychometric tools
  - interested in how the brain operates when carrying out different (academic) activities – processing speed and memory in particular
  - explores deficits in relation to the general population.
- Metacognitive
  - takes into account the individual's cognitive and learning styles
  - examines the strategies the individual uses to carry out activities
  - focuses upon processes.
- Diagnostic
  - adopts an analytical approach to performance.
- Behavioural
  - explores the behaviours and feelings of the individual in relation to performance.
- Dynamic
  - interested in the relationship between instruction, feedback and the individual's performance
  - adopts a socio-cognitive approach reflecting Vygotsky's Zone of Proximal Development (ZPD) which explores the individual's potential for performance with assistance from an expert.

Debates often revolve around the efficacy of using standardised tests and measurement of the individual versus the more affective methods which rely upon a subjective approach whereby the student's learning styles and feelings drive decisions about identification. Such dichotomous discussion can be damaging and fruitless. An holistic, eclectic approach which combines all of the above will reflect the principles of adult education, encompassing a developmental continuum of performance.

3. Differential diagnosis – is this student dyslexic or not?

Making a decision about whether an individual is dyslexic or not relates to the current theories about dyslexia: they provide the back-drop to the criteria used by SDTs during assessment. This results in the need to find evidence of specific aspects of an individual's functioning and performance. As we saw in Chapter 1, under *Definitions and Research*, there is a growing synergy of knowledge which informs assessment practice. Using Frith's causal framework (1985, 1999), the SDT can explore cognitive and attainment performance. Thus she will draw upon tests and activities which will provide an individual profile to inform her decision. Delving deeper and deeper (layers of assessment) requires knowledge of what information a test will give you – will it answer your questions? Patterns of behaviours will emerge as a profile – does this match with simple checklists and theory?

The crux of this complex process **is differential diagnosis**. This means that an individual's performance is constantly compared within the confines of an assessment framework and structure. Thus the SDT will examine both test scores and informal assessment activities, looking for differences. For example, a student who demonstrates comprehension ability yet scores poorly under timed conditions would have differentials in performance which would have to be explained in some way. This will result in further questions (hypotheses) which might result in finding out the student's speed of processing information and working memory capacity (see Figure 1: Cycle of Assessment).

An understanding of the strengths and weaknesses of the test tools, together with a knowledge of psychometric measurement and its role in identification are essential to accurate conclusion. If someone gets a reading score of 6/20, is this good compared with others of the same age? Is this what would be expected of this individual, given other performance factors?

4. Why is measurement helpful?

One of the most obvious things about people is that we are all different. Not just in terms of height, colour of eyes and hair but also in terms of strengths and weaknesses, our abilities and the way we behave. Our uniqueness is an essential quality which is celebrated. It would be very boring if we were all the same. However, as human beings we do have things in common. So there are similarities and differences between people. Psychological testing was developed to gain an understanding of the person and how she differs from others. The study of individual differences underpins the principles adhered to in this book. Thus testing is concerned with measuring the difference **between** individuals or **within** the same individual.

This begs the question of what we should measure. Statistical measurement is concerned with the probable significance of correlations between variables and can help the assessor to recognise patterns of performance. Statistical significance, described as 'P', provides information about the probability of something occurring in the population. Thus, 1 in a 1000 displaying a specific characteristic or score would be written as $P < 0.001$. 1 in 100 is $P < 0.01$, and 1 in 10 $P < 0.1$. The DfES guidelines (2005) rightly state that the effect of an SpLD can be 'evaluated more effectively' when underlying ability is considered. However, this is but one aspect of differential diagnosis: using knowledge of underlying ability can help the SDT assess whether performance in other areas, such as attainment, is unexpected or part of a dyslexic profile.

5. Psychometric measurement

....dyslexia is a contrast ...it is identified not by a measure but by the distance between 2 measures. IQ and achievement merely provide the most obvious of these contrasts ... We will undoubtedly wish to move beyond this most obvious contrast, but we will not wish to move back from it. ... Dyslexia is still a contrast, a distance between two measures, and we refine our techniques in the light of this unvarying principle. (Turner, 1997:246)

Turner's notion of the contrasts within dyslexia sit well with eliciting information about an individual's underlying ability. Psychometric measurement is the measurement of the individual's cognitive profile and usually involves finding out a person's intelligence. It is a statistical application and is based upon probabilities of occurrence in a population.

The normal distribution curve describes how ability is distributed within a population. The Bell Curve is most frequently used to demonstrate this distribution, whereby the majority of the population will perform in a similar way in response to IQ tasks, for example. Tests are standardised on a specified population, hence the lower and upper age limits.

What you will notice is that the Bell Curve representation of distribution shows that 50% of the population fall on either side of the mean in the centre.

The Bell Curve is symmetrical and the mean can be seen at '0', right in the centre. Deviations from the mean on the left are negative figures and deviations from the right of the mean are represented as positive figures.

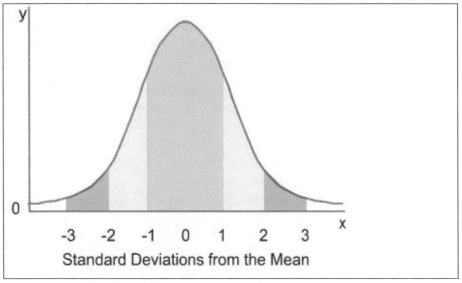

Image accessed from: www.duncanwil.co.uk/norm.html March, 2007

68.26% of the population will fall within one standard deviation (SD) of the mean (+/-1SD); 95.44% will fall within two standard deviations of the mean (+-2SD) and 99.74% will fall within three standard deviations of the mean (+/-3SD).

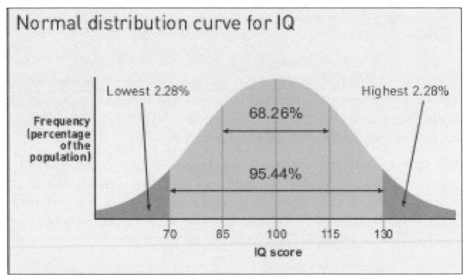

Figure 4: The Bell Curve

Image accessed from: www.makingthemodernworld.org.uk/.../?section=3 March, 2007

6. What is intelligence?

Professionals in this field need to have a firm understanding of what they mean by intelligence; how it is defined; and an awareness of the debates which surround this subject. Some of the current debates which the SDT needs to feel secure about are:

- Is there a single, general intelligence which controls action and thought?

- Is it more appropriate to consider multiple intelligences within an individual?

- Is intelligence inherited?

- Is intelligence gender-specific?

- Is it possible to measure intelligence?

- What does neuro-psychology have to offer in terms of understanding cognitive functioning?

There are many opposing theories. The notion of a single, general intelligence was developed at the turn of the last century with Spearman's (1973) description of the 'g' factor or general ability. Cattell's model of intelligence (cited

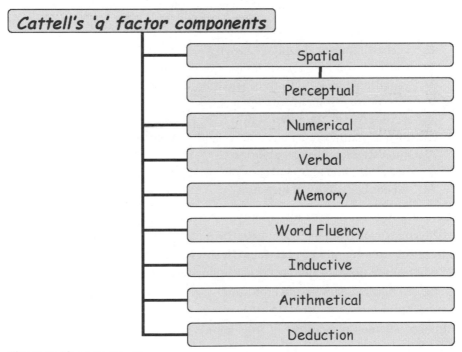

Figure 5: IQ components

75

in Eysenck, 1982) contained many of the aspects of performance which can still be seen today in the test activities contained in psychometric tests and clearly embodies a definition of intelligence which has lasted for many years.

Proponents of this model of intelligence posit that intelligence is something which can be measured and that Cattell's components can be divided into two types of intelligence: crystallised and fluid. Crystallised intelligence is that which can be developed throughout life and can be reliant upon ex-posure to an educational system which extends specific knowledge and skills and individual experiences. Fluid intelligence, on the other hand, is often highly dependent upon such cognitive features as memory capacity and speed of processing and deteriorates with age.

> Intelligence is a very general mental capability that, among other things, involves the ability to reason, plan, solve problems, think abstractly, comprehend complex ideas, learn quickly and learn from experience. It is not merely book learning, a narrow academic skill, or test-taking. Rather, it reflects a broader and deeper capa-bility for comprehending our surroundings – 'catching on, ' making sense' or 'figuring out' what to do next. (Deary, 2001:17)

Gardner (1993) put forward a controversial view of intelligence, suggesting the possibility of people having not one but multiple intelligences. Since the inception of this theory, the number of intelligences has grown from seven to nine.

- verbal/linguistic: language based
- musical: ability to recognise tone and rhythm
- visual/spatial: visualisation and mental imagery
- interpersonal: social intelligence
- intrapersonal: the inner self
- logical/mathematical: inductive and deductive reasoning
- kinaesthetic: physical abilities
- naturalist: awareness of the environment
- existential: ability to question

There are many critics of this theory. Sternberg (1985) declares that it is a 'psychometric nightmare'. Others have suggested that Gardner's 'intelli-gences' are merely abilities and skills (Hernstein and Murray, 1994; Coffield *et al*, 2004). Often the arguments of those opposing psychometric measurement are flawed because they use an emotional response to IQ *testing* as a reasoned argument for the abolition of IQ measurement. It is common to see muddled thinking between definitions of intelligence and problems associated with testing tools. It is useful for the SDT to have thought through her own definition of intelligence, as SDTs may have to defend the use of IQ tools so need to be quite clear about what intelligence consists of so they can critically evaluate testing tools.

Haywood (2004) presents a 'transactional perspective' of abilities which could be considered to be the catalyst which may bring together these opposing views of intelligence. He suggests that intelligence is 'multi-faceted' (p.233) and brings together three main components: cognitive processes, meta-cognition and motivation. He suggests that these aspects interact to produce 'intelligent' action and thought. His interpretation may be useful for SDTs.

7. The value of IQ tests: uneven cognitive profile
IQ tests also fuel debate. However, the experienced and knowledgeable SDT should be able to consider the strengths as well as be aware of the weaknesses of these particular tests. The IQ test can be useful because it provides a general picture of the student's cognitive abilities, which in the case of a dyslexic student is often an uneven profile. It provides a baseline against which other tests and performance can be measured to explore differentials. Many assessors prefer not to quote a general ability score in their reports because the unevenness of the profile might well give a misleading impression about the student's ability. The IQ test also highlights strengths as well as weaknesses. It will show a differential between performance on tasks that rely heavily on working memory and performance on tasks which do not (McLoughlin *et al*, 1994). The dyslexic profile often shows high scores on verbal reasoning but poor scores on short-term memory and visuo-motor tasks (Reid and Kirk, 2001).

IQ results should, however, always be treated with extreme caution. Some adults will have difficulty with some of the items in IQ tests because of their dyslexic difficulties and a general IQ result might well be an under-representation of their abilities. Reid and Kirk (2001) point out that some adults might perform badly on a particular sub-test not because they lack understanding 'but because they have a difficulty in dealing with symbolic material at speed, fail to remember instructions or have difficulty recalling facts from long-term memory' (Reid and Kirk 2001:28).

There is no single test for SpLD. SDTs have to bear in mind that the test materials they choose have not been designed specifically to identify whether SpLD is present. Choice of test materials is of paramount importance and relies upon the ability of the SDT to evaluate tests effectively.

8. How are tests standardised?

They are constructed so that the scores produced fall within the normal distribution curve for the population, giving normative, standardised scores.

Test questions or activities are tried out on a given population. The pool of questions has to be fairly large to ensure that the results have a normal distribution curve. This is why questions start off easy and develop in difficulty; only the top 2.28% of the population would be expected to answer the final questions correctly. To get this right, the questions have to be tried out on sizeable numbers, and population samples are used. If a test designer only tried out the questions on a small number of participants they might not be considered representative of the normal distribution. This is a lengthy and costly process but necessary to ensure the robustness of the outcomes of the test.

Differential diagnosis, to identify whether or not an SpLD is present, relies substantially upon the evidence used by professionals. So it is vital that test materials are chosen because they provide statistically robust information. In order that the SDT can evaluate tests the following need to be taken into consideration: how reliable and how valid is the test? These are crucial elements in decisions about which tests to use.

8.1 How to evaluate standardised tests?

The SDT needs to take into account many aspects of a test to evaluate a) the quality of the test and b) its suitability for purpose. These are crucial elements in decisions about which tests to use during the assessment process. They will also influence the credibility of the test scores and ultimately affect decisions about identification. Robust tests should be statistically reliable and valid.

Reliability is the ability of a test to give nearly the same result each time a person takes the test or an alternate form of the same test

Validity: does the test measure what it is designed to measure?

SDTs are advised to look closely at the test manual and to find out about how the test was developed. It is necessary to think about the following questions:

- What age group was used to standardise the scores of the tool?
- Are there any flaws or gaps in the type of population used for developing the tool? For example, there are some criticisms of the Wide Range Intelligence Tests (WRIT) because it was not tried on an Hispanic population in the USA and therefore does not reliably represent that country's population.

▨ If the tool has been tried out on a large population (over 1000) in the development and design, it is more likely to give the same scores each time it is used because any gliches will have been eliminated.

When examining the various sub-tests the SDT needs to consider the following factors which can affect the accuracy of tests:

▨ How was the test designed and constructed? (look at the spread of questions/tasks/activities for spread of difficulty)

▨ Population of standardisation – size, constituency eg. ethnic groups etc

▨ Date of design – have there been any up-to-date revisions? Language changes over time and the language tested can become dated in some verbal reasoning tests. This can affect scores.

▨ Correlation with other tests: this is an important factor when conducting a differential diagnosis because the assessor is constantly weighing up performance in different activities. If the tests have been similarly standardised then it is possible to be more accurate when relating scores from different tests.

▨ Test/re-test facility: this is an important feature if the test is intended to be used as a 'before' and 'after' comparison of performance. Using the same test questions may produce skewed scores because the testee has remembered the test and may provide a false score.

▨ Is the content of the activity/activities relevant to the age group?

▨ Do the activities measure what they say? For example, if any activity's purpose is to measure non-verbal reasoning, and the instructions have to be read by the testee, then it could be said that the results are not a true reflection of non-verbal reasoning alone but also rely upon the testee's reading comprehension skills.

▨ Could the results of the activities give too many false negatives and false positives (Reference to causal theory)?

Many inexperienced SDTs evaluate new tests using inappropriate criteria for judging the test: they simply look at whether the test is easy for them to use. This is not a sound method for selecting a test.

9. Types of tests

What is a test? Cronbach (1990) defined a test as a systematic procedure for observing behaviour and describing it with the aid of numerical scales or fixed categories, while Anastasi (1982) hinted at the advantage of objectivity in certain types of tests.

Various tests are available: standardised or norm-referenced tests; criterion-referenced; informal/diagnostic; ipsative (which literally means 'within self' and compares performance with own earlier performance. This can be applied to standardised tests and is useful for reflecting upon a teaching strategy). It is useful for the SDT to be aware of what tests are available, but the reality is that when assessing adults within the DfES guidelines (2005) the choice will be mainly from standardised tests.

9.1 Standardised or norm-referenced tests

These include tests of ability, achievement and personality. They are constructed to produce a normal distribution curve and to give normative, standardised scores. Such tests allow for comparison with other adults in the same population. It is essential that the SDT reads the manual carefully and administers the tests in strict accordance with the instructions. This ensures that the test is carried out in the same way by each assessor and so results will be consistent. It is important to use the most up to date version of a test to ensure that current norms are used. Some tests have ceilings which make them unsuitable for use with some of the older students, although sometimes they can be used diagnostically, without quoting a standardised score. Most tests provide percentiles as well as standard scores. See the next chapter for an explanation of this. Most of the tests from the DfES guidelines fall in this category.

9.2 Criterion-referenced tests

Criterion-referenced tests are frequently used by subject departments to assess knowledge and understanding of the curriculum. These tests are based on narrow, curriculum-related learning objectives and focus on quality of performance in specific, defined tasks. Therefore they are not used by SDTs. However, the results of these tests may provide further insight into performance related to the underlying skills required for the curriculum. This information may be useful when considering the most appropriate support for a student.

9.3 Informal/diagnostic tests and assessment

These tests or assessments, such as miscue analysis, are part of the repertoire of the SDT and can provide a systematic observation of individual behaviours. They enable the assessor to generate hypotheses about strategies and the strengths and weaknesses of the testee. They can be used by expert assessors in conjunction with standardised tests to provide an in-depth picture of the individual. For example, when a single word reading test or a reading comprehension test is administered, a standardised score is also obtained. Miscue analysis of the decoding and comprehension skills and strategies will give a fuller picture of the functional literacy of the student. Critics of this approach have suggested that informal and diagnostic data cannot be measured and are subject to interpretation by individual assessors – hence they lose objectivity in the eyes of some. Nevertheless, this type of information might be used to provide evidence for support internally within institutions rather than providing a full diagnostic assessment which can also be used for funding purposes.

In conclusion...

This chapter has provided an overview of the assessment process. It has explored many of the issues which the SDT should consider when undertaking a full diagnostic assessment. In making a decision about the nature of the student's difficulties, it is vital that the SDT is aware of the strengths and short-comings of the various tools so that appropriate tests are chosen to elicit information to provide as true a picture of the testee as possible. The chapter has, therefore, given consideration to the many underlying questions which are an essential part of the evaluation process.

Further reading

Elliott, J (2003) Dynamic Assessment in Educational Settings: realising potential. *Educational Review,* 55(1), 15-32

Feuerstein, R, Feuerstein, R S, Fakik, L and Rand, Y (2002) *The Dynamic Assessment of Cognitive Modifiability.* Jerusalem: The ICELP Press

Thomson, M (2002) *The Psychology of Dyslexia.* London: Whurr Publishers

Turner, M (1997) *Psychological Assessment of Dyslexia.* London: Whurr Publishers

6

The assessment process

This chapter looks at the different aspects of assessment which the SDT will need to consider in a full diagnostic assessment. It provides a guide to interpreting the DfES guidelines.

Using this chapter
This chapter will enable you to:

4. Cognitive processing tests: phonological processing; speed of processing; perceptual difficulties

    4.1 Symbol digit modalities test

    4.2 Comprehensive Test of Phonological Processing

    4.3 Perin Spoonerism Task

    4.4 Tests for perceptual difficulties

    4.5 Developmental Test of Visual Perception

    4.6 Test of Auditory Processing Difficulties

    4.7 Test of Visual Perceptual Skills 3

5. Cognitive processing tests: memory

    5.1 Digit Memory Test

    5.2 Wide Range Assessment of Memory and Learning

    5.3 Issues to consider when interpreting cognitive processing tests

6. Underlying ability: the Wide Range Intelligence Test

    6.1 Issues to consider when interpreting ability test results

B   Consider the different elements of assessment when making a final decision about whether a student is dyslexic or has another SpLD.

7   Interpreting the results of the assessment tests

    7.1 Compensated dyslexic students

    7.2 Persisting difficulty

    7.3 History of difficulty with acquisition of literacy skills

    7.4 Exclusion of other factors

    7.5 Student with English as an additional language

    7.6 Co-existence of more than one specific learning difficulty

    7.7 Dyscalculia

    7.8 Consideration of secondary characteristics

C   Provide feedback to the student

Many students are assessed for the first time in HE. This could be because of the increasingly rigorous demands of academic study. Singleton (1999) refers to the 'special demands' that HE places on the learner: the greater depth and breadth of study; the increased volume of work, particularly reading; the increased technical and conceptual difficulty of the material; the switch to independent learning and self-reliance in the organisation of study (Singleton, 1999).

It is important to build up a rapport with the student before commencing any assessment or test results will be unreliable (Thomson, 2002). This is particularly true when assessing adults who might be feeling very vulnerable and lack confidence in themselves and their abilities.

1. Assessment framework

The DfES Working Party Guidelines (2005) identify what the SDT should be looking for in an assessment, suggest which tests to use and propose a proforma for the assessment report. Most assessments at HE will be carried out not only to establish the presence of dyslexia and set up appropriate teaching support but also to provide evidence for funding bodies to enable the student to apply for the Disabled Students' Allowance (DSA). It is important therefore for all SDTs to follow the DfES guidelines closely to ensure that they gather appropriate evidence of dyslexia. These guidelines have been drawn up by professionals in the field, so the principles and suggested tests are sound and provide an essential aid for the SDT rather than limiting their choice.

The DfES Working Party Guidelines (2005) suggest the following diagnostic criteria as a basis for the diagnosis of dyslexia:

- A history of difficulty with the acquisition of literacy skills
- Persisting difficulty
- Evidence of an underlying cognitive deficit (e.g. slow phonological processing speed; weak phonological awareness; weak visual and auditory working memory; visual perceptual difficulties; motor difficulties).
- Underlying ability/achievement differentials
- Exclusion of other factors (e.g. English as an additional language; poor educational experience).

1.1 Carrying out a full assessment

The full assessment is often carried out after a screening assessment has established the possibility of dyslexia. As Chapter Four has shown, the screening assessment is a valuable tool, giving the assessor the opportunity to build up an initial picture. The SDT should ideally have access to the results of the screening assessment. In a full diagnostic assessment, there might not be the time to maintain a sustained dialogue with the student. It can take up to three hours (or more) to carry out all the relevant tests, which can be quite tiring for both student and SDT. However, if it has not been possible to carry out a full screening interview, the SDT will need to take some time at the beginning of the assessment to question the student about her past history and difficulties before commencing the battery of tests. (See Chapter 4: *The identification process*.)

In HE institutions many students will arrive with a full educational psychologist's or specialist teacher's assessment report which is out of date or not wholly relevant to Higher Education. Sometimes it is possible to carry out a 'top-up assessment' or what used to be called a 'Performance Attainment Assessment'. The underlying ability tests will not necessarily need to be repeated. If dyslexia has already been established the purpose of a 'top-up assessment' is slightly different from the usual full assessment. What the SDT is looking to do is to establish the existing strengths and weaknesses and determine how the dyslexic profile will relate to the student's current course. Many of the tests used in the full assessment will still be relevant, depending on the individual case.

1.2 Selecting appropriate tests

The DfES Working Party (2005) looked at all the tests currently standardised for adults and has published a list of acceptable tests which will be regularly updated, (See Appendix 1). The guidelines state that a range of tests should be used. In most cases an appropriate assessment would require one test from each of the following categories:

Attainments in literacy

- reading: single word reading; non-word reading; comprehension; oral prose reading (including reading rate); silent prose reading (including reading rate)

- listening comprehension

- spelling

■ free writing and copy writing

Underlying ability

Cognitive processing

■ working memory

■ phonological processing

■ speed of processing

■ other relevant tests if appropriate: numeracy; motor control; perceptual difficulties

The working party (2005) state that assessors may use alternative tests on occasion but if they do, they will need to provide justification within the report. It is the job of the SDT to ensure that suitable tests are selected which are appropriate for the individual. This chapter looks at a *sample* of tests which, taken together, would provide an appropriate assessment. SDTs might well choose alternatives.

2. Reading tests

SDTs are expected to use a variety of different tests to assess different aspects of the reading process. The results from the different tests can be analysed to give an overall assessment of a student's reading ability. Some students are able to achieve average or above scores on non-timed tests of word reading but will find timed tests more difficult because of slow processing speeds. Some students will achieve average scores on word reading tests but will find non-word reading tests more difficult, which can point to an underlying phonological weakness.

2.1 Single word reading tests

Untimed: Wide Range Achievement Test 3 (WRAT3), Wilkinson (1999)
This is available in two parallel forms: Tan and Blue. Individual words are read from a card, giving an indication of the student's decoding skills. The test is co-normed with the Wide Range Intelligence Test (WRIT) (2000), so it is useful for SDTs who are using the WRIT to establish underlying ability. It is easy to score, giving standard and percentile scores. However, it has recently been updated to the **WRAT4** which is not co-normed with the WRIT.

Timed: Test of Word Reading Efficiency (TOWRE), Torgesen et al, (1999)
This is standardised to age 24.11 but guidelines state that it could be used qualitatively for older students. It measures fluency of reading real words

and provides a Reading Efficiency Measure with the Phonemic Decoding Efficiency Test. It is an extremely useful test to use with compensated dyslexic students who will often achieve an average score on untimed tests of word reading or text reading, but will achieve a much lower score on this test, indicating a lack of automaticity and fluency.

2.2 Non-word reading tests
Timed: Test of Word Reading Efficiency (TOWRE): Phonemic Decoding, Torgesen et al (1999)
This is standardised to 24.11 and provides a measurement of fluency in decoding non-words. Together with the Towre Sight Word Efficiency Test above it provides an overall reading efficiency measurement. It could be used qualitatively for older students. If difficulties are shown up on the Phonemic Decoding Efficiency Test, phonological processing can be tested further by using the Word Attack sub-test from the Woodcock (see below).

Untimed: Woodcock Reading Mastery Tests: Word Attack, Woodcock (1998)
This is standardised to adult level and tests decoding skills for non-words. It is very useful for establishing a student's phonological skills and ability to decode non-words. It is often possible to see a pattern when analysing the student's errors.

2.3 Comprehension tests
The SDT will also need to provide an assessment of comprehension skills, using both oral reading tests and silent reading tests as well as measuring oral and silent reading rates.

WRAT4 Sentence Comprehension Test, Wilkinson(2006)
This test measures an individual's ability to gain meaning from words and to comprehend ideas and information contained in sentences through the use of a modified cloze technique. It can be combined with the word reading test to give an overall reading efficiency score.

Woodcock Reading Mastery Test: Passage Comprehension, Woodcock (1998)
An alternative to the WRAT4, this consists of a series of short paragraphs with a word missing. The student has to read each passage silently but provide an appropriate word orally which the assessor notes. It is suggested that it would not be sufficient to use this test or the similar test in the WRAT 4 as a total measure of reading comprehension and that a longer piece of text comprehension should be used as well.

2.4 Oral prose reading

Students are required to read a passage aloud without rehearsal and to answer questions without further access to the text. It is generally considered that 150 words per minute is an adequate speed for academic purposes. Oral tests can bring out underlying difficulties with phonological processing. SDTs should note the kind of mistakes students are making and whether the reading is fluent or hesitant, whether words are missed out or substituted and whether this affects the comprehension of text.

The SDT could choose from a variety of non-standardised passages such as those in Cynthia Klein's Diagnosing Dyslexia (1995) or other appropriate passage at an adult level. An alternative would be to choose one of the passages in the Adult Reading Test (ART), Brooks *et al* (2004). This is a fairly recent test, devised for adults in further and higher education. It consists of a series of oral tests which would be very time-consuming to incorporate in their entirety but can be used in a non-standardised way to provide a reading rate and a consideration of reading fluency. Passage Five and the extension test are the most appropriate for HE level. Questions are provided for comprehension.

2.5 Silent prose reading

The student is required to read a passage once only and then to answer questions on it, usually with access to the text. It is generally considered that 200 to 250 words per minute is adequate for academic purposes. The SDT could choose an appropriate non-standardised academic passage or choose from one of the DfES Working Party Guidelines (2005) listed tests (see Appendix 1). The majority of reading which takes place at HE is silent research reading so this test is essential. It will establish slow reading speeds and weak comprehension skills. One suggestion would be to use a passage from the Gray Silent Reading Test (GSRT) (Wiederholt *et al*, 2001). It is standardised to age 25 and can be useful within a battery of tests as it can provide a standardised score (if sufficient passages are used) which is useful for comparison with other reading scores.

2.6 Issues to consider when interpreting reading test results

■ Are the results surprising in view of the student's ability levels?

■ Is there a difference between word reading and reading comprehension or between oral and silent reading? What is the reason for this? Is it significant?

■ Is there a difference between timed and untimed tests?

■ Does the student appear to be a compensated dyslexic reader? Is there evidence of underlying difficulties in phonological processing and non-word reading even if word reading and comprehension are at expected levels? Is the speed of reading unexpectedly slow in comparison with other test results? Does the student read adequately but cannot decode at speed? Is there a lack of automaticity in literacy despite possible adequate scores?

■ Is there any evidence of visual stress from oral reading? The SDT might already have an indication that visual stress might be present from answers in the initial screening or when questioning the student at the beginning of the assessment.

3. Writing Tests

The SDT will need to look at spelling skills as shown in a test of individual words and in free writing where the student is concentrating on content rather than individual words as well as establishing writing speeds.

3.1 Spelling: Wide Range Achievement Test 3 (WRAT3) Wilkinson (1993)

This is a test of individual words. Two alternative forms (Tan and Blue) are available. It is standardised to adult level and co-normed with the WRIT. It is useful for SDTs who are using the WRIT to establish underlying ability. It is easy to score, giving standard and percentile scores. However, the updated WRAT4 is now available and is similar in format, but it is not co-normed with the WRIT.

3.2 Free writing

The DfES guidelines (2005) suggest that the student should undertake a timed free writing test which should be a minimum of fifteen minutes. This should test writing speed as well as the ability to organise and present ideas at speed. The average adult academic writing speed is generally considered to be 20 to 30 words per minute. The SDT should analyse the writing for spelling errors, sentence structure, punctuation, organisation, legibility and use of vocabulary.

3.3 Copy writing

This is not listed in the DfES guidelines (2005), but can be useful in that it stimulates copying from overheads/board. A speed of 30 to 40 words per minute is considered adequate for academic purposes. Any appropriate short passage could be chosen. One option would be to use the one-minute passage from the Dyslexia Adult Screening Test (DAST).

3.4 Issues to consider when interpreting writing test results

- Is the level of written literacy skills below expectation?

- Is there a difference between spelling achieved on individual word spelling tests and spelling used in free writing?

- Is there any evidence that the student deliberately chooses words she knows how to spell in the free writing test?

- Is there a pattern of spelling errors?

- Is there any evidence of weakness in fine motor control? Is the handwriting messy or difficult to read?

4. Cognitive processing tests: phonological processing; speed of processing; perceptual difficulties

The SDT is also expected to carry out tests to establish whether there is an underlying deficit in working memory or a slow processing speed. The student's performance in phonological processing speed; phonological awareness and visual and auditory working memory can be assessed using tests such as the Symbol Digit Modality Test (SDMT), Comprehensive Test of Phonological Processing (CTOPP), the Digit Memory Test (DMT) and the Wide Range Assessment of Memory and Learning (WRAML2).

4.1 Symbol Digit Modalities Test (SDMT), Smith (1973)

This is standardised to adult level. It is quick to administer (90 seconds plus short practice items) and produces a standard and percentile score, which is useful for comparison with attainment and ability tests. It measures clerical speed, visual search and memory, fine motor control and concentration. It also measures a student's capacity for multi-tasking.

4.2 Comprehensive Test of Phonological Processing (CTOPP), Wagner et al (1999)

This is standardised to 24.11 years only but could be used qualitatively for older students. It assesses phonological awareness, memory and rapid naming. SDTs can use appropriate sub-tests. The most useful at this stage would be the Rapid Naming Tests.

Rapid naming tests measure efficient retrieval of phonological information from long-term or permanent memory. Such tests measure speed and processing of visual as well as phonological information. Individuals who show poor performance on rapid naming tasks are expected to have difficulty reading fluently. Each of the four subtests (Rapid Digit Naming, Rapid Letter

Naming, Rapid Object Naming and Rapid Colour Naming) is quick to administer but it would be appropriate to use just two, such as Rapid Object Naming and Rapid Colour Naming.

4.3 Perin Spoonerism Task (Perin,1983)

This is not in the tests suggested by the DfES Guidelines (2005) but it can provide some useful information about phonological skills and the student's ability to manipulate sounds, although it is not standardised to adult level. It is relatively quick and easy to administer. A student might be able to complete all or most of the items correctly but not within the five second time limit and this might indicate a lack of automaticity in phonological skills.

4.4 Tests for perceptual problems

Making sense of what is seen and heard contributes to the way in which a student can perform academically. Visual and auditory perceptual problems can have an impact upon performance in reading and spelling (Brown *et al*, 2003), and this may be one of the reasons why an individual's standardised scores in these areas are low.

4.5 Developmental Test of Visual Perception – Adolescent and Adult (DTVP-A) (Reynold et al, 2002)

This suite of six subtests measures visual-perceptual and visual-motor abilities. The test is useful not only to find out if there are specific difficulties in visual perception but also to explore visual motor skills to find out, for example, if a student is at risk for dyspraxia.

The subtests include:

- Copying: Individuals are shown a simple figure and asked to draw it on a piece of paper. The figure serves as a model for the drawing.

- Figure-Ground: After being shown stimulus figures, the student is asked to find as many of these figures as she can on a page. The figures merge into the background and the testee has to be able to sort out information while being distracted by the background information.

- Visual-Motor Search: The individual is shown a page covered in numbered circles randomly arranged on the page, and has to connect them in numbered sequence as quickly as possible.

- Visual Closure: This activity tests an individual's ability to select exact information from a series of figures.

■ Visual-Motor Speed: Students are shown (a) four different geometric designs, two of which have special marks in them, and (b) a page filled completely with the four designs, none of which have marks in them.

■ Form Constancy: This activity tests a person's ability to pick information which may be a different size and slightly hidden within a busy background.

As well as obtaining a general visual perceptual index the tests provide an indication of eye-hand co-ordination.

Currently, many of the available tests are outside the parameters for students in Higher Education. However, it is worth considering the following tests which can be used qualitatively to provide an analysis of performance.

4.6 Test of Auditory-Processing Skills – 3rd Edition by Martin and Brownell, 2006

Although this test has a ceiling of 18 years, it provides the SDT with detailed information about auditory functioning. It is an updated version of a test devised by Gardner. As the test says, '[it] measures what a person does with what is heard'. It explores in depth: Phonological Segmentation, Phonological Blending, Auditory Comprehension, and Auditory Reasoning. It is used diagnostically to delve into these areas which are often considered root causes of dyslexia.

The sub-tests are:

Word Discrimination
Word Memory
Phonological Segmentation
Sentence Memory
Phonological Blending
Auditory Comprehension
Numbers Forward
Auditory Reasoning
Numbers Reversed

The entire untimed test usually takes 90 minutes. However, experienced SDTs can isolate specific subtests to pin-point specific difficulties.

4.7 Test of Visual Perceptual Skills 3 by Martin, 2007

This test also has a ceiling of 18 years but is worth consideration. This 3rd edition is a re-vamped version of the original Gardner tests and combines all age groups into one test. It uses black and white line drawings as stimuli for all the perceptual tasks, so that colour blindness difficulties are eliminated.

The subtests consist of:

Visual Discrimination
Visual Sequential Memory
Visual Memory
Figure-Ground
Visual Spatial Relationships
Visual Closure
Form Constancy

Whilst these tests have been normed on an extensive American population, they remain useful tools.

5. Cognitive Processing tests: working memory

It is important to distinguish between different aspects of memory, particularly between short term memory and short term working memory. Short term memory is very transient and brief. It is not designed to hold lots of information but will deal with auditory and visual information for a short period of time and does not store information. It is believed that it can hold seven items of information for 15-20 seconds at a time. Working memory (sometimes called short term working memory) could be considered as the multi-tasking component of memory. It has limited capacity. Working memory is concerned with manipulation of information – doing one thing while storing and using parts of information. On the other hand, long term memory has limitless capacity in principle.

Two tests which SDTs can use to assess memory are:

- Digit Memory Test
- Wide Range Assessment of Memory and Learning2 (WRAML2)

5.1 Digit Memory Test, Turner et al (2002)

This short test assesses forward and backward span and provides a standard and percentile score which is useful for comparison with attainment and ability tests. A low score on this test can indicate difficulties with all aspects of literacy, particularly reading and note taking. It is generally considered an essential component of any assessment.

5.2 Wide Range Assessment of Memory and Learning (WRAML2)
Sheslow and Adams, 2001

This is standardised to adult level. It provides the SDT with a valuable and comprehensive tool for analysing various aspects of memory function. The General Memory Index is obtained from the analysis of three sub-indices: verbal memory, visual memory and attention-concentration.

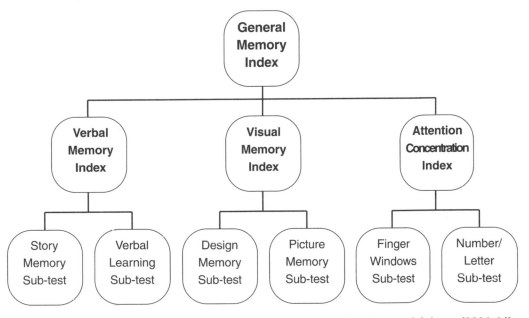

Figure 1: Overview of the WRAML2 adapted from Sheslow and Adams (2001:14)

These core tests are quite lengthy and time-consuming to administer when taken in the context of a battery of tests. However, some of the sub-tests can be administered independently and can provide valuable information for the SDT as a way of establishing visual and verbal memory difficulties. If the SDT suspects that the student may have attentional problems it is worth while administering the Attention-Concentration battery of tests to provide evidence for referral to other professional bodies. The working memory index is particularly useful for adults. This consists of two subtexts: Verbal Working Memory and Symbolic Working Memory.

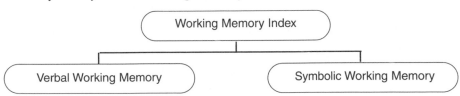

Figure 2: Overview of test battery for Working Memory Index

In the **Verbal Working Memory Test** participants are given a list of words some of which are names of animals, some objects, and are asked to repeat the list back to the assessor, recalling the animals in size order for the first level; at the second level the participant has to recall animals in size order, followed by objects in size order.

In the **Symbolic Working Memory Test** the assessor dictates a series of numbers and the participant has to point to the numbers in correct numerical order on the Number Stimulus Card. For the second task, the examiner dictates number-letter sequences and the participant has to point out the dictated numbers followed by the dictated letters in correct numerical and alphabetical order.

5.3 Issues to consider when interpreting cognitive processing tests

- Is there any discrepancy between ability and working memory?

- Is there any discrepancy between ability and speed of processing?

- Is there evidence of phonological difficulties? It is worth comparing performance on Perin's spoonerisms test with results from non-word tests such as Woodcock Word Identification.

- Is there a difference between short term working memory as shown on the WRAML2 and the Digit Memory Test and reported difficulties with long term memory and sequencing (days of week/months/tables)?

- Is there any evidence of a lack of automaticity with learning common sequences such as the alphabet or multiplication tables?

- Are there any reported organisational difficulties? How does this affect the course?

6. Underlying ability: The Wide Range Intelligence Test (WRIT) Glutting *et al* (2000)

This is the teacher equivalent of the Wechsler Adult Intelligence Scale 3rd Edition (WAIS-III), (Wechsler, 1999). It is standardised to 85 years. It is also co-normed with the WRAT3 which is useful for comparison. There are two non-verbal/visual subtests (Matrices and Diamonds) which give a performance scale and two verbal sub-tests (Verbal Analogies and Vocabulary) which give a verbal scale.

The **Performance** scale examines the manual and visual abilities. The participant performs tasks such as observations and pattern construction, which do not require explicit use of verbal skills.

Matrices

In this subtest the participant has to select a picture from several alternatives in order to complete the design. It is intended to assess non-verbal reasoning, analogic reasoning, sequential reasoning, spatial ability, figure/ground perception, visual acuity, visual problem-solving and the ability to see a pattern as a whole, rather than in sections. This also examines co-ordination of the hands and eyes. This visual (fluid) ability is less influenced by education and culture and is considered to measure potential innate ability. Low scores on Matrices tests may indicate a possible weakness with spatial ability and visual memory or working memory.

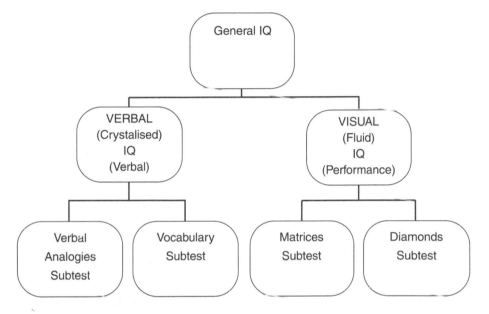

Figure 3: WRIT Overview

Diamonds

In this subtest the participant has to reproduce a two and three dimensional pattern. It is intended to assess spatial visualisation, spatial perceptual relationships, figure/ground perception, visual acuity, short-term visual memory, attention to detail and visual problem-solving. It also examines co-ordination of the hands and eyes.

The **Verbal Scale** assesses the development of language, vocabulary, verbal reasoning, general knowledge and auditory sequential memory. It is the scores on this scale which best correlate with academic achievement.

Verbal Analogies

In this subtest the participant has to find common elements between two objects presented orally. It is intended to examine categorical thinking, how things link together, abstract reasoning and verbal concept formation. These skills are acquired through school learning, reading and general interest.

Example: Wheels are round and boxes are...

Vocabulary

In this subtest the participant has to explain the meaning of words presented orally. It is intended to assess language development, knowledge and expression. Vocabulary is acquired through reading, school learning, environmental and cultural opportunity.

Example: What does illuminate mean?

The sub-tests are presented in a set order. The manual states that the Matrices sub-test was chosen first because it 'facilitates rapport building' and allows participants 'to become comfortable' (Writ Manual, page 59). This might well be the case for some students, but the SDT needs to be aware that there are some students who find this kind of test quite stressful.

Dyslexic and dyspraxic students usually have an uneven pattern of scores both within the sub-tests and between the different scales. Many students find the Verbal Analogies subtest more challenging than the Vocabulary sub-test as they are not limited to one word answers. Many score more highly on the Performance tests, showing strengths in non verbal reasoning skills, than on the Verbal sub-tests, though this is by no means always the case. Dyspraxic students are likely to score more highly on the verbal sub-tests and find the performance tests more challenging, particularly the Diamonds subtest.

6.1 Issues to consider when interpreting underlying ability test results

- Are all the test results reliable? Did the student experience particular difficulty with any one element of the test?

- Is there an uneven cognitive profile? What is the significance of this? Is there a statistical difference between Verbal and Visual ability? The Writ Manual is useful for providing information about the statistical difference between Verbal and Visual ability. (See Writ Manual: Table 6.3, page 68). If there is a higher visual score does this show strength in visual ability or is there an underlying cause for a weaker verbal score such as difficulty with language due to poor education or English as an additional language? If there is a higher verbal score does this indicate a strength for language or might there be other causes for the comparatively weak visual score such as visual/spatial difficulties, or visual perceptual difficulties? Is there any indication of dyspraxia? A dyspraxic student might find particular difficulty with the Diamonds sub-test.

- Is there any difference between the results of individual sub-tests? What is the importance of this? (WRIT manual: Table 6.6, page 76)

- How unusual are the test results? The WRIT manual provides prevalence tables which can be very useful. (WRIT Manual: Tables 6.4, page 64 and Table 6.7, page 77)

- Are there any discrepancies between achievement and ability scores, ability and reading, ability and reading comprehension, ability and speed of processing, ability and spelling?

- If there are difficulties on the WRIT Visual subtest, how do these relate to any indications of visual stress/ visual perceptual difficulty?

The DfES Working Party Guidelines (2005) state that assessors are expected to assess whether there appears to be any discrepancy between the student's underlying ability level as shown on the WRIT and levels of achievement shown in the literacy tests. A difference between ability and achievement has long been considered to point to a dyslexic difficulty, although this discrepancy model has largely been discounted by recent researchers (Stanovich, 1991). Compensated dyslexic students will often achieve average or above average scores on tests of reading and spelling but still have underlying phonological difficulties. Sometimes this can be determined by differences between scores achieved on untimed tests and those achieved on timed tests and whether there is a weakness in memory and processing speed.

7. Interpreting the results of the assessment tests

The Patoss Guide to Assessment (Backhouse and Morris, 2005) stresses the importance of close observation during assessment in order to produce an accurate diagnosis. Kindersley (2005 in Backhouse and Morris) cites the difference between two students who achieve a standard score of 105 on a standardised spelling test. One achieves it effortlessly whereas the other achieves the same result only through much thought and many attempts at the word. Similarly, she points to the importance of noting the effort required during a free writing test. She considers it might be appropriate to use test behaviour of this sort as evidence of a difficulty.

The SDT needs to look at the whole picture of test results, history and other significant factors when reaching a decision about whether or not the student is dyslexic. She will need to consider the strengths that have been identified as well as the weaknesses. Other factors which are of significance are evidence of language difficulties – the use of vocabulary and word retrieval difficulties.

It is sometimes useful to put the tests results in the form of a graph as visual representation will illustrate the differences between individual test results quite well and will be helpful in reaching a decision. It will also be helpful when feeding back later to the student. The diagram in Figure 4 shows a typical dyslexic profile. The student has an uneven cognitive profile with relative strength in non-verbal reasoning. Weakness is shown in working memory and processing speed, which affects attainment scores.

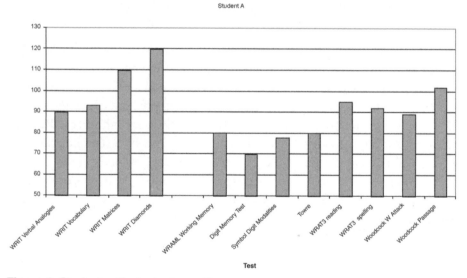

Figure 4: Student with dyslexic profile

Figure 5 shows an example of a compensated dyslexic student who has a more even profile. Attainment is on a level with verbal ability but she has a very weak working memory as shown on the Wide Range Assessment of Memory and Learning2 (WRAML2) and the Digit Memory tests, and slow processing speeds as shown on the Symbol Digit Modalities Test (SDMT). Scores on untimed reading tests (WRAT3) are on a level with **verbal** ability on the WRIT but much lower on timed tests such as Towre. Scores on the Woodcock Word Attack indicate a phonological processing difficulty.

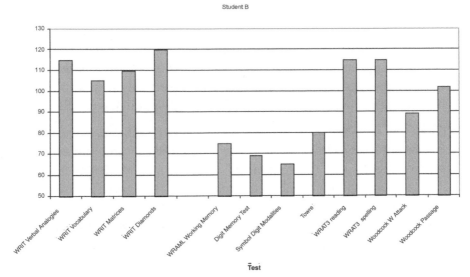

Figure 5: Compensated Dyslexic Student

7.1 Compensated dyslexic students

Singleton (1999) believes that assessors should provide evidence that there is still a significant discrepancy between a student's predicted and actual attainment and that dyslexia will still therefore impair the learning process even though the student has been able to compensate to some extent (Singleton, 1999). It is noted in the DfES Working Party Guidelines (2005) that 'both the severity of the impairment and the effectiveness of compensatory strategies vary widely'.

Many adults have largely overcome literacy difficulties and will achieve average levels when tested in reading, writing and spelling. Other tests which rely on working memory might continue to cause difficulty such as mental calculations or tasks involving sequencing. However, even if an adult has developed strategies to cope with most of the difficulties, other factors might still be present, such as 'low self-esteem and poor self-confidence' (McLoughlin *et al*, 1994). Such factors would usually be apparent from the initial screening interview, and the SDT needs to take these into account when reaching any conclusions.

The development of compensatory strategies can mask the original difficulty (McLoughlin *et al*, 1994). When tested, adults might appear to have a good memory but this could be because their poor working memory has affected them greatly on a daily basis and they have developed strategies to improve it and consequently through strong motivation and determination have developed 'an above average ability to recall material'. They would, however, still have difficulty with other aspects such as phonological memory (McLoughlin *et al*, 1994:27). SDTs can often tell by observation whether an adult is experiencing particular difficulty with a sub-test. Questions about how the sub-test was approached can be illuminating. If unexpected results are reached such as a high speed of processing which is not usual in an SpLD profile, the SDT might find it helpful to question the student about how she tackled the task.

If a student achieved average or above average scores on untimed reading tests, timed tests such as the Towre will be useful in showing any underlying deficit. The student might have adequate skills when time is not an issue but under time pressure such skills might begin to break down. Similarly, phonological processing tests might indicate adequate skills but timed tests such as the Towre non-word sub test could show that these skills are not automatic and only achieved slowly.

Scores on untimed word spelling tests again might reveal average or above average ability but spelling on free writing tests where students are being asked to think about what they are writing and organise their ideas at the same time, might reveal more spelling errors. However, questioning might well establish that students will use words they are confident of spelling and their writing appears surprisingly simplistic when compared to their performance orally and/or on the Vocabulary test in the WRIT.

7.2 Persisting difficulty
The DfES Working Party Guidelines (2005) describe the areas of persisting weakness as slow, possibly inaccurate reading, poor spelling and punctuation and difficulty putting ideas across in a written form. Again, many of these difficulties will have been discussed in the initial screening assessment but some students will be likely to minimise their own difficulties because they do not like to admit to a weakness, whereas others with a poor self-image might consider their difficulties are more severe than they actually are. The assessment will establish the level of current difficulties; if a student demonstrates weakness in reading and/or spelling it is reasonable to suppose that these difficulties have always been present.

7.3 History of difficulty with the acquisition of literacy skills
The DfES Working Party Guidelines (2005) state that dyslexic adults might have a history of poor reading and spelling at school as well as finding second language learning difficult. Much of this information will have been established at the initial screening assessment through the interview questions.

However, the compensated dyslexic adult might appear to have no such history or might have coped adequately until HE level.

7.4 Exclusion of other factors

▓ Family history

▓ Strengths as well as weaknesses. Many dyslexic students will have good visual-spatial skills, creative thinking and/or intuitive understanding (Singleton, 1999).

Other barriers to learning also need to be eliminated: sensory impairment; English as an additional language; environmental factors such as educational experience and reduced opportunities for learning. As the Working Party point out in the DfES guidelines (2005) 'it is the role of the assessor to attempt to tease apart possible causes of persisting literacy difficulties'. It is important for the assessor to determine that any identified difficulties are not due to a lack of motivation, emotional causes, or poor general health or medical condition (Singleton, 1999:97).

7.5 Students with English as an additional language (EAL)

There is a lack of research about how EAL affects the assessment process in HE and this is an area where research is badly needed. Ideally students whose first language is not English should be assessed in their first language, but in practical terms this is not always possible. Not every SDT can hope to be an expert in languages but she can have an awareness of the issues that are likely to affect a particular student and if possible find out more about the student's first language if the differences are particularly significant. Chapter Four, *The Identification Process*, gives examples of the sort of questions it is appropriate to ask. The DfES Working Party Guidelines (2005) advise the SDT to be aware of and make allowances for any linguistic or cultural variations that could affect the individual tests such as lack of familiarity with timed assessment and a limited English vocabulary. They alert the SDT to the need to be aware of cultural bias in many of the standardised tests which have been developed for English-speaking populations. They suggest that some adjustments are justifiable but warn that this could affect the reliability of the results.

Shulman (2002) looks at different methods of dynamic assessment (an adjustment to the assessment procedure) which she sees as being a fairer way of establishing the presence of a specific learning difficulty. She suggests that this can be done by allowing extra time to complete tests; by giving additional explanations or cues if the student does not understand instructions or permitting a second attempt at a task; taking into account how the student approaches the task and allowing the student to explain her approach or in changing the modality of the administration by letting her respond orally or verbally rather than in written format.

The DfES guidelines (2005) advise the assessor to find out how the student approaches the test, as this could also affect the result. A student who translates into her first language before replying is likely to produce an unreliable result, particularly if the test is untimed. Non-verbal tests are likely to be more reliable and less culturally biased than literacy tests.

7.6 Co-existence of more than one specific learning difficulty

As already seen Chapter Four, *The Identification Process*, there is considerable overlap between different types of specific learning difficulty. Although current thinking is that SDTs should assess for dyslexia only, they should still be aware of other SpLDs when reaching a conclusion about whether a student is dyslexic or not. The important point for the SDT is that the common indicators can cause confusion when reaching a decision about a specific difficulty (Deponio, 2004).

Dyspraxic students usually have high scores on spelling and reading tests, but might report that they lose marks for weak written coursework despite this and also experience difficulty with structuring and organising ideas in written form. Results from tests of phonological processing are likely to be average or above, but working memory and speed of information processing test results are likely to be below average. They are quite likely to find Visual subtests on the WRIT difficult, particularly the Diamonds, while scoring quite highly on the Verbal subtests. Similarly, their performance on the Symbol Digit Modalities Test is likely to be depressed. Copy writing and free writing tests might reveal poor, messy handwriting.

During the course of the assessment, it may appear that a student has AD(H)D rather than dyslexia. She might find it very difficult to concentrate on the battery of sub-tests; she might ask for instructions to be repeated or she could take a considerable time on untimed tests because of loss of concentration. Similarly, she might appear restless and uncomfortable in the assessment situation. In such cases, she should be referred on to the appropriate professional for a diagnosis of the condition. The diagnostic assessment of AD(H)D would be carried out by a medical professional.

7.7 Dyscalculia

There is controversy about the nature of dyscalculia and the difference between dyscalculia in its purest form and simply a difficulty with mathematics. Many students with dyslexic difficulties such as weak short term working memory and sequencing difficulties might struggle with some aspects of mathematics but not be dyscalculic.

The DfES Working Party Guidelines (2005) define dyscalculia as:

> ... a learning difficulty involving the most basic aspect of arithmetical skills. The difficulty lies in the reception, comprehension, or production of quantitative and spatial information. Students with dyscalculia may have difficulty in understanding simple number concepts, lack an intuitive grasp of numbers and have problems learning number facts and procedures. These can relate to basic concepts such as telling the time, calculating prices, handling change.

Robertson (2005) points out that difficulties with mathematics are common even among the non dyslexic population. This could be due to a number of factors including maths phobia and poor teaching.

There are currently no published tests available for the assessment of dyscalculia at adult level and the SDT will find it difficult to refer the student to a suitably qualified professional for a diagnosis of dyscalculia. Beacham and Trott, researchers at Loughborough University, are in the process of trialling a screening tool, Dyscalculium, which will be very useful for the SDT.

7.8 Consideration of secondary characteristics

There are many 'secondary characteristics' of dyslexia which need to be taken into account during the assessment process. Hales (1994) points out that the assessor should consider the emotional and personal element as well as looking at clinical results. 'Professionals must be sensitive to the emotional as well as the cognitive aspects of dyslexia'. Many adult dyslexics experience a lack of self-esteem and low self-confidence, due to a history of failure. Others suffer from high levels of anxiety and stress which affects their performance on many tasks. Many experience the cumulative effect of tiredness and their performance on academic tasks varies from day to day.

8. Final feedback

It is good practice for an SDT to discuss the assessment results with a colleague before writing up the final report. This is useful as it enables the SDT to clarify her own ideas as well as having a second objective viewpoint. Of course, the final decision as to whether or not a student is dyslexic must be the assessor's. This consultation is particularly useful for borderline cases, where the SDT must weigh up all the evidence very carefully to decide whether the difficulties are due to dyslexia or some other cause.

Students are often extremely relieved to discover that they have a specific learning difficulty as this gives them a reason for their previous struggles and possibly failures. Other students are rather bitter and angry about the results, feeling that they have been treated unfairly in the past and that their lives might have been different had they known earlier that they were dyslexic. The SDT needs to be extremely sensitive to the student's reaction and offer appropriate advice and guidance. Occasionally, the feedback session can turn into something of a counselling session. The SDT also needs to be able to recognise when the depth of the student's feelings are such that referral to a counsellor would be advisable.

The dyslexic profile should be explained and the strengths commented on as well as the weaknesses. The SDT and student should then be able to plan a programme of support to help the student with the highlighted weaknesses. The SDT can agree appropriate special examination arrangements (see Chapter 7: *Recommendations for support*) as well as academic study skills support and will need to inform the student's department about the recommendations and any action that is required.

In conclusion ...

This chapter has looked at some of the assessment tools which can be used to assess a student's attainment skills, processing skills and underlying ability. It has discussed different aspects of assessment and performance which need to be considered before reaching a final decision about whether an SpLD is present.

Further reading

Backhouse, G and Morris, K (eds) (2005) *Dyslexia? Assessing and reporting – the PATOSS Guide*. London, Hoddon-Murray

McLoughlin, D, Leather, C and Stringer, P (2002) *The Adult Dyslexic: Interventions and Outcomes*. London, Whurr Publishers

Thomson, M (2002) *The Psychology of Dyslexia*. London, Whurr Publishers

Robertson, J (2005) Maths and Dyslexia in Further and Higher Education in Pollak, D (Ed) (2005) *Proceedings of a joint conference: Supporting the dyslexic student in HE and FE: strategies for success*. De Montfort University, University of Hull

Appendix One: DfES Working Party Guidelines (2005)

List of Suitable Tests for the Assessment of Specific Learning Difficulties (SpLD) in Higher Education

Categories:	Name of Test	Closed/ Open	Age Range	Admin. Time	Publisher and Distributors	Components	Comments
ATTAINMENTS IN LITERACY Reading:							
Single word recognition	Wide Range Achievement Test 3 (WRAT3)	Open	5-75 years	5-10 mins	Psychological Assessment Resources, Inc., USA/Harcourt Assessment/Dyslexia Institute		Co-normed with WRIT
	Woodcock Reading Mastery Tests (WRMT-R)	Open	5-75+ years	Approx 10 mins	American Guidance Service, USA/Dyslexia Institute	Word Identification	
	Test of Word Reading Efficiency (TOWRE)	Open	6-24.11 years	5 mins	Pro-Ed, USA/Taskmaster/ Dyslexia Institute/Harcourt Assessment	Sight Word Efficiency subtest with alternate forms.	This is a timed test that provides a measure of fluency reading real words Together with the TOWRE Phonemic Decoding Efficiency test it will yield an overall Reading Efficiency measure. Can be used qualitatively for ages over 24.11 years.

List of Suitable Tests for the Assessment of Specific Learning Difficulties (SpLD) in Higher Education

Categories:	Name of Test	Closed/ Open	Age Range	Admin. Time	Publisher and Distributors	Components	Comments
Continuous text reading Oral Reading	**Spadafore Diagnostic Reading Test (SDRT)**	Open	6-Adult	Varies	Academic Therapy Publications, USA/ Ann Arbor		An appropriate passage can be used for miscue analysis purposes
	The Adult Reading Test (ART)	Open	16-55 years	30 mins	Harcourt Assessment	Reading accuracy; reading comprehension; speed of reading and speed of writing	Reading is assessed by reading aloud only Memory, factual and inferential comprehension questions. It is advisable in the case of dyslexia to carry out a piece of free writing over a longer time than 2 minutes.
	Gray Oral Reading Test Fourth Edition (GORT-4)	Open	6-18.11 years	15-45mins	Pro-Ed, USA/Harcourt Assessment	2 parallel forms; 14 paragraphs; 5 comprehension questions per paragraph.	Rate; Accuracy; Fluency; Comprehension; Oral Reading Quotient. Student is not allowed to refer back to the passage for answers to comprehension questions. Can be used qualitatively for ages over 18.11 years.

List of Suitable Tests for the Assessment of Specific Learning Difficulties (SpLD) in Higher Education

Categories:	Name of Test	Closed/ Open	Age Range	Admin. Time	Publisher and Distributors	Components	Comments
Silent Reading	**Gray Silent Reading Test (GSRT)**	Open	7-25 years	10-15mins	Pro-Ed, USA/Harcourt Assessment	2 parallel forms 13 paragraphs 5 comprehension questions per paragraph	Different types of comprehension questions; can be administered as group test. Multiple-choice format.
	Spadafore Diagnostic Reading Test (SDRT)	Open	6-Adult	Varies up to 30 mins	Academic Therapy Publications, USA		An appropriate passage can be used. Literal recall and inference comprehension questions. Student is not allowed to refer back to the passage for answers to comprehension questions. Comment on reading speed.

List of Suitable Tests for the Assessment of Specific Learning Difficulties (SpLD) in Higher Education

Categories:	Name of Test	Closed/ Open	Age Range	Admin. Time	Publisher and Distributors	Components	Comments
	Advanced Reading Comprehension Test (ARC)	Open	Adult	20 mins	Department of Psychology University of Hull	Two Versions (M & C)	Norms collected under timed conditions & based on sample of students which, in terms of intelligence & educational attainment, is probably slightly above the average for the UK HE sector as a whole. Version M slightly easier than Version C. Literal & inferential comprehension questions – in multiple-choice format. Further standardisation using students from a wider range of HE Institutions currently in progress and new norms scheduled to be published in 2006.
	WRAT-Expanded Group Assessment (Form G) Reading Comprehension Test	Open	7-18.11 years	50 mins	Psychological Assessment Resources, Inc., USA/Harcourt Assessment/Dyslexia Institute		Multiple-choice; can be used individually. Can be used qualitatively for ages over 18.11 years.

List of Suitable Tests for the Assessment of Specific Learning Difficulties (SpLD) in Higher Education

Categories:	Name of Test	Closed/ Open	Age Range	Admin. Time	Publisher and Distributors	Components	Comments
	WRAT-Expanded Individual Assessment (Form I) Reading Comprehension Test	Open	7-24.11 years	Approx 15 mins	Psychological Assessment Resources, Inc., USA/Harcourt Assessment/Dyslexia Institute		Multiple-choice; can be used individually. Can be used qualitatively for ages over 24.11 years.
	Woodcock Reading Mastery Tests (WRMT-R)	Open	5-75+ years	Approx 15 mins	American Guidance Service, USA/Dyslexia Institute	Passage Comprehension	Modified cloze procedure
Non-word reading	Test of Word Reading Efficiency (TOWRE)	Open	6-24.11 years	5 mins	Pro-Ed, USA/Taskmaster/ Dyslexia Institute/ Harcourt Assessment	Phonemic Decoding Efficiency subtest with alternate forms.	This is a timed test that provides a measure of fluency of reading nonwords. Together with the TOWRE Sight Word Efficiency test it will give an overall Reading Efficiency measure. It can be used qualitatively for ages over 24.11 years.

List of Suitable Tests for the Assessment of Specific Learning Difficulties (SpLD) in Higher Education

Categories:	Name of Test	Closed/ Open	Age Range	Admin. Time	Publisher and Distributors	Components	Comments
	Woodcock Reading Mastery Tests (WRMT-R)	Open	5-75+ years	Approx 10 mins	American Guidance Service, USA/Dyslexia Institute	Word Attack	
	Non-word Decoding Test	Open	Non-standardised use	5-10 mins	Dyslexia Institute		
Listening Compre—hension	Spadafore Diagnostic Reading Test (SDRT)	Open	6-Adult	Varies	Academic Therapy Publications, USA		An appropriate passage can be used.
Spelling: Single word	Wide Range Achievement Test 3 (WRAT3)	Open	5-75 years	5-10 mins	Psychological Assessment Resources, Inc., USA/ Harcourt Assessment/ Dyslexia Institute		Co-normed with WRIT.

List of Suitable Tests for the Assessment of Specific Learning Difficulties (SpLD) in Higher Education

Categories:	Name of Test	Closed/ Open	Age Range	Admin. Time	Publisher and Distributors	Components	Comments
	Helen Arkell Spelling Test (HAST)	Open	5-19+ years	Approx 15-20 mins	Helen Arkell Dyslexia Centre	Includes high and low frequency, and regular and irregular words.	Standardised on UK population. Can be used for group or one-to-one testing.
	British Spelling Test Series (BSTS)	Open	15.6-24+ years	30 mins	NFER-Nelson	Series 5 (X/Y forms)	Can give information about dictation abilities and proof reading abilities.
Writing:	**Free Writing**	Open	Non-standardised	Up to 15 minutes			Timed – up to 15 minutes. Writing speed score can be obtained; comparison of spelling usage and single word spelling. Comment on: structure, punctuation, spelling in context, organisation, legibility & use of vocabulary. Student can either: (1) choose a topic to write about, (2) write about a topic in his/her area of study or (3) write about a passage he/she has read, putting in the key points. (1) & (2) can be used for the Speed of Writing Prose Task.

List of Suitable Tests for the Assessment of Specific Learning Difficulties (SpLD) in Higher Education

Categories:	Name of Test	Closed/ Open	Age Range	Admin. Time	Publisher and Distributors	Components	Comments
UNDERLYING ABILITY							
	Wide Range Intelligence Test (WRIT)	Open	4-85 years	20-30 mins	Psychological Assessment Resources, Inc., USA/Dyslexia Institute	Verbal (Vocabulary & Verbal Analogies); Visual (Matrices & Diamonds).	High correlation with WAIS-III & WISC-III; co-normed with WRAT3. Published 2000.
	Wechsler Adult Intelligence Scale, 3rd Edition UK version (WAIS-IIIUK)	Closed	16-89 years	75 mins	Harcourt Assessment.	Indices: Verbal Comprehension (Vocabulary, Similarities, Information); Perceptual Organisation (Picture Completion, Block Design, Matrix Reasoning); Working Memory (Arithmetic, Digit Span, Letter-Number Sequencing); Processing Speed (Digit Symbol Coding, Symbol Search).	Published 1999 (superseded WAIS-R).

List of Suitable Tests for the Assessment of Specific Learning Difficulties (SpLD) in Higher Education

Categories:	Name of Test	Closed/ Open	Age Range	Admin. Time	Publisher and Distributors	Components	Comments
	Wechsler Abbreviated Scale of Intelligence (WASI)	Closed	6-89 years	30 mins	Harcourt Assessment	Verbal Scale (Vocabulary, Similarities); Performance Scale (Block Design, Matrix Reasoning)	Published 1999
COGNITIVE PROCESSING							
Working Memory	**Wechsler Memory Scale, 3rd Edition UK version (WMS-III)**	Closed	16-89 years	75 mins	Harcourt Assessment.	Immediate Memory (Auditory & Visual); General Memory (delayed) (Logical memory; Verbal Paired associates, Faces, Family Pictures); Working Memory (Spatial Span; Letter-Number Sequencing)	Published 1999
	Wide Range Assessment of Memory and Learning Second Edition (WRAML2)	Open	5-90 years	20+ mins	Psychological Assessment Resources, Inc., USA/ Harcourt Assessment	6 core tests; 2 optional delay recall tests; 4 optional recognition tests; 3 optional memory tests	The factor structure contains verbal memory, visual memory and attention/concentration information. Excellent range of memory tests.

List of Suitable Tests for the Assessment of Specific Learning Difficulties (SpLD) in Higher Education

Categories:	Name of Test	Closed/ Open	Age Range	Admin. Time	Publisher and Distributors	Components	Comments
	Wechsler Adult Intelligence Scale, 3rd Edition UK version (WAIS-IIIUK)	Closed	16-89 years	10-15 mins	Harcourt Assessment.	Digit Span; Letter-Number Sequencing	
	The Digit Memory Test	Open	6-Adult	5-10 mins	Dyslexia Institute	Digit Span forward and backward	
Phonological Processing	**Comprehensive Test of Phonological Processing (CTOPP)**	Open	5-24.11 years	30 mins	Pro-Ed, USA/Taskmaster	Phonological Awareness Quotient; Phonological Memory Quotient; Rapid Naming Quotient; Alternative Phonological Awareness Quotient; Alternative Rapid Naming Quotient.	Can be used qualitatively for ages over 24.11 years

List of Suitable Tests for the Assessment of Specific Learning Difficulties (SpLD) in Higher Education

Categories:	Name of Test	Closed/ Open	Age Range	Admin. Time	Publisher and Distributors	Components	Comments
Speed of Processing	Symbol Digit Modalities Test (SDMT)	Open	8-Adult	90 secs	WPS, USA/Dyslexia Institute	Matching number with symbol	Similar to Digit-Symbol Coding sub-test of WAIS III; administered as written and/or oral test; measure of speed of processing
	Comprehensive Test of Phonological Processing (CTOPP)	Open	5-24.11 years	30 mins	Pro-Ed, USA/Taskmaster	All Rapid Naming subtests & Quotients	
	Wechsler Adult Intelligence Scale, 3rd Edition UK version (WAIS-IIIUK)	Closed	16-89 years	10 mins	Harcourt Assessment.	Processing speed index (Digit-symbol coding & Symbol search)	
	Speed of Writing Prose Task	Open	Adult	Up to 15 mins			Timed – up to 15 mins. Student can choose topic to write about. Provides words per minutes and indicates speed of processing. Can also be used for the Free-Writing Task.

List of Suitable Tests for the Assessment of Specific Learning Difficulties (SpLD) in Higher Education

Categories:	Name of Test	Closed/ Open	Age Range	Admin. Time	Publisher and Distributors	Components	Comments
OTHER RELEVANT INFORMATION Attainments in numeracy (where appropriate)	Wide Range Achievement Test 3 (WRAT3)	Open	5-75 years	15 mins	Psychological Assessment Resources, Inc., USA/ Harcourt Assessment/Dyslexia Institute		Timed test; quick to administer; only tests arithmetic skills; presentation of items is in an American format
	WRAT-Expanded Group Assessment (Form G) Mathematics Test	Open	7-18.11 years	45 mins	Wide Range Inc, USA/ Harcourt Assessment/ Dyslexia Institute		Can be used individually; multiple-choice; assesses understanding of concepts, computation and problem solving. Can be used qualitatively for ages over 18.11 years
	WRAT-Expanded Individual Assessment (Form I) Mathematics Test	Open	7-24.11 years	Approx 15 mins	Psychological Assessment Resources, Inc., USA/ Harcourt Assessment/ Dyslexia Institute		Multiple-choice; assesses understanding of concepts, computation and problem solving. Can be used qualitatively for ages over 24.11 years.

List of Suitable Tests for the Assessment of Specific Learning Difficulties (SpLD) in Higher Education

Categories:	Name of Test	Closed/ Open	Age Range	Admin. Time	Publisher and Distributors	Components	Comments
	Mathematics Competency Test	Open	11.6 – Adult	30-40 mins	Hodder & Stoughton	Using & Applying Mathematics; Number & Algebra Space & Shape Handling Data	Useful for students who have difficulty with mathematics; gives percentile scores only; can be used qualitatively.
Attainments in motor control	Morrisby Manual Dexterity Test	Open	14-49 years	5 mins	The Morrisby Organisation		Fine motor control indicators for dyspraxic-type difficulties

Accessed from: www.dfes.gov.uk/studentsupport/uploads/SPLDG%20Final%20report.doc

7

Writing the report

Report writing is a vital component of the assessment process. Not only does it inform the student of her strengths and weaknesses but also provides recommendations for support. Thus, it helps to inform practice. This chapter will look at how to approach the writing of the report, following the latest DfES guidelines and how to interpret test scores and performance.

Using this chapter

This chapter will enable you to:

Write up the assessment results according to DfES guidelines and consider the issues related to the interpretation of test scores for accuracy of identification.

1. Reporting information

    1.1 Cover sheet

    1.2 Summary

    1.3 Background

    1.4 Test conditions

    1.5 Reporting on the tests

    1.6 Attainments in literacy

    1.7 Cognitive processing

    1.8 Underlying ability

    1.9 Other relevant information

    1.10 Conclusions

    1.11 Recommended support

    1.12 Assessor's statement

1. Reporting information

The SDT needs to be aware that a report not only provides evidence of dyslexia and justification for reasonable adjustments but also provides evidence for funding bodies that support is necessary for the student. The report should therefore be written in such a way as to be easily understood by these different audiences. The DfES Working Party Guidelines (2005) set out a suggested proforma. The reason given for this is to make it easier for Local Authorities (LAs) and other funding bodies to understand and act on the evidence. The working party recognised that individual SDTs must be allowed to exercise professional judgement in the choice of tests and conclusions but nevertheless insist on a consistent standardised format.

The guidelines set out the core components of the report:

- Cover sheet
- Summary
- Background information
- Test conditions
- Reporting on the tests: Attainments in Literacy; Cognitive Processing; Underlying ability
- Other relevant information
- Conclusion
- Recommended support

1.1 Cover sheet

The front page of the report should contain the testee's personal information, together with a statement providing information about the assessor. An example is provided below opposite.

1.2 Summary

- Statement of the findings of the assessment
- Statement as to whether or not the student has dyslexia
- Summary of the evidence that led the SDT to reach the diagnosis
- Summary of the main effects of the SpLD on student's skills at university, including strengths as well as weaknesses
- Any difference between underlying ability and achievement should be highlighted if relevant

Confidential Assessment

Name:
Date of assessment:
Home Address:
Date of birth:
Age at assessment:
University attended:

Course of study:
Year:
Author of this report:

Contact details:

This report represents a professional opinion based on information available at the time of assessment. The report is set within the context of such information as derived from assessment data, observation of behaviour, consultation and other reports as available.

The author of this report holds a current Practising Certificate and certifies that this assessment has been conducted in accordance with the SpLD Working Group 2005/DfES Guidelines for Assessment of SpLDs in Higher Education.

Signed: Date:

A teacher, MA, Diploma SpLD
Practising Certificate number:
Issuing body: Patoss

Contact address:

1.3 Background
- Reasons for the assessment and summary of the presenting difficulties

- Family history

- Educational history and any previous support

- Summary of any previous assessment including information provided from an initial screening assessment

- Any other relevant factors such as English as an additional language

1.4 Test conditions
- Conditions of the room setting e.g. whether the student was disturbed by external factors such as noise

- Comments about motivation/anxiety which might affect the results

1.5 Reporting on the tests

The SDT should give a brief description of each test in the report – i.e. what it is testing – as well as the results of the tests, together with comments about the individual student's performance for each section (Attainment/Processing/Underlying Ability). This description can also be included in an appendix as required by the DfES, but it is sometimes easier for the student to have the explanation for a particular test alongside comments about her results.

The question often asked is how can test scores be communicated? It should be borne in mind that the reports are multi-purpose and will be used by the student and, in some cases, other professionals. Therefore it is important that the report has credibility professionally and yet is clear and easily understandable to the student. It must be appropriate for two ends of the spectrum: those with a deep knowledge of psychometrics and those who feel threatened by technical terminology. This is a tall order.

Standardised scores provide accurate statistical evidence and are appropriate for those with a depth of knowledge, for example, SDTs and psychologists, while percentile scores are crude but more easily understood and explained to students. The student can grasp her position when the test score is related to the notion of a score out of 100. Thus it is best to provide both types of data in the report. It is not appropriate to quote an age equivalent score for adults. It is useful to include a sentence to explain this.

> *Results are usually given as standard scores and percentiles. Scores at the 50th percentile are exactly average. Scores between the 16th and 84th percentiles are within the average range.*

Sometimes it is useful to also include the equivalent description 'below average'/'average'/'high average' for all tests in the report as well. The assessor can then comment on any discrepancies or patterns emerging from the different tests (see Appendix 1). A student may often find it helpful to see a visual representation of the results in the form of a chart, particularly if her profile is spiky or uneven. This can be included in the body of the report or in the appendix (see Chapter 6: The assessment process, for a sample chart).

1.6 Attainments in literacy

The guidelines state that literacy attainments can be subdivided under headings for reading, spelling and writing. The SDT is required to comment on a summary of the student's overall reading performance in relation to her course of study and in relation to her dyslexic difficulties. Similarly, the SDT is expected to comment on the student's spelling skills as indicated in the free writing task as well as spelling tests and dictation if necessary.

1.7 Cognitive processing

The SDT can comment on whether there are any unexpected weaknesses or differences between cognitive processing and other elements of the assessment.

1.8 Underlying ability

Information about a student's underlying ability is useful in that it gives a baseline against which other scores can be judged. For example, underlying ability and attainment test scores and performance can be compared. These comparisons might or might not result in unexpected behaviour and performance. Standard and percentile scores are given for general ability as well as for verbal and non-verbal ability. If there is a large discrepancy between the verbal and non-verbal ability the SDT might consider omitting the general ability score as this could under-represent the student's ability level.

1.9 Other relevant information

- This section allows the SDT to include any additional test results and justification for using the tests
- Comments on visual perceptual difficulty
- Comments on dyspraxia checklists and/or other factors

1.10 Conclusions

The SDT will need to state her conclusions as to whether a specific learning difficulty is present, the reasons why she has reached this conclusion and whether there are any other factors to be taken into consideration such as an indication of language difficulties or lack of education. It often helps to quote a definition of dyslexia in this section to help the reader understand why the final conclusions have been reached.

(See Section 1.2 in Chapter 1: *Definitions and research*)

1.11 Recommended support

The SDT is expected to give a brief statement about the type of support that might be relevant, concentrating on academic needs rather than any technological support (which will be covered in an Assessment of Needs). The SDT will need to consider how and to what extent any difficulties or discrepancies are likely to affect the student's performance on her particular course. She will need to look at any reported difficulties with coursework and consider to what extent these are typical of HE students as a whole or whether the difficulties are unexpected given the overall pattern of test results and therefore related to SpLDs.

The SDT can make recommendations for a programme of tutorial support, stating what areas of academic study skills will be needed. The support should be tailored to the student's individual needs as shown in the test results and also take into consideration the nature of the student's course. It would be appropriate here to make recommendations for suggested support for students on placement and field trips.

The SDT will be expected to comment on the most appropriate special examination arrangements needed to ensure that the student is not disadvantaged by her SpLD. It might be enough for the SDT to state that extra time for examinations would be appropriate and leave it to the institution to determine how much should be allowed. Many institutions, however, rely on the recommendations made in the diagnostic report, so it is fitting to include a specific recommendation.

See Chapter 7: *Recommendations for support*, for a discussion of appropriate special examination arrangements and reasonable adjustments.

1.12 Assessor's Statement

The SDT will need to include a statement to declare that the assessment report has been prepared in compliance with the DfES regulations. She will need to date and sign the report and include an appropriate practising number. This provides verification of the professional status and is increasingly becoming a requirement for DSA applications to demonstrate that the evidence of an SpLD has been evaluated by a qualified professional. See chapter 3: *Training and the SDT.*

1.13 Appendix

The appendix should include:

- a list of tests used in the assessment
- a summary of scores together with an explanation of what standard and percentile scores mean
- a chart of the test scores
- a chart of the student profile

(See Chapter 6: *The Assessment Process* for a sample chart.)

In conclusion ...

This chapter has looked at the current guidelines with respect to producing reports for students within HE.

Further Readings

Thomas, ME, (1990) *Developmental Dyslexia*. London: Whurr Publishers

Thomson, M (2001) *The Psychology of Dyslexia: A Handbook for Teachers*. London: Whurr Publishers

Turner, M (1997) *Psychological Assessment of Dyslexia*. London: Whurr Publishers

Appendix 1

Chart to show standard scores, percentile range and equivalent descriptions

Standard Score	Percentile Range	Description
130 & above	more than 98	Very high
115 – 129	85 – 97	Above Average
110 – 114	75 – 84	High Average
90 – 109	25 – 74	Average
85 – 89	16 – 24	Low Average
70 – 84	3 – 15	Below Average
69 & below	1 – 2	Very Low

8

Reasonable adjustments: recommendations for support

This chapter examines different forms of reasonable adjustments that HE institutions can provide to take into account individual students' needs for examinations and coursework.

Using this chapter

The chapter will enable you to:

1. Consider individual reasonable adjustments

2. Make decisions about the most suitable recommendations for special examination arrangements

    2.1 Extra time

    2.2 Flagging of scripts

    2.3 Use of a computer

    2.4 Use of an amanuensis or voice activated software

    2.5 Multiple choice examinations

    2.5 Alternative assessments

3. Advise academic departments about reasonable adjustments for coursework; lectures, tutorials etc

    3.1 Handouts

    3.2 Assignments

    3.4 Tutorials

    3.5 Reading

4. Consider recommendations for marking dyslexic student's work

1. What are reasonable adjustments?

The Disability Discrimination Act (1995) states that institutions and organisations are expected not to treat students with disabilities 'less favourably' than other students and to make 'reasonable adjustments' to ensure a level playing field. Dyslexia is classified as a disability, though many professionals in the field and most students prefer to see it as a 'learning difference'. Nevertheless, students with dyslexia and other specific learning difficulties are entitled to expect recognition of their difficulties in the form of reasonable adjustments.

A reasonable adjustment is 'an accommodation or alteration to existing academic programmes' which is deemed necessary for students to be able to demonstrate their abilities (ADSHE, 2004). Reasonable adjustments will affect all areas of teaching and learning from special examination arrangements to adjustments for tutorials and fieldwork. The 2004 annual conference of the Association for Dyslexia Specialists in HE (ADSHE) set out to draw up a series of guidelines which they hoped would provide national consensus to enable all HE institutions to work towards the same model. These guidelines are available on their website www.adshe.org.uk.

It is the responsibility of all HE staff to make reasonable adjustments. The role of the SDT is to advise staff and make recommendations. When a student registers with the university's dyslexia service or is assessed for the first time, it is usual practice for the SDT to discuss support with the student and make recommendations to the student's academic department. The form of the recommendations will depend on the student's dyslexic profile, the nature of her course and the institution's policies. Learning outcomes will need to be considered as well as any extra professional considerations on courses which lead to a professional qualification in addition to the academic award. Subjects such as Social Work, Education, Medicine and other health related courses (nursing, podiatry, radiotherapy, occupational therapy and physiotherapy) have to take Fitness to Practise issues into account when agreeing to any reasonable adjustments to the student's programme. Some adjustments such as note-takers and/or readers might be 'reasonable' in the academic setting but would be inappropriate in placement situations. Students would need to demonstrate they had the skills to write legibly and clearly on practice, as that is a 'fitness to practise' issue. However, that skill should be tested within the placement setting rather than in the academic setting.

(See Chapter 12: *Supporting students on placement and fieldwork* for a further discussion about reasonable adjustments for students on placement.)

2. Special examination arrangements

The main special examination recommendations which can be considered are:

- Extra time, in a separate room

- Flagging of scripts

- Use of a computer (which has been checked to ensure that it is does not have any word files available for the student to use)

- An amanuensis – usually with extra time in a separate room or voice activated software and additional extra time, depending on the expertise of the user

- A reader

- Consideration of format of questions papers, particularly for multiple choice examinations

- Alternative assessments: short answer formats instead of essay questions; open book exams; seen exams; a viva examination; an informal interview following on from the examination; oral presentations or video assessments; extended essay

Other special examination arrangements include:

- Papers provided in alternative formats – e.g. enlarged font or coloured paper

- Spare paper for planning answers and for rough working out; coloured overlays

- A recording of the examination paper in a separate room – sometimes with the provision of some extra time to account for the manipulation of the machine

- Use of a dictaphone/recorder to produce responses which are later transcribed into text by a typist for marking

- Where examinations exceed three hours because of additional time, consideration may be given to offering the examination in two or more parts (e.g. morning and afternoon, or on two successive days) in order to reduce disadvantage to the student because of fatigue

- Extra time for printing out answers

2.1 Extra time

Most students with dyslexia or other specific learning difficulties will be eligible for extra time in a separate room (along with other students receiving extra time) so that they are not disturbed when the majority of students leave the room.

Dyslexic students are likely to make more mistakes than usual when writing under timed conditions. It is widely accepted that stress makes any difficulties worse (Scott, 2004). Students with dyslexia often process information more slowly and all aspects of the learning process take longer. While many students can spend hours writing and re-writing drafts for coursework assignments and take perhaps up to four times longer research reading, this is not possible during timed conditions. Students often rely on technological aids to help with coursework, such as specialised proof reading or planning software and will therefore find writing without these aids more difficult than their non-dyslexic peers. Students with dyslexia will need the extra time to read and re-read the question paper to make sure that they do not misread or misinterpret the questions as well as longer to plan and organise their ideas and to write down their answers.

ADSHE guidelines establish that it is not a 'reasonable adjustment' to allow unlimited time. The usual recommendation is for 25% extra. However, sometimes recommendations are made for less or more than this depending on the severity of the dyslexia or the particular dyslexic profile. It is also worth considering that in some examinations students will require more time than in others. This could be the case for multiple choice exams which involve substantial reading, or where there is a long list of options and the student has to keep re-reading as short term memory difficulties mean that she cannot retain all the relevant information for long enough to decide on the correct answer. Similarly, in some examinations, for example in some Medicine examinations, the student is expected to read long sections of unseen text. With such examinations, time additional to the usual 25% would be more than justified.

The SDT will sometimes have to decide whether or not to make recommendations for extra time for practical examinations. Students on language courses often take regular assessments in schools. It might be appropriate to allow extra time for oral examinations which involve an element of reading and writing as well as for listening comprehension assessments. Extra time for practical examinations in health related courses, however, are not always compatible with professional regulations.

2.2 Flagging scripts

Even with extra time provided, examinations are likely to be more difficult for students who have dyslexia and an allowance for sympathetic marking is also more than justified to help to achieve a level playing field. As we have seen, dyslexic students will often spend hours and hours on coursework, going through several drafts, and consulting SDTs to help with proof reading skills which of course they cannot do under timed conditions. Students with specific learning difficulties will usually have their scripts identified in some way, often by a coloured sticker, which is meant to ensure that in blind marking, a dyslexic student is not unduly penalised for typical dyslexic spelling and syntax errors. The sticker is simply to bring to the attention of the marker that dyslexic students have difficulty expressing themselves under timed conditions. It is important that dyslexic students are not penalised for errors that have nothing to do with the understanding of the subject. Unless language skills are being assessed specifically, simple errors of spelling or punctuation should be discounted when marking dyslexic students' scripts. Some academic tutors are uncomfortable with the use of stickers because they feel they are not qualified to judge whether a mistake is related to dyslexia or not. While it is very difficult to offer definitive guidance on how to approach such scripts, some generic pointers can be given. (See Appendix 1: *Types of written error*). Some institutions prefer not to use the sticker system but take dyslexia into consideration after the examination, during the Exam Board meetings.

2.3 Use of a computer

Many students would prefer to take their examinations on computer as that is their usual way of working. It is vital that students with specific learning difficulties are not given an undue advantage, so the use of a computer should only be recommended when the student would be substantially disadvantaged without it. Dyspraxic students are often permitted the use of a computer because of the combination of organisational and motor difficulties which result in poor handwriting. As with all reasonable adjustment recommendations, the individual profile should be carefully considered. Usually evidence in the form of a recommendation from an Educational Psychologist or an SDT will be required.

2.4 Use of an amanuensis or voice activated software

Some students with severe dyslexia might be allowed the use of an amanuensis (a reader and a scribe) if they are able to organise their thoughts in this way. It has to be noted that this skill can be difficult for some dyslexics and will need considerable practice in support sessions. If a student is skilled at dictating ideas orally, an alternative would be to use voice activated software. Again, the SDT would need to be confident that the student was competent at using this method and would not in fact be disadvantaged. Provision for support sessions to practise this skill is also useful (see Appendix 2: *Guidelines for the use of an amanuensis*).

Some students will only need a reader (see Appendix 3: *Guidelines for the use of a reader*).

2.5 Multiple choice examinations

Multiple choice examinations can cause dyslexic students great difficulty, although some prefer them because of the limited writing. A student with a slow processing speed and working memory deficit will have difficulty retaining the question and then reading through the answers. If a multiple choice question involves a lot of reading together with several different choices of answer, it might well be that the student becomes overloaded with information and would have to read through the question several times before being able to answer it. Depending on the number of answers she might well have forgotten the question by the time she reaches the last option. Other students will struggle with the practical filling in of the paper. Sometimes an alternative layout of the paper can be negotiated with academic departments in order to make it as accessible as possible. An SDT might offer tutorial sessions to help the student develop strategies and skills to cope with this type of exam.

2.6 Alternative assessments

The Quality Assurance Agency (1999) set out guidelines for HE institutions to follow to ensure compliance with the Disability Discrimination Act. They stress the need to consider 'flexibility in the balance between assessed course work and examinations' as well as allowing 'demonstration of achievement in alternative ways'.

Sometimes students can demonstrate understanding of the subject and learning outcomes in alternative assessments through:

- coursework in place of timed assessment
- oral assessment
- alternative assignments, such as reports, portfolios
- informal interviews following on from the exam. The student would take the examination in the usual way and afterwards have a short interview with one or two people from the academic department to

give them an opportunity to prove they do in fact have adequate subject knowledge. If both interviewer and student have a copy of the exam script in front of them, the student can be asked questions about what she has written which will provide the opportunity to fill in details and give explanations which she might not be able to do in written form.

3. Other reasonable adjustments

As well as discussing reasonable adjustments with the student, the SDT is increasingly expected to provide academic schools with information about how the department can make reasonable adjustments for coursework. The following is a suggestion of possible adjustments for all aspects of academic study. It is worth noting that adjustments which are helpful for dyslexic students are usually beneficial for all students and are often part of normal departmental practice anyway.

3.1 Handouts

The style in which information is presented greatly affects students' comprehension. Dyslexic students often have difficulties with visual perception and easily accessible text is vital. They often have difficulty keeping their place in the text; the more complex the text, the harder this becomes. Minor adjustments to the presentation of material have clear benefits for all students.

Font and writing style

■ Use a sans serif font such as Comic Sans, Arial, Verdana, Helvetica, Tahoma or Trebuchet of at least 12 pt

■ Avoid Times New Roman as the mixture of broad and narrow strokes can be confusing

■ Use the same font throughout the document as this makes it easier to read

■ Use bold to highlight key words instead of italics or capitals (which can be difficult to read); box of key words

■ Avoid underlining as it can make the words seem to run together.

Page layout

■ wide margins make tracking easier and allow space for notes

■ plenty of spacing between paragraphs and sections

■ justified left hand margin only

- headings for different sections

- minimum text; no excessively long sentences; bullet points or numbered points are easier to read than continuous prose

- no background graphics, as this can make the text difficult to read.

Paper

- Many students find black print on white particularly difficult to read. A lower contrast between the print and background is easier (e.g. blue text on white)

- Alternatively, pastel coloured or cream paper, matt paper or off-white is preferable if no coloured paper is available. Avoid paper with a shiny finish

- Coloured overlays can sometimes help with the reading process.

3.2 Assignments

- Consider alternative formats such as reports, portfolios, tapes

- Assignment titles should be given as soon as possible

- Provide a sample of the standard of work expected, perhaps from a previous year's intake

- Provide a sample of an appropriate academic style of writing

- Provide clear guidelines about departmental systems for referencing and preferred layouts, such as the use of subheadings

- Give positive feedback about assignments and guidance about how to improve

- Oral feedback about written work is helpful as well as clear, written feedback

- Extensions should not automatically be granted because of specific learning difficulties, but if the student has good reason to require an extension, it would be hoped that academic departments would look on the request favourably.

3.3 Targeted tutorial time

Dyslexic and dyspraxic students appreciate short (ten minute) tutorials before the start of an important assignment. An initial tutorial might allow dyslexic students the opportunity to discuss an A4 outline of their ideas. This ensures that the typical dyslexic error of misinterpreting the language of the essay title is avoided. A second tutorial might allow students to show the tutor a brief sample of their writing – again to reassure them that they are on the right lines.

3.4 Reading

- Students should not be expected to read a paper instantly. As well as having a slow reading rate a dyslexic or dyspraxic student will often need to read a passage of text several times in order to understand it fully

- Avoid asking a student to read aloud

- Provide a checklist of key words and terminology at the beginning of a new unit or module to aid web searches

- Give 'guided' reading lists with indications of essential and additional readings

- Permit students to record tutorials

- Provide written references as well as verbal

- Provide an overview for the whole course

- Present an introductory or concluding summary of what will be covered in a lecture

- Allow enough time for copying. The justification for this is that dyslexic students often cannot multi-task efficiently and cannot listen and take notes simultaneously

- Put notes on a website or Blackboard

- Provide copies of OHTs or lecture notes (if appropriate) in advance so the student has an overview of what the lecture will be about

- Allow the use of a recording device or lap-top computer in lectures

- Permit students to use note-takers

- Provide references and key terminology in written format.

4. Marking policies

Some universities have adopted institutional marking policies for coursework as well as for examinations. Coursework assignments are flagged in the same way as examination scripts and academic departments are expected to mark accordingly for content rather than style, not penalising for dyslexic type errors. Often tutors are asked to read scripts twice in order to make it easier to pick up on content. It can be very tricky to implement such policies and academic tutors are often uneasy about being expected to differentiate between dyslexic type difficulties and careless errors. Sometimes the difficulties are such that meaning becomes lost, but if a student cannot convey her meaning clearly then she is unlikely to be able to meet the learning outcomes. Reasonable adjustments during the drafting stage are a way round this. The SDT can read work aloud to the student so that she can hear whether what is written is what she meant to say. Tutorials can provide support with writing style and proof reading skills (see Appendix 1: *Types of Written Error*).

In conclusion ...

This chapter has looked at recommendations for reasonable adjustments for examinations, alternative forms of assessments and reasonable adjustments for all aspects of study.

Reasonable adjustments are intended to give dyslexic students the opportunity to demonstrate their subject knowledge clearly whilst still meeting learning outcomes and achieving the same standard as other students. They are not intended to lower academic standards. Adjustments to coursework and assessments which are beneficial for dyslexic students are often of benefit for all students.

Further reading

Learning Differences Centre, University of Southampton, *A Guide for Tutors*

Staff-Student Partnership for Assessment, Change and Evaluation Project (SPACE), (2007) *Inclusive Assessment in Higher Education: A Resource for Change. Disability Assist Services*, University of Plymouth,

Appendix 1: Types of written error

Some students give cause for concern because of the unexpected, poor quality written work. The main features tutors may question are:

Inconsistencies in spelling

- a specific word misspelled in many different ways on one page

- simple, high frequency words such as *who* and *how* misspelled or muddled

- parts of multi-syllable words in incorrect order

- letters within words out of sequence e.g. **flied/feild** for **field**

- a tendency to use phonetic spelling

- capital letters used in the wrong place

- substituting less effective words because of worries about spelling

Weak sentence construction

- words missed out of sentences

- phrases not in the correct order

- meandering construction – too many ideas telescoped together

- lack of sophisticated use of punctuation

- punctuation muddled e.g. *the boys hats'* for *the boys' hats*

- lack of sound, grammatical construction

- inconsistent use of tense

- poor essay structure

- weak sequencing of ideas, paragraphs and sentences

- cause and effect in incorrect sequence

- lack of confidence in using abstract language

- lack of awareness of writing genre

The above points are not intended to be an exhaustive checklist, just examples of typical difficulties which are observable when marking written work.

Appendix 2: Guidelines for the use of an amanuensis

An amanuensis is a scribe who, in an examination, writes down, types or word processes a candidate's dictated answers to questions and reads for the student.

■ Additional time should be permitted for the use of an amanuensis. This will normally be an extra 10 minutes per examination to allow for printing out typed scripts for checking by the students.

■ An amanuensis will normally be a responsible adult who is able to produce an accurate record of the student's answers; who can write legibly, type or word process at a reasonable speed; and, should ideally, have a working knowledge of the subject and terminology.

■ Some students may prefer to draw their own diagrams/charts, when they are required for the answer. These should be indicated as an appendix in the question by the amanuensis and should be clearly labelled by the student on a separate answer book, indicating number of appendix, question number being answered and a title. Students who have poor co-ordination can request the amanuensis to draw the diagrams to their dictation.

■ An amanuensis is responsible to the department examination officer, and the person appointed to act as the amanuensis must be acceptable to the department examination officer. The student cannot nominate the amanuensis but should be given the name of the amanuensis prior to the examination.

■ An amanuensis should not normally be one of the student's subject tutors. On no account may it be a relative of the student.

■ A student should, wherever possible, have adequate practice in the use of an amanuensis.

■ A student using an amanuensis must be accommodated in such a way that no other student is able to hear what is being dictated.

■ The amanuensis may also act as the invigilator.

■ It is the student's responsibility to direct the amanuensis regarding the appropriate layout of the response.

During the examination an amanuensis

■ must neither give factual help to the student nor offer any suggestions

■ must not advise the student regarding which questions to do, when to move on to the next question, or the order in which the questions should be tackled

■ must write down, type or word process answers exactly as they are dictated

■ must write, type or word process a correction on a typescript or Braille sheet if requested to do so by the student

- may, at the student's request, read back what has been recorded

- must not expect to write throughout the examination because the student will be expected to carry out some form of planning for each response. This will be conducted by the student in the answer book provided by the School examination officer and any rough workings crossed through before it is handed in at the end of the examination

Appendix 3: Guidelines for readers' use

A reader is a person who, on request, will read to the student:

- the entire (or part of the) examination paper

- any part of the student's answers

When students require a reader and an amanuensis, the same person may act as both.

- Additional time should be permitted for the use of the reader. This will normally be an extra 30 minutes for a two hour examination with additional 10 minutes for each subsequent 30 minute period, provided in a designated room. However, if a reader and an amanuensis are both used the time allocation will be as in the 'Guidelines on the use of an Amanuensis'.

- A reader will normally be a responsible adult who can read accurately and at a reasonable rate and who has a working knowledge of the subject and the terminology.

- A reader is responsible to the department examination officer, and the person appointed to act as the reader must be acceptable to the department examination officer.

- A reader should not normally be one of the student's subject tutors. On no account may a relative of the student be used as a reader.

- A student should, wherever possible, have adequate practice in working with a reader.

- A student using a reader must be accommodated in such a way that no other student can hear what is being read.

- The reader may also act as the invigilator.

During the examination a reader:

- must read accurately

- must only read the rubrics and questions, not explain or clarify

- must neither give factual help to the student nor offer any suggestions

- must not advise the student regarding which questions to do, when to move on to the next question, or the order in which the questions should be done

- can only repeat instructions given on the examination paper when the reader is specifically requested to do so by the student

- can read the responses when specifically requested to do so by the student

- must, if requested, give the spelling of a word which occurs in the question paper – otherwise spellings must not be given

- must not expect to read throughout the examination because the student will be expected to carry out some form of planning for each response.

Candidates must do all rough workings in the answer book and cross it through before it is handed in at the end of the examination

9

Supporting students on their courses

Supporting learning differences relates to the needs of dyslexic students undertaking a variety of courses. This chapter explores the underpinning skills which are needed to perform effectively. It examines what is meant by higher order skills' teaching and the development of criticality. Suggestions for pinpointing difficulties are provided, together with solutions for effective time management and organisation.

Using this chapter
This chapter will enable you to:

> 5. Understand support strategies for managing lectures and seminars
>
> 5.1 *Note-making techniques and their uses*
>
> 6. Explore the use of technology in the development of academic skills.

1. Supporting learning differences

The dyslexic learner's experience of HE revolves around coursework and examinations. These two aspects of study are potentially the most stressful aspects of gaining a degree. The SDT has to provide guidance and support for a range of problems with which the student is presented. However, there are generic skills which are needed for the elements which make up the day-to-day life of a dyslexic student. All students have to attend lectures and seminars as part of their studies. Some students will find themselves attending sessions where they have to give a presentation to their peers. These essential components provide a back-drop to examinations and the production of assignments.

2. Course demands and skills

A survey conducted at Southampton University (Price, 2001) elicited perceptions from the academic and student bodies – undergraduate, postgraduate and research students. The results of the academic, departmental surveys revealed:

- the academic skills required for the study of the subject discipline
- which of the skills were explicitly taught within the curriculum
- which of the skills were embedded within the course curriculum
- how academic study skills are delivered to undergraduate and post-graduate students.

Four skills were identified by **all** departments as essential:

- library search skills and use of e-resources
- referencing skills
- research reading skills – particularly inference and synthesis of information
- oral presentation skills

Six further skills were identified by **90%** of the departments as important:

- time management and organisation

- critical analysis and logical argument

- taking notes in lectures and seminars

- listening and comprehension

- making notes from research reading

- reading skills – specifically skimming, scanning and selection of information

The following were recognised by 83% of departments as important for their subject discipline:

- selecting and prioritising information for written work

- summary skills

- developing appropriate written style

A closer inspection of these skills demonstrates that many dyslexic students experience difficulties in the majority of the above at some time in their studies because of the nature of dyslexia. However, students do not come for support with the same starting points, and for this reason it is vital that the SDT responds to the differences in learning.

2.1 Criticality in the HE environment

When a group of experienced educationalists was recently asked to define criticality, the responses were breath-taking. The question was punctuated with a heavy silence, followed by mutterings such as 'ah well, that's an interesting question!' There was a sense of exasperation at not being able to provide a quick and succinct reply. Terms such as critical thinking and higher order skills were most frequently used. It is ironic that there is fuzziness in thinking about criticality, for critical thinking has been defined as 'purposeful, reasoned and goal-directed' (Halpern, 1997:4). Perhaps this paradox has emerged because of the 'multiple meanings' (Jones, 2004:167) associated with the term. Yet, the notion of critical thinking is fundamental to educational aims in HE, not only in the UK but in the USA and Australia. For some, the term criticality has encompassed not only critical thinking and higher order thinking skills but also reflective thinking and metacognition. The dimension of metacognition brings with it a sense of declarative knowledge, conscious control, self-monitoring and regulation. This is a cognitive perspective of skill utilisation. Thus, critical thinking and critical skills are two elements of criticality. However, the debate is not whether criticality should or should not be part of the objectives of HE but rather when and how critical skills can be developed.

University staff 'recognise that many of the features described above are not necessarily peculiar to dyslexic students' (Singleton, 1999: section 2.7.8:39). These findings demonstrate the skills which *all* students are expected to develop over the course of their studies. Many of the skills are associated with the development of criticality on all levels: critical thinking, reflective thinking and analytical thinking (Barnett, 1997) linked to reading and writing activities. However, once the dyslexic, cognitive profile is superimposed, the duality of skill acquisition and functionality becomes apparent.

The most invasive aspect of specific learning difficulties (dyslexia/dyspraxia) is the lack of automaticity of processing either spoken or written language. This greatly affects the student's ability to carry out aspects of research reading and writing, and requires the student to spend more time than the non-dyslexic student on many aspects of study. A reading activity which would take the average student one hour might take the dyslexic student four (Price, 2003). A similar comparison can be made with written assignments. Dyslexic students can be anxious about study and may require more sympathetic support than non-dyslexic students. Dyslexic students usually spend more time at each stage of study – taking notes, research reading and writing essays. The dyslexic profile can have a cumulative effect upon the student's ability to manage the learning environment effectively.

The combination of the widening entry gate and the impact of dyslexia upon academic study results in another layer of skill development of which the SDT must be watchful. For some students entering university, ability in the ten categories mentioned above is such that the SDT may need to take a step back and address basic skills difficulties – i.e. sentence structure and construction, grammar and syntax knowledge and how to write prose appropriate to the HE required levels – in conjunction with higher order and critical skill acquisition. In addition to the aspects of academic skills mentioned earlier, the pressures with which the student with dyslexia also has to cope are:

- remembering facts and terminology
- personal organisation
- working to gruelling deadlines
- monitoring progress

As can be seen by the above, the support provided by the SDT goes beyond literacy and encompasses contextualised functionality and effectiveness. As Hunter-Carsch (2001a) states, it is the notion of meta-affectivity which the SDT has to address with the student.

3. Higher order skill development

We cannot teach people anything;
We can only help them discover it within themselves.
(*Galileo Galilei*)

The development of higher order skills is part of a developmental continuum. If viewed in this way, the SDT is able to incorporate all the fundamentals of the teaching framework elucidated in Chapter Two. Appropriate, collaborative guidance will provide a learning environment whereby the following principles are included:

- thinking skills engaged
- interactive, collaborative working
- controlled experimentation to develop a toolkit of skills
- scaffolded guidance
- 'Steps to Mastery' approach to skill acquisition
- 'Diversity of Needs' through individual support.

A metacognitive approach will empower the student to be aware of the skills which are fundamental to HE study:

- retrieving information efficiently
- searching/selection of information
- skimming
- scanning
- categorising information
- organising/mapping information
- summary skills
- planning
- knowledge of texts
- linguistic knowledge
- critical thinking skills.

These elements of study form part of the glue needed for success. The skilled SDT will have this framework in mind so that the individual's needs can be identified to ensure that there is progression and not just an ad hoc approach to support. It makes the difference between personalised learning and simply responding to crisis management.

The Skill Framework, in Appendix 1, provides a break-down of the underpinning skills required. It divides the skills into three main categories:

- basic skills
- transferable/key skills
- academic/higher order skills

The development of effective reading strategies is seen as the glue which binds many academic activities in HE. There are many reasons why a student might not be efficient, and the SDT should be able to pinpoint the difficulties.

3.1 Pinpointing the difficulty

The causes of ineffective reading are multifarious. The SDT needs to explore the routes of failure to help make decisions about the needs of each student and the type of guidance and support she will provide.

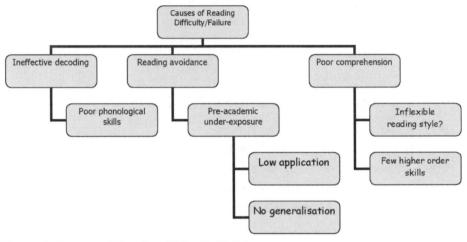

Figure 1: Causes of Reading Difficulty/Failure

To a greater or lesser extent each of these components mitigates against students' ability to cope with the demands of HE. The skills to research or do background reading for any course requires the students to have knowledge of the following:

- navigation of texts: knowing where specific information can be found, e.g. abstracts for summary information etc.

- critical analysis

- management and organisation of the process.

The SDT has to assess the student's level of working in these four areas in order to ensure that she develops the range of higher order skills needed for HE study. Reading and note-making are two sides of the same coin and incorporate many of the generic study skills so will be included in this process.

When teaching higher order skills it is important to remember that these are to some extent hierarchical. For example, scanning is easier than skimming for dyslexic readers. Scanning involves searching text for specific words or phrases whereas skimming hinges upon visual techniques in conjunction with a syntactical knowledge of language. Skimming takes more confidence because the reader does not say each word in her head but lets her eyes flow quickly over a text, searching for nouns, verbs and adverbs in the first instance.

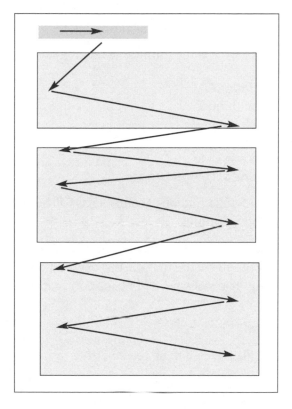

Figure 2: Example of eye movements during skimming

3.2 Reading with your mind

Most students will express concerns about the volume of course reading and their inability to keep up. Many have not had exposure to the text genre and, as a result of dyslexic difficulties, do not absorb the rules of reading experiences – they have to be explicitly taught. Comprehension is an additional problem. That is not to say that the dyslexic student does not have the innate ability to comprehend but rather that she may not have the appropriate higher order skills she needs to tackle the level of reading for her course. By observation and careful prompting the SDT can quickly assess a teaching starting point.

Successful, expert readers go about the task in an entirely different way from those who are struggling. First and foremost, they often operate on automatic levels of processing so are unaware of the underlying skills which they tap into at speed. They adopt an interactive method of reading texts which supports comprehension by self-questioning and self-monitoring. To do this effectively, an expert reader draws upon knowledge of:

- task analysis – what is the purpose of reading this text?
- text layout
- overview techniques
- prediction techniques
- paragraph rules
- use of language
- choice of reading style
- self-monitoring of comprehension

Deconstruction and re-construction of course texts will help students to learn about most of the above features.

If the assessment process shows a student's functional reading performance to be weak, the SDT has to ensure that she has been exposed to the elements of successful reading. The skills needed to support reading comprehension are:

- inference skills

- selection skills: selection of reading style as well as selection of information

- summarising skills

- knowledge of difference between different pieces of information: information weightings

- monitoring comprehension

- monitoring when comprehension breaks down.

The expertise of the SDT enables her to weigh up where comprehension is breaking down; the skills the student brings to this activity; the appropriateness of the current compensatory strategies and the selection of appropriate solutions to meet the student's immediate demands. Many students are unaware of when comprehension is breaking down and may not have been taught a range of techniques from which to choose a relevant solution. If a student is struggling with a text it may be due to inappropriate reading style. Such students read a text from beginning to end and need to be taught the use to which expert readers put the following:

- title
- sub-headings
- bold print
- key words

However, it is the connectivity of these elements which is vital for the HE student:

- making the connections between titles and text

- making the connections between pictorial/graphical information and text

Asking students to explain how they go about tackling a new text provides the SDT with information about the gaps in knowledge and skill, and this enables the SDT to model how to make use of text features to gain quicker access to information with the students' current text,. Similarly, finding out the strategies students use when they come across a blockage which results in the break-down of comprehension is valuable diagnostic information for teaching support. Some students may need to have explicit explanations about the strategies expert readers use. They will:

- pass over the word and read on

- pick up clues from the text

- go back and re-read a section

- leave it out for the time being

- sound out the letters – phonological strategy which is only used if all the above fail

- ask someone – which requires confidence or learned helplessness!

Breaking the cycle of weak strategy use is essential to efficiency and time management.

3.3 Reading systems and solutions

The infrequency of the pattern of student support at HE results in the need to introduce students to systems which can be tried as part of the coursework experience. The Five Point Plan is a method of covering all the skills discussed. This system develops independence in reading whilst providing a practical solution. The Five Point Plan develops the following higher order skills:

- Self-questioning techniques
- Prediction skills

- Clarification
- Effective use of key words
- Summary skills
- Decision-making skills – matching reading style to reading purpose.

This system encourages students to get the gist of a text and then to explore the detail. It has the advantage of flexibility: each 'point' can be demonstrated independently or the student can be taken through all five 'points' in the system. The Five Point Plan handout can be found in Appendix 2 at the end of the chapter. A word of caution: such a mechanistic system is open to abuse. Unless the SDT ensures that the student reflects upon when to use each of the components of the system and monitors usage, the student will not generalise the skills effectively.

There are other methods which students may have come into contact with before university: a popular method is the SQ3R method. It stands for:

- Survey
- Question
- Read
- Recall
- Review

First of all the student needs to get a taste of the chapter/article chosen to read. She will need to skim the text to see if it is suitable for purpose (SURVEY).

Next, she has to ask why she is reading the text and what she wants to get out of it, so that she reads with a specific focus. The student should be encouraged to actively search for answers to questions (QUESTION), so that comprehension is enhanced and self-monitoring takes place.

Then she should read carefully, breaking up the reading into small sections, looking for main ideas (READ).

After this, the student is encouraged to go through the ideas and pick out the main points, while checking that answers to initial questions have been found. She will need to check that the ideas have been summarised or assimilated. How much can be remembered (RECALL)?

3.4 Critical readers

Once the basic higher order skills are in place it is appropriate to help the student to develop critical reading skills. Critical reading is the ability to make judgements about the way a text has been constructed. It is dependent upon an awareness of how language can be manipulated, i.e. the nuances of language needed; and questioning what the author has said in relation to other authors' views. It is particularly difficult for dyslexic readers because of their weak linguistic experiences and the demands placed upon working memory to hold and synthesise information from different sources. However, that is not to say that dyslexic students cannot be taught how to develop these skills. The SDT can steer students towards developing routine questions to interrogate a text which will help to cultivate a critical approach.

To develop a critical approach to reading these generic questions should be asked:

- What are the central claims/arguments of the text?

- What is the main evidence provided?

- How is the evidence substantiated?

- Is the substantiation credible?

- What assumptions are there behind the ideas/claims/arguments?

- What are the weaknesses in the threads of the claim?

- What are the strengths in the threads of the claim?

- Are the claims opposed or validated by other people?

Some students need to be shown explicitly how to find this evidence while others can sharpen up their reading skills by using the checklist.

3.5 Reading list management

Dyslexic students are not alone in worrying about what to do with course reading lists. There are cultural as well as cognitive issues which the SDT should be aware of. Students who are not confident of their reading proficiency are often overwhelmed by a long reading list and are unsure of the 'best' books to choose. Students from the Far East, for example, will expect to read every single book on the list because in their culture that is what is assumed. The dyslexic reader will need to be strategic in her choices and plan her reading appropriately. If the academic tutor responsible for the unit has not differentiated the reading into 'essential' and 'additional', the SDT may need to act as an advocate for the student to find out which texts are required reading. At times, it is difficult for students to find this out because the academic tutor may think that they are trying to get out of reading or to do the bare minimum. There is conflict of intention because the academic tutor wants each student to read as much as possible about the subject, while the reality for the dyslexic reader is that speed and fluency may mitigate against this ideal.

4. Students' needs in coping with the academic life cycle
4.1 Organisation and time management

Life at university through the eyes of the student with dyslexia may appear chaotic at first. Each new year brings new routines, new and increasingly difficult academic demands as well as the need to get used to the teaching styles of another set of lecturers. Although the type of teaching delivery for each course varies within disciplines and departments, the student will have to learn to juggle the individual teaching style of numerous lecturers and different learning environments. The SDT has to bear in mind that this experience hinges upon internal factors such as individual differences and cognitive styles, that is a person's thinking make-up and the preferred and habitual way of mapping information internally. It is also vital to be mindful of how the learning environment is perceived by the *dyslexic* learner. Students provide powerful accounts of painful experience:

> I arrived late for the first main lecture in Unit 703 because I lost my way and couldn't find where I was supposed to be. Worse than that was the fact that I entered the room by the wrong door and ended up standing next to the lecturer. I felt as if everyone was looking at me and laughing. There were hundreds of students there. (Michelle, a first year student nurse)

> My first lecture was a nightmare. There were thousands – well probably hundreds – of students and I couldn't see a single person that I recognised or knew. The noise was deafening: whisperings, paper rustlings, clicking from laptops and students shuffling and fidgeting. I couldn't concentrate on what (the lecturer) was saying. (Andrew, First Year Biological Sciences)

Diversification and widening participation have brought into question the traditional mode of delivery in HE – the lecture. An increasing interest in the teaching and learning environment in the academic community has resulted in a variety of pedagogical approaches. The most common modes of delivery tend to be:

- lectures
- seminars
- tutorials
- laboratory work
- e-learning

Organisation and time management are the keystones to successful course completion and are all-pervasive. Effective students give consideration to preparing for these and ensuring that there is sufficient time to fit everything in satisfactorily so that quality is not compromised. It has been said that some dyslexic people 'cannot see the wood for the trees' (Hunter-Carsch, 2001:5 a) and have difficulty with all aspects of organisation. Working out priorities for long, medium and short-term direction is an essential starter. SDTs can discuss coursework essentials with the student and get her to identify deadlines and tasks to help her reach the point of 'doing'. Appendix 3 provides a planning prompter which can be used with students and adapted for individual use. It enables students to obtain an overview of priorities, linked to timelines.

The SDT should be mindful that not all dyslexic students' needs are the same. Some manage their lives with a type of military precision, whereby everything is organised to the highest degree. One of the ways in which they cope is to ensure that everything is prepared in advance. Others adopt a more laid-back approach! Those dyslexic students who have come through the school system with the bonus of additional support will, no doubt, be used to following carefully prepared weekly time and planning sheets. Planning, scheduling and using 'to do' lists are now part of life in the 21st century.

4.2 Lectures

As would be expected, there is often a disparity between the lecturers' and the students' *initial* knowledge entry-point during lectures. Moreover, the lecture presents tensions: the gap between the students' and the academics' perceptions of the role of the lecture is well documented. The formality and rigidity of the lecture can be a positive feature for the dyslexic learner by providing security and a degree of routine. However, the advantages of a lecture can only be realised once the student understands the game-plan and the ground rules. Many students are not aware that most academics use the lecture as a vehicle for disseminating content information. A lecture is renowned for being:

- a traditional method of imparting information to large numbers of students in a cost-effective manner

- a didactic approach

- the global overview for a series of seminars within a unit

- a monologue style of delivery, with many lecturers reading from a set of notes, interspersed with PowerPoint slides

- a lack of interactive learning – students are not expected to be able to ask questions in this formal environment

- a method of providing a foundation or skeletal framework for a unit/course of study

- a passive approach to learning

- large classes (In some Health Professional courses there can be anything up to four hundred students in a lecture theatre).

The impersonal nature of the lecture can be threatening to the students who learn best by questioning and spontaneous interaction. Many students find the lecture style of delivery frustrating because there is little chance of experiential learning. However, it is the speed of delivery which causes most difficulty for dyslexic students. The ephemeral nature of the information in a lecture depends upon abstraction of concepts and language. For a student who experiences difficulties with language retrieval, word matching problems and difficulties with language visualisation linked to semantic knowledge, this poses problems because there are few hooks upon which to place the new knowledge other than language – the very source of the language processing frustrations. A single lecture, therefore, places demands upon concentration, listening skills and internal concept mapping.

The reality of student life is that many students have to cope with three or four such lectures per day. The passivity of this approach does not support the *constructivist* paradigms which are frequently adopted by dyslexic students who like to *build up* knowledge or *construct* an internal concept map to ensure full understanding Many dyslexic students adopt a semi-passive role during lectures. In one sense they allow the information to flow over them, because they are locked into the mechanistic mode of taking down information almost verbatim. They worry that they must take down the lecturer's every word in case they miss something. This is because their summary skills are weak, and they are not able to perform this type of task at speed before executive resources in memory are overloaded.

4.3 Seminars

I had done all my preparation for the seminar. I had spent hours doing all the reading, trying to figure out what all these people had to say. I felt very strongly about the subject of the seminar and was really looking forward to it so that I could have my say. I was totally deflated within about ten minutes of the seminar. I had my say but the only problem was that everyone had moved on to something else and looked at me as if I was mad. I also found that when I said certain things other students didn't latch on to what I was getting at. Then a few seconds later someone said exactly what I had said – admittedly it came out much clearer than mine – but it was still my point and everyone was congratulating them and saying 'how perceptive'. I wanted to scream at them that I had just said that. So all that hard work was for nothing because either I couldn't keep up with the speed of the discussion or my ideas were misinterpreted. So from being really prepared and looking forward to being able to shine because of my ability to talk, I felt stupid and here is another thing I can't do. (Sarah, Second Year Sociology student)

Seminars present different tensions for the student with dyslexia. Although they are more interactive, they require automaticity of language retrieval and an ability to assimilate verbal information at speed in order to respond appropriately. The mismatch between students' and lecturers' expectations of seminars is apparent. Lecturers assume that students have prepared fully for the discussion which will ensue yet students are at times ill-prepared for their role in the seminar and consequently do not get as much out of it as they might. The seminar offers:

- a more interactive approach to learning

- a smaller size of group (These can vary from twenty-five to ten students)

- detailed examination and discussion of a specified theme or topic

- the expectation that students will have carried out specific, prepared reading(s) prior to the seminar session so that they can contribute to ideas and discussions

- the expectation that students may have to give a brief, prepared presentation to the group (which might involve PowerPoint).

Whilst it is recognised that smaller class sizes are beneficial for all learners, this comes with a caveat for dyslexic learners. The reduction in group size in seminars results in greater individual interaction, and this can have far-reaching consequences for them.

The dynamics of the seminar revolve around *spontaneous* interaction, and students have to be able to *respond quickly* to the dialogues but also to be able to *think on their feet*. Participation in the discussions relies heavily upon preparatory reading. More and more frequently students are expected to take a lead role and to direct the discussion with a preliminary presentation. Such a presentation is expected to *summarise* key information, thinking and research in the seminar topic. Students are provided with reading lists and are expected to *select* from the titles, chapters and journal articles to prepare for the seminar discussion. The words and phrases in italics highlight the stumbling blocks many dyslexic students might encounter. The skills needed for this type of learning environment place great pressure upon language processing, speed of processing and working memory capacity: all factors which are fragile in the cognitive profile of the dyslexic student. Added to this, it must be recognised that the students are working at the edge of their conceptual knowledge in these circumstances, trying to grapple with new terminology and complex and difficult concepts. This compounds the problems dyslexic students face.

4.4 Tutorials

Students often don't know how to get the most out of tutorials. The SDT can help the students prepare for them by developing efficient coping strategies, discussed later in the chapter. Some departments run individual tutorials while others organise groups of two or three students for a session. The shift in emphasis to research in HE institutions has meant that tutorials are precious for both students and tutors. The procedures for tutorial supervisions vary substantially between institutions and even between departments in the same institution. Nevertheless, it is important that the SDT is aware of the student entitlement so that she can direct the student appropriately, to get the most out of this type of academic support.

> I had a meeting with my tutor because he is *the* world expert on the subject of my assignment and I thought, like, it would be cool to get his ideas. He sat looking at me which was a bit unnerving. 'Well, Joss, what do you want?' That stumped me. I thought he was going to give me the information for my assignment. I asked a vague question and he answered that really quickly and waited for me to ask another question. I could feel the words vanishing from my memory and I blurted out something stupid. I left his office feeling really, really silly. Do you know what I think: I think he's got that Apserger's thingy. He can't deal with ordinary talking. (Joss, First Year Psychology student)

Students are often unaware of the shift in power presented by the tutorial environment and do not realise that they are expected to lead the discussion and go with prepared, targeted questions.

Of course, this assumes a capacity for metacognition, and the ability to formulate pertinent questions to ensure that the answers meet the individual's needs. Accordingly, the student may require help not only in posing the right questions but more importantly in being able to monitor progression during learning.

4.5 Laboratory work

In laboratory work students have to be skilled in observation and in recording results of the observations. Accuracy of recording both numerical and language information is of paramount importance. In some subjects students are expected to write up the method and results during the session and are not given the opportunity for revision. This can pose obvious problems for dyslexic and dyspraxic students. Notes will need to be accurate and clearly dated.

Students will need to be aware of the style and format that is expected in the writing of any laboratory report. All departments have slightly different expectations, some expect notes or bullet points, others expect a more formal style.

Students with a severe form of dyspraxia might find some difficulty with managing the equipment in a laboratory, and if this is the case, the SDT will need, with the agreement of the student, to alert the department about the difficulties in a sensitive way, making sure that the department is aware that the student does not pose a safety hazard, but might merely need to be shown more than once how to use a particular piece of equipment. However, a student whose dyspraxia means that she has a tendency to be clumsy and possibly drop equipment needs to build up personal strategies to make sure that she is safe. Most students in higher education with dyspraxia, however, will manage as well as any other student.

Laboratory time-table schedules are harsh, due to space and equipment allocations which are at a premium for most departments. Thus, students have to ensure that they are well organised so that they do not miss *their* allocated slot. Often, laboratory space is cramped and students have to work effectively in confined environments. To get the most out of laboratory work requires careful pre-preparation, clarity of focus and efficient organisational skills, on top of the academic writing skills already mentioned. For many dyslexic students, working in these conditions puts pressure upon the individual cognitive profile and leads to stress and anxiety.

5. Support strategies for managing lectures and seminars

Many students, not only dyslexic students, fail to prepare effectively for lectures and seminars, with the consequence that they do not make the most of the opportunities provided. Time spent before and after the lecture or seminar will reap many benefits for the dyslexic learner. The '*Before, During and After*' framework provides flexibility and adaptability to individual academic and course needs:

Before: the warm-up

The student needs to prompt the mind by considering what the lecture is to cover; and take stock of what is already known. Some dyslexic students are so immersed in the message of the lecture that they fail to take steps to organise their filing systems before going to lectures. Buying file dividers and labelling them; numbering pages; putting titles and dates can save much grief later on.

During: the work-out

The active approach to learning is to be encouraged. This enables the student to take control of her own learning and to ensure that she is receptive to incoming information (this will be achieved by sound pre-lecture preparation). In addition, she needs to be sufficiently organised to take down the information in a way which can be easily accessed later and which will jog the memory. This relies upon well organised note-taking and note-making techniques.

After: the control and management of information

Some dyslexic students find the volume of information they have to manage overwhelming because they have faulty or inappropriate file management strategies or because their notes are unclear when they return to them for essays or revision for examinations. The SDT may need to explore with the student the methods used to manage the filing system in order to provide appropriate advice and support.

Memory weakness is part of everyday life for most dyslexic students. Supporting memory difficulties can be achieved by simple routines. Time taken to read through notes on a daily basis, and getting into a habit of annotating the lecture notes can save much time and hardship later. Appendix 4 provides prompts which can be shared with students. Appendix 5 provides suggestions for equipment for file management. For some students recording lectures may be one of the options which is discussed with the SDT. It could encourage students to become passive learners, shelving responsibility for listening efficiently (for listening skills guidelines, see Appendix 6). It takes twice as long to make notes from a recording, so with time at a premium this may not be the most effective way of organising time.

5.1 Note-making techniques

Many dyslexic students use techniques with which they feel comfortable and which suit their own preferred cognitive and learning styles. However, such students may have missed out on an important part of the equation which would ensure greater efficiency and more effective notes: the role of the context in which they are operating. That is to say, the subject and the context of the note-making. There is an urban myth which suggests that dyslexic learners are all visualisers. Taking this a stage further it would imply that visual techniques for note-making are best. There is no research which backs up this notion and experienced SDTs would maintain that dyslexic students are like most non-dyslexic students in that a variety of note-making techniques should be part of their academic tool kit.

Exposing dyslexic learners to this range of techniques is a vital part of support. However, the crucial factor is the student's reflection of the use of the techniques so that realistic decisions can be made about future choices.

Ensuring that students follow broad, general principles for note-making can increase efficiency in essay writing and examination success. One of the greatest difficulties for dyslexic students is summarising information, because this relies upon good language skills and knowledge, word retrieval and comprehension skills. However, mechanistic techniques can be used to support the dyslexic difficulties. Extracting key information, eliminating subsidiary and exemplary detail, and putting key ideas into one's own words are the skills which the dyslexic student has to perform. Highlighting and colour coding will support the first two parts of the above list. Encouraging students to put aside the original text and imagine trying to explain the key points in their own words will sharpen their summary skills.

Styles of note presentation

Students often think that one style is better than another. Yet it is the content which is being summarised which should dictate note style. However, it is true to say that individuals have preferences which they use to produce quick notes. The essential element is that the notes are of use when accessed at later stages.

Linear/bullet points/listing

This type of note-making style is the most traditional format. It shows a hierarchy of information. It can incorporate bullet points and numbered lists. This style is often adopted because many lecturers produce information in this format.

Grids/tables

These are a useful way of categorising information. To see a worked example, see Chapter 10, *Supporting students' written work.*

Diagrams and hierarchies

These formats provide a quick visual overview of how information is related and, depending upon the format, can make links between ideas, concepts and information clear. For example, historical information can be presented in a time line, while political hierarchies can be laid out in a pyramid shape.

Cycle diagrams and flow charts

These are useful when summarising processes and procedures.

Concept maps and mapping structures

These methods of presenting notes are often complex. They provide visual notes as memory joggers and to help build up the relationships between different aspects of a topic. They can incorporate colour and shape as ways of classifying and categorising information. They use branches, arrows and lines to show relationships. Appendix 7 gives an example which was generated using Inspiration software.

The Cornell System

This incorporates the 'Before (A), During (B) and After (C)' framework and provides students with a format which will support organisational difficulties. If students make notes directly onto a laptop then the Cornell templates can be set up in advance. Similarly, templates can be printed out in preparation for lectures and seminars.

A. Lecture Title:	
Date: Lecturer's Name:	Notes page number

B. Space for information taken down **DURING** lecture	C. **After** Lecture:
	Additional information which is remembered from the lecturer's talk.
	e.g.
	          key words
	          key concepts
	          key theorists/names

D. Follow-up: Questions/commentary (to aid memory and comprehension later)	

Figure 3: Sample of Cornell System Notes Lay-out

6. Using technology to develop academic skills: E-Learning and management

One of the goals of HE institutions is to encourage student autonomy and to develop independent and life-long approaches to learning. E-learning is an example of institutional innovation which promotes self-regulated study. The explosion in the use of information technology is now taken for granted. Email, the Internet, intranets, and multimedia provide students with learning environments which are differentiated. Virtual learning environments are increasingly being developed by academics as a way of involving students more actively but also as a method of rationalising the balance between contact time and research.

Mediated learning environments (MLEs), such as Blackboard, provide a useful tool for the student with dyslexia. She is able to access information when she needs it; can change the appearance of the information to suit her individual needs (font style and size, background colour etc.); and can download notes in advance to help prepare for lectures and seminars. Although visitor status on Blackboard courses can be requested from the departments, this is not practical for SDTs whose student load is considerable and whose students are drawn from many departments and different year groups. It is more appropriate to view these resources with the dyslexic student present so that instructional support can be given to enhance her use of this learning environment.

This multi-modal learning environment can be both friend and foe, depending upon the cognitive and learning styles, previous experiences and level of key and academic skill development of the individual student with dyslexia. It is not the purpose of this chapter to analyse the pedagogical paradigms chosen by academic tutors, departments and institutions but rather to highlight the tensions, frustrations and pressures which each can place upon the student with dyslexia. One of the stumbling blocks for dyslexic students is that getting into these systems relies upon sequential procedures which have to be mastered.

There are many electronic gadgets which can not only help with meeting deadlines but also provide electronic reminders. Students have to make decisions about whether they prefer electronic helpers or paper and pencil supporters. Electronic devices can be simple mobile telephones or sophisticated machines which combine telephones and cut-down mobile computing facilities. Personal Digital Assistants (PDAs) can be used as weekly and monthly schedulers; provide reminders of deadlines; store electronic information downloaded from departmental intranet sites; be used for brief note-taking in lectures; be a repository for collecting and sending email; contain contact information such as useful websites; act as a memory jogger by storing contact information, telephone and email numbers/addresses; and help the user to plan time efficiently. However, technology is only as good as its human user! If inaccurate information is put into the machine, it will not perform miracles and change and adjust items. For students who like to be in control they are worth the investment.

In conclusion...

It cannot be stressed too strongly that the student life cycle is more than the component parts which have been discussed in this chapter. Whilst the student experience can be delineated in terms of the temporal and physical learning environments, and dissected according to skill aspects of the social learning environment, the essential part of the jigsaw which is missing is the role of reflection, metacognition and self-regulation which have to be developed and nurtured by the SDT to ensure that the student with dyslexia is able to access her curriculum efficiently. In partnership, the SDT can help the student to be one step ahead of the game in all the learning environments in which she finds herself.

Further Reading

Cottrell, S (2001) *Teaching Study Skills and Supporting Learning.* Basingstoke: Palgrave

Goodwin, V and Thompson, B (2004) *Making dyslexia work for you: a self-help guide.* London: David Fulton

Price, G A and Maier, P (2007) *Effective Study Skills.* Harlow: Pearson Educational

Appendix 1: The Skill Framework

CONTEXT	SKILL	LEVEL[1]
Lectures	Listening skills	B
	Legible handwriting	B
	Ability to write at speed	B
	Ability to recognise key terminology at speed on screen	B/T
	Knowledge of a variety of note formats	
	Taking down information accurately and at speed	B/T
	Ability to carry out multiple tasks simultaneously (multi-tasking: drawing upon working memory capacity and short term sequential memory)	T/A
	Summary and language synthesis skills	T/A
	Automaticity of internal concept mapping	T/A
Seminars	Listening skills	B
	Communication skills	T
	Word retrleval skills	B
	Summary and language synthesis skills	A
	Automaticity of responses in discussions	T
Essays	Ability to concentrate for long periods	T
	Functional decoding skills for background reading	B
	Knowledge of text layouts	B
	Knowledge of significance of emboldened text	B
	Sentence construction	B
	Knowledge of grammar and syntax	B
	Knowledge of spelling	B
	Vocabulary skills	B
	Keyboard skills	T
	Knowledge of word processor facilities	T
	Key word identification for topic	T/A
	Search skills: internet, library, journal articles	A
	Critical reading skills	A
	Knowledge of genre rules for discipline	A
	Ability to organise and structure ideas in logical manner	T/A
	Recursive planning skills	
	Summary and paraphrasing skills	A
	Ability to present an argument	A
	Ability to differentiate between main ideas and detail in	

[1] B = Basic Skills

T = Transferable/key skills

A= Academic/higher order skills

CONTEXT	SKILL	LEVEL[1]
	Ability to differentiate between main ideas and detail in	A
	both input (reading) and output (writing)	A
	Editing skills	A
	Proof-reading skills	A
	Referencing rules appropriate to discipline	B
Examinations	Knowledge of variety of revision techniques	B
	Organisation of notes and files	B
	Legible handwriting under timed conditions (Use of	B
	computer may not be automatic for dyslexic students)	
	Basic spelling, grammar and punctuation knowledge	B
	Reading fluency	B
	Reading accuracy	B
	Ability to communicate knowledge and information	B
	effectively under timed conditions	
	Ability to interpret questions	B
	Ability to re-shape knowledge map and synthesise	A
	information according to task requirements	
	Time management	B/T
	Stamina	B
Laboratory Reports		
Dissertations		
	Essay skills and additionally:	
	Problem-solving skills – selection of research topic	A
	Self-questioning skills – establishing research questions	A
	Seeing connections between research questions,	A
	research methods and findings	
	Objectivity	A
	Selection skills – selecting topic and appropriate	A
	research from reading	
	Conducting a literature review search	A
	Ability to carry out multiple tasks simultaneously	A
	Expert planning skills – inter-connective management of	A
	global and detailed planning aspects of writing	
	Ability to transform information of others into own	A
	concepts/ideas/points	
	Ability to evaluate information	A
	Time management	T/B

CONTEXT	SKILL	LEVEL[1]
Group Work	Listening skills	B
and	Communication skills	B
Oral	Articulation of key and multi-syllabic terminology	B
Presentations	Word retrieval skills	B
	Ability to work collaboratively	T
	Time management	T/B
	Presentation skills	T
	ICT skills – use of PowerPoint	T
	Automaticity of responses in discussions	B
	Ability to act as a scribe for a group – note-making skills; automaticity of synthesis of verbal information	T/A
	Maintaining deadlines within the team's schedule	T

Appendix 2: Five Point Plan Guidance Sheet

Five Point Plan
Procedures for Use

Getting the Gist

1. Look at the title, sub-titles, any bold/italics text

    ■   Try to work out or predict what the whole section or chapter is about
        from these clues.
    ■   Link this information together to give you the global/big picture.

2. Look carefully at pictures, diagrams or graphical information

    ■   What additional information do they give?
    ■   Read any accompanying captions or titles
    ■   How does this type of information link to the global/big picture?

3. Look for a summary or a conclusion

    ■   Often found in the final section of a chapter.
    ■   Or found also in the Abstract at the beginning of a journal article.
    ■   Fit this information into what you have already accumulated in Points 1
        and 2.

Getting the Focus

4. Now think about what you want to find out
        Where can you locate the information in the text?

5. Decide upon the most appropriate reading method to get hold of your
    information:

    Scan?   Skim?   Read in detail?

    Highlight the information you need.

Appendix 3: Planning Prompter: A student *Aide-Memoire*

LONG TERM PLANNING	MID TERM PLANNING	SHORT TERM PLANNING
SEMESTER PLAN	**WEEKLY SCHEDULE**	**DAILY TO DO LIST**
Identify your academic goals for this semester.	Work out a weekly schedule/planner.	This is your present time perspective. Apart from your time-sensitive slots, you should prioritise your other activities.
Read unit descriptions to see what is expected of you.	Ensure items identified in your semester plan get transferred to appropriate weekly planner.	
Select options.		Start your day by setting your to-do list
Note assignments and hand-in dates for your courses.	Enter your time-sensitive items like lectures, tasks/events that satisfy your key goals and those urgent things that just must get done.	PDAs usually have a 'to-do list' function – you may want to use that.
Find out who you need to see regarding possible work placements, Erasmus exchange etc.		Highlight the high priority tasks.
Note any software you need to learn or be expected to know and find out how you can train yourself.	Make sure your weekly schedule/planner includes your whole life and not just your studies. Many people are increasingly turning to electronic means for this through mobile phones or PDAs*.	
Promise yourself to complete your personal development profile as this will enable you to articulate what you are learning and identify where your strengths and weaknesses are.	Carefully estimate the time it will take you to complete tasks. This takes experience, but it is a characteristic of good time management.	

Adapted from Price, G. A. and Maier, P. (2007)

*PDA is a personal digital assistant. It can be integrated in your mobile phone or be a standalone tool. There are also several desktop tools that can be used like a PDA, e.g. Google has a selection of tools and Microsoft's Outlook has a PDA-like function built into it.

Appendix 4: Student Guidelines for Managing Time

(Our grateful thanks to the SDT Team at Southampton University's Learning Differences Centre for allowing this to be included.)

Priority-setting checklist:

■ make a list of everything you need to do

■ identify the most urgent tasks on the list

■ highlight urgent tasks in one colour and items that can wait in another colour

■ work out how long you should spend on each task

■ think about items that depend on other people, e.g. research visits

Plan your days, weeks, terms using a wall planner

■ write in dates, times and rooms of all lectures, seminars and tutorials. Include assignment deadlines, exams and any other meetings or appointments you have.

■ now block out a realistic amount of time for eating, sleeping, seeing friends, leisure, etc.

■ organise the time you have left for private study

■ think about time patterns that suit you. Do you work best first thing in the morning or late at night? Do you prefer to study in short bursts with lots of breaks or to settle down and concentrate for a few hours?

Set mini-goals

■ Then you can always do something and feel good when it is completed.

■ break assignments into short tasks such as 'read pages 20-24'; 'make notes on chapter 1'; 'write first paragraph of essay'.

■ set a realistic start and finish time for each mini-task.

■ put the mini-goals for the each day into a diary that you always keep with you and tick them off when completed. (Very satisfying!)

■ make the mini-goals as specific, realistic and measurable as possible.

Finally: Save time and avoid last-minute panics by recording references, and colour coding your notes as you go along.

Appendix 5: Equipment for file management

- a4 loose-leaf files
- lever arch files
- concertina files
- computer
- boxed cards
- notebook per topic – often used for laboratory work
- coloured file dividers – so that topics can be quickly located
- coloured highlighter pens
- coloured lined paper – useful for categorising topic notes
- labels for all files
- coloured Post-It notes

Appendix 6: Effective listening – The PISAN Method

Predict and anticipate what is going to be said. Think about

P   *What, Where, When, How?*

Think of some questions you would like answered – this will help you with the next step.

Ideas

I   Listen for important **ideas**. What are the main ideas? What is the point the lecturer is making? Is it a main or supporting idea? What is the speaker doing – explaining, giving an example, categorising, giving an outline, developing an idea?

Signals

S   Listen for **signal** words which will give you clues about what the information is about and where the speaker is going. S/he may signal that the next few things you hear are supporting information.

Active listening

A   This is not something which happens to you. You must weigh up what is being said and not just take down words in automatic, mechanical mode. You must decide what is important and what can be left out.

Note

N   You should **note** down the important information as a memory jog for further work and learning. Make sure you organise your notes well.

Appendix 7: Mapping Style of Note-Making

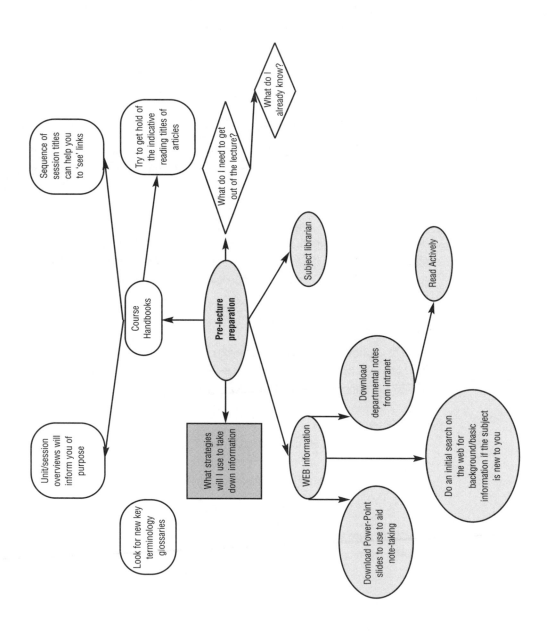

10

Supporting students' written work

Writing causes dyslexic students the greatest anxiety. It is vital to understand the cognitive components of writing in order to provide an intervention programme which meets the needs of the individual's profile and the course demands. This chapter will give you an insight into many approaches to teaching dyslexic writers to become more expert. The chapter considers teaching methods which give practical solutions. It also provides suggestions for supporting doctoral students with dyslexia.

Using this chapter
This chapter will enable you to:

1. Understand what makes writing so difficult for the dyslexic student

    1.1 What is writing?

2. Support coursework: written assignments/essays

    2.1 Support session preparation

3. Examine cognitive strategy instruction

    3.1 A metacognitive teaching approach to the writing process

    3.2 Metacognitive interrogation

    3.3 Using metacognition to develop writing skills: the BUG technique

    3.4 The role of metacognition

    3.5 Support solutions for gathering information for the written assignment

    3.6 Organisational grids

    3.7 Support for the drafting process

    3.8   Support for the editing process

    3.9 How to avoid plagiarism

4. Consider the issues related to proof-reading

5. Explore practical solutions to support laboratory report writing

6. Consider the support issues for dissertation work

7. Consider the support issues for doctoral students

    7.1 Funding pathways

    7.2 Types of doctoral study

    7.3 Support issues

8. Examine the use of technology for dyslexic writers

    8.1 Planning

    8.2 Gathering information

    8.3 Drafting

1. What makes writing so difficult for dyslexic students?

Writing has two specific purposes at university: firstly, writing as a tool to develop students' thinking and understanding; and secondly, to demonstrate knowledge and understanding in a way which can be assessed and examined. Written work constitutes a great proportion of a student's time and effort at university. Surveys of students (Price, 2001) always highlight their anxieties about coping with the written components of their studies. It is vital that the SDT is aware of what is involved in writing and the cognitive components needed to make the activity effortless. This chapter explores the type of support some students would benefit from, although not all students will need every aspect of support.

1.1 What is writing?

Writing is a highly complex set of procedures involving many cognitive processes. Most of what is considered writing in academic terms in HE is composition (Grabe and Kaplan, 1996). The writer has to operate on various levels. Students are expected to be 'expert' writers, and the mark of a good student is the ability to use writing as a tool for thinking. On the one hand they are expected to 'transform', or synthesise information (Bereiter and Scardamalia, 1987) from a variety of sources; to wrestle with the ideas; to develop personal constructs, synthesising information from study; while on the other hand this cognitive network is overlaid with the conventions of writing: knowledge of language and linguistic structures such as sentence and paragraph construction; genre; syntax and semantics. Working under time constraints is often the straw which breaks the camel's back for dyslexic students.

The way in which dyslexic writers processes language, the speed at which this is performed and the way in which their cognitive control box is used may make a difference to performance and production. The cognitive control box is rather like the operational mastermind and relies largely upon memory capacity to provide speed of working and the amount of information which can be held at any given time.

Cognitive psychologists have described writing as a problem-solving activity (Bereiter and Scardamalia, 1987; Flower *et al*, 1992; Torrance and Jeffery, 1999). However, to be able to construct text, the writer has to be able to manipulate many language features:

- syntactic structures
- semantic senses and mappings
- cohesion signalling
- genre and organisational structuring to support coherence interpretations
- lexical forms and relationships
- stylistic and register dimensions of text structure
- non-linguistic knowledge bases (Grabe and Kaplan, 1996:62)

This list in itself is daunting but it is overlaid by the writing process which consists of the following components:

- defining the task
- selecting information (content) during reading
- drafting ideas
- editing
- proof-reading and checking.

If writing were a linear process, it would place considerable demands on the cognitive deficits allied to dyslexia. As research has demonstrated, writing is much more complex and is not a matter of completing one stage before going on to the next in a 'do this, do that', manner. It is a recursive activity. This results in starting points being constantly modified in the light of new and incoming information and ideas. This type of process is more demanding of cognitive capacity and puts greater strain upon working memory. Therefore it is even more important that some of the low-level activities operate on automatic pilot.

Interest in dyslexic writers in HE is growing. It helps the SDT to understand why dyslexic students experience difficulty. Studies of speed of text production (mechanical and compositional), analysis of dyslexic spelling and grammatical errors and assessment of lexical choices made by dyslexic students in HE are emerging (Singleton and Aisbitt, 2001, Hatcher, 2001, Farmer *et al*, 2001.). Other studies relating to dyslexic students' writing in HE have demonstrated a) structural weaknesses with dyslexic students' text (Farmer *et al*, 2002); b) that dyslexic students' essays are shorter than their non-dyslexic peers' (Sterling *et al*, 1998); and c) that dyslexic students' use of the spelling checkers on computers helps them to identify errors during proof-reading stages (McNaughton *et al*, 1997). This all points to the fact that dyslexic writers in HE will require support for these aspects of writing. Steering the dyslexic writer through the process requires expertise and a knowledge of the pressure points for a dyslexic writer.

The teaching of writing comes under the three wide categories (Table 1 below) which encompass lower and higher order skills. To make sure that students develop expertise in writing, it is important to assess levels of experience and skill in the categories shown in Table 1.

Processes	Forms of Writing (Genre)	Conventions of Writing	
Organisation	Descriptions	Left	Right
Task Analysis	Reports	Top	Bottom
Planning	Summaries	Spacing	
Research	Instructions	Sentences	
Drafting	Letters	Punctuation	
Editing	Narratives	Spelling strategies	
Proof-reading	Poetic forms	Paragraphs	
Conferencing	Comparisons	Vocabulary usage	
	Making an argument	Grammar	

Table 1: Features of Writing Development

It is not always possible to provide a teaching programme which will give exposure to genre writing – highlighted in the middle column of the table above. However, this column can be used by the SDT to assess the writing needs of the individual matched to subject demands. Similarly, the right-hand column contains the lower order skills which are often taken for granted by academic tutors when students enter university. These may need to be assessed so that the SDT ensures that the individual is provided with opportunities for learning these skills as and when they arise in coursework writing.

For many dyslexic students at university, much time will have been spent upon the conventions and mechanics of writing, to the detriment of provision for higher order skill acquisition. Consequently, dyslexic adult writers may not have been exposed to opportunities to learn how to manipulate and control the actual process of writing.

The luxury of time to teach dyslexic writers the mechanical as well as the higher order aspects of writing is not open to most SDTs, so a pragmatic approach to teaching has to be made and priorities have to be clear. The starting point and progression for the student will be individual, thus making the support for writing personalised.

Nevertheless, organisational difficulties are, in a sense, the over-arching problem for the dyslexic writer and affect every aspect of performance. Linguistic processing difficulties, allied to weak retrieval and faulty language mapping processes, slow down the systems and not only have an impact upon time on task and text generation but also create anxiety. There are a number of elements of the writing process over which the students have little or no control: the task environment (the writing task), the writing deadlines and the discourse community in which they find themselves. Nevertheless, many of the students have developed compensatory strategies which were either intuitive or strategic. The SDT has to assess the quality of these to ensure that the student is optimising compensatory ways of working but also that she is exposed to new techniques to increase efficiency and improve grades.

2. Supporting Coursework: written assignments and essays

In a student-led environment, dyslexic students will bring along to a support session coursework with which they are struggling. It is important to ascertain where the difficulties lie so as to provide targeted, relevant support. Some students are in such a state of panic that they cannot see the wood for the trees and give garbled descriptions of what they have to do, while at the same time demonstrating high levels of panic in terms of what they should write about. The inexperienced SDT could fall into the trap of concentrating upon content when the anxious dyslexic student comes to a session with an assignment task. This is not the role of a support tutor.

Dyslexic students are likely to require support for coursework in the following areas:

- Management of the whole writing process
- Organisation of various components of the writing process
- Where to get the required information
- Keeping to deadlines
- Drafting, editing and proof-reading

In an ideal world the student would arrive having just been given an assignment, so that the SDT can start at the very beginning and take the student through a structured teaching programme which builds up writing skills and takes her through the experience of the process. However, many students seek help at the point of crisis management, when the deadline is looming, and it has become obvious that their strategies are not working and that they are unlikely to complete the assignment to meet the deadline. At this stage the experienced SDT will quickly assess the situation, the student's immediate needs and choose a starting point for teaching which will provide skill development and progression yet provide information to enable the student to get the written work done. This type of first aid approach is short term and can work. The student is helped to produce the required written work but, in terms of developmental progression and long term goals, she may not learned to manage the learning process. Critical self reflection is vital if the student is to take a more active part in the learning process. This can be sensitively guided by the SDT.

2.1 Support session preparation

One of the drawbacks of a student-led model is that it relies upon the student bringing complete information to a support session. This requires organisation and forward planning, two skills for which the dyslexic student is not renowned! Often well-intentioned SDTs will spend valuable time working on skills with dyslexic students, guiding them to formulate written work, only to find that they have presented a partial picture. If the SDT had had all the jigsaw pieces she could have helped them make more effective choices. But the SDT has to prepare in advance for such eventualities. Unlike the dyslexia tutor in secondary school, who can prepare for each session and gather the necessary resources for teaching, the SDT in HE might never know what to expect in advance of a session. However, she can conduct more generic planning. Departments provide coursework guidance, deadlines and even assignment titles in electronic format. So the SDT can download vital and accurate information from subject sources as a back-up in case the individual student forgets to bring such vital resources to the session. In this way, organisation, management and time-planning can be supported through an accurate framework. This will ensure that the guidance is more relevant.

Students have to be encouraged to bring along specific information if they require support with coursework. Providing a memory jogger in the form of a shopping list will support weak memory and provide a practical checklist for work management for the dyslexic student. A generic list might contain:

- the title of the written assignment

- word limits

- deadline

- any departmental guidance on how to approach the assignment

- notes made by the student during lectures relating to tips and hints given by the academic tutor who has set the assignment

- departmental guidance about stylistic features (genre issues)

  - preferred referencing style for bibliographic management

  - use of sub-headings

  - use of footnotes

  - use of first-person singular and third-person singular

  - use of lists and bullet points within the text

  - use of diagrams, pictures and web images

  - preferred fonts

  - regulations about student information to be contained on each assignment – student name and/or number etc.

- notes and information about the content which may be used for the assignment

- any notes on background reading already carried out

- lecture handouts

- books and journal articles already chosen as possible sources for the content of the assignment.

Supporting written work is not only about ensuring that the student can get the assignment written and handed in on time. It is also about an individual's development as a writer. To help the student to become a more reflective learner, interpreting feedback on the assignment from an academic tutor is essential and helps to set new student targets for the future. However, it is not always easy to obtain such information. There may be a departmental policy which states that students can look at the feedback report sheets but that they cannot have a copy for themselves. The SDT may need to liaise with academic tutors so that this information can be brought to support sessions by the student.

3. Cognitive strategy instruction

It is vital that SDTs reflect upon the teaching methods they use to support writing. All the activities should be set within the interactive, scaffolded framework to help increase metacognitive strategy development, as discussed in Chapter 2, *Demands upon learning in the HE Context*. The SDT should be clear about the distinction between 'authors and secretaries' (Beard, 1993:181) so that the objective of the support session is clarified, and the SDT is aware of when to teach the lower order skills needed as a secretary and the higher order skills of the author. The layer which pervades all of this is the ability to manipulate the whole writing process with ease. In this way the *how* of writing is emphasised, not the *what*. Healy Eames' (2002) research points out that well-meaning educational support can miss the mark because there is a lack of engagement of metacognitive strategies. She posits that writing gains can be increased by a teaching environment in which the learner is actively monitoring progress, i.e. is learning to manage the experience. Thus, the role of critical literacy, a combination of literacy skills and metacognition, requires more attention in the development of dyslexic writers. This will enable them to make strategic decisions in planning and organisation to ensure greater efficiency and effectiveness and reduce low self esteem. It is about not only the ability to construct grammatically correct sentences with correctly spelled words but also the ability to make choices from an understanding of one's own literacy practices. Self-monitoring systems need to be *explicitly* taught to dyslexic writers. It is not sufficient to tell them to 'check your work to make sure it makes sense'. Even if the dyslexic writer has the time to edit and check (proof-read) her work, she may not be able to spot her own errors in construction and spelling.

Cognitive strategy instruction (cognitive education) helps to bring the thinking skills to the surface so that the dyslexic writer can see how expert writers manage the process. Teaching students self-questioning techniques will provide long-term gains and develop a metacognitive approach to learning. It offers the reflective self-monitoring which is the vital metacognitive component.

3.1 Metacognitive teaching approach to the writing process

For the SDT knowledge of the pitfalls which the dyslexic writer could experience is a key to relevant support. The pressure points in the writing process for the dyslexic writer are:

- knowing what to do or what is expected in the written assignment

- knowing whether the information selected from reading is appropriate

- overcoming writer's block

- controlling writing style

- managing time constraints

These aspects are compounded by weak working memory capacity and difficulties with language processing and speed of working. Armed with this knowledge the SDT can tackle each component of the process to meet the dyslexic writer's needs while at the same time providing opportunities for strategy instruction, self-monitoring and reflection.

> I know what I want to say, but it never comes out right. I don't understand why my teachers can't understand what I'm getting at. They always tell me that the essay is not well organised. (Jason, 2nd Year History Student)

> I'm often told that I haven't answered the question. Yet I thought I had and I don't understand why he (the academic tutor) made that comment. (Michelle, 1st Year Nursing Student)

These comments exemplify the gulf which exists between learners and lecturers. Students have expressed their exasperation and embarrassment at their inability to work out what was expected of them, despite numerous explanations from academic tutors (Herrington, in Hunter-Carsch and Herrington, 2001). Typically, many dyslexic students require more detailed explanations about the process as well as the essay content requirements because of their inability to read between the lines of essay title language. Often these students are provided with content information by academic tutors rather than information on how to go about the management of the process – that is, the skills aspect of writing.

3.2 Metacognitive Interrogation

Interrogation Rationale	Student Internalisation
PURPOSE	Why am I doing this?
OUTCOME	What is required at the end?
STRATEGY	What is the best way to do it?
MONITORING	Was it successful?
DEVELOPMENT	How can it be improved?
TRANSFER	Can I use it in different situations?

These questions can be used as a practical prompt by the student to manage and organise the writing process (Haller *et al*, 1988).

3.3 Using metacognition to develop writing skills: The BUG Technique

The BUG technique, which stands for Box, Underline and Glance-Back, is a task analysis framework. Task analysis enables dyslexic students to gain experience in untangling the language of the activity. It also affords the SDT the opportunity to introduce collaborative and internal dialogues as a step to independence and control. The essence of the 'interactivity' of the model evolves from the combination of the bottom-up and top-down concepts. Because the starting point is the dyslexic conceptualisation of abstract language, in this sense it is a bottom-up model which is student-driven. However, the teaching methods employed use explicit modelling to develop metacognition, meta-language and meta-skill performance in an environment which promotes success by scaffolding the learning and breaking skill acquisition into manageable steps. In this way, the SDT says aloud the decision-making processes which are involved in understanding the abstraction of the language of the task environment, and the connections between task language and the management and organisation of the drafting and editing processes. It is dictated by the individual's different writing demands, which become increasingly more complex. In this way the concept of a developmental continuum can be achieved through a model which makes skill acquisition explicit, to ensure that the dyslexic writer learns the features of control of the process.

With this in mind, it is vital to devise a task analysis system (TAS) which meets these specific needs:

- to unravel language by using non-language stimulators

- to provide bridges between the task language and effective systems for organising data/information collection (note-making systems)

- to link task language to a visualisation of the finished product

- to develop a system of self-monitoring which will increase meta-cognition and enable better transferability of skills.

For students who are unable to crack the code of abstract language, anxiety and frustration are often just below the surface. The BUG technique aims to reduce some of the stress by providing a practical tool for untangling the language of the question. Thus, a multi-sensory approach is utilised in the following way:

Verbal: Collaborative dialogues to bring the decision-making and thinking skills to the surface. The tutor-modelling can adopt a problem-solving approach, getting the students to develop their own internal dialogues to enable them to function independently.

These dialogues can help the students to develop language selection techniques. They become familiar with the type of language which is used in this environment. By means of familiarity and reinforcement, they learn to develop a wider sight vocabulary for task language.

The collaborative dialogues show the students how to interrogate and make connections between a word such as 'Explain' and the expected shape of the essay with its paragraph structure. Thus, the internal web of language connections is forced by demonstration and over-learning.

Kinaesthetic: Students are directed to selecting and isolating key features of the language of the task environment by having to physically box and underline aspects of the question or task. This procedure not only develops decision-making and problem-solving interactions to language but also defuses the anxiety related to unravelling abstract language with no apparent hooks.

Students are encouraged to develop their own memory hooks to help them to link language and action. For example, drawing a simple weighing scale above the word 'Evaluate' can trigger the type of essay which is expected. This, in turn, can loop back to the collaborative and internal dialogues which help to make the connections explicit and enable students to move from stand-still to action with a visualisation of the structure of the paragraphs.

Visual: Colour-coding language provides the dyslexic reader with a quick way of locating significant words in the task environment. This part of the procedure also develops metacognitive knowledge of language and meta-language usage. It builds upon the problem-solving approach to decision-making which will ultimately help the students to work independently.

The BUG procedure:

A closer examination of this procedure demonstrates its pedagogical features. For example, using the following essay title provided by a year 1 Arts undergraduate as part of a coursework assignment, the SDT would say aloud the different thought processes which are involved in making decisions about boxing and underlining. The SDT would model the self-questioning techniques which are employed in this process.

'Evaluate the connection between language and game according to *Saussure*.'

Procedural steps:

1. The student is asked to put a box around the word(s) which directs her to 'what *to do*' for the written task i.e. the written operation: 'Evaluate' (knowledge of language)

2. The student is then directed to ask herself the question 'what' in conjunction with the boxed word: in this example: 'Evaluate what?' (problem-solving approach to self-questioning, developing and utilising internal dialogues). The answer provides a method of problem-solving and helps the student to work out which are the key features. This leads to the underlining process.

3. The 'Glance Back' is an essential aspect and should not be overlooked. It provides the student with a self-checking strategy to ensure that words which are important to the task are not overlooked and to help clarify the task (self monitoring).

3.4 The role of metacognition

The above procedure makes explicit what the experienced reader does subconsciously, viz. interact with language. The 'expert' reader makes decisions about the significance of the individual word on different levels. She can relate the words in a sentence to each other, while at the same time eliminating some words which are not crucial to the written task. She can also weigh up which word(s) gives clues to the shape and structure of the written task. Thus, the 'expert' reader is able to make decisions about words in text while beginning to plan the macro structure of the writing.

This ability to multi-task within a recursive language activity is problematic for those with working memory difficulties that writers with dyslexia experience. By breaking the cognitive language functioning into manageable chunks, the dyslexic reader does not overload her system, and at the same time she is able to use a logical, step-by-step deconstruction and reconstruction of language. When students understand the rationale for generating self-questioning techniques to unlock the language of the task, they begin to generalise the techniques. A toolkit of questions can be constructed so that, with growing expertise, students can choose the best tool from their individual toolkit for the task in hand. Giving students this framework for self-questioning empowers them to engage in active self monitoring – a skill used subconsciously by expert readers and writers (Palincsar and Brown 1984; Wray, cited in Gains and Wray, 1995).

Some students tend to skip over the 'Glance Back' element of the procedure, stating that '... don't have the time for all that checking and going over things. I need to get on with my essay'. However, reading inaccuracies are often related to the small, everyday glue words which can be overlooked by dyslexic readers. Such words often appear insignificant, but may significantly change the inferential meaning of a sentence. Getting dyslexic readers to weigh up and take notice of language may appear to be anathema. Studies have shown that competent dyslexic readers pay more attention to the context than to the use and analysis of language (Reid, 2003, Hunter-Carsch, 2001). Nevertheless, this is the skill the tutor can model to bring to the surface the nuances of language for the benefit of those for whom language is not dynamic.

Instruction words are vital clues for students to understand how the assignment has to be tackled. Helping students to make mental bridges between the language of the title and the shape of the essay is vital for those with dyslexia. (See Appendix 1 for a list of commonly used instruction words with suggested descriptions. It is, however, more effective to use the student's own words so that they are more easily remembered.)

3.5 Support solutions to gathering information for the written assignment

Dyslexic students often spend far too long on this part of the writing process, and their working methods are inefficient and ultimately time-consuming. So students need to try new techniques which can be generalised and used in the future. This enables the SDT to expose the student to various techniques which are explored later in the chapter. Effective task analysis, using The BUG technique, will provide the foundation and a bridge to move onto the next stage of the writing process. Managing the collection of data relies upon selection of information just as much as organisation of good notes. This is yet another pressure point in the process for the dyslexic writer, and the SDT can guide her through this mine-field. The selection of information will be much easier if she has a clear understanding of the task through the use of The BUG. In other words the student is much more aware of what is needed and what to be on the alert for in her reading. The dyslexic writer will function more efficiently if she has a data collection system which will help her to organise her thoughts when she comes to the drafting process.

3.6 Operational grids

One such system is operational grids. These are methods of harnessing the random thought processes of the dyslexic learner whilst moving towards a linear structure. They act as bridges and smooth the organisation of decision-making processes. They act as a buffer to enable the student to control the content which will be used in the drafting component of writing.

Using the important words identified in the task question, the student can set up an organisational framework which will help to focus the background reading and categorise the information as she carries out the collection component of the writing process. This is divided into two stages. First, the student makes decisions about locating the information in the grid. Secondly, once all the information has been collected, the student can group this and put it into order of writing priority. Such organisational grids support working memory deficits by chunking and staging the overall complexity of the process. In the same way as writing templates are useful for laboratory reports, so grids are valuable to prompt more focused reading.

Let us imagine that the student has come to the session with the following essay title:

Essay Question: 'Prepare a report to use as a discussion document for the Board of Directors of the engineering company about the use of slip gauge accessories; plug gauges; and air gauges. Your report should make reference to the following points:

a) the design features or principles used in each system

b) the equipment or components that form the measuring system

c) the procedures that are followed when component dimensions are checked.'

To avoid straying from the point, wording from the question forms the basis for headings in the grid below.

	slip gauge accessories	plug gauges	air gauges
design features or principles used in each system			
equipment or components that form the measuring system			
Checking procedures			

Initially the SDT might explicitly model how to set up a grid or matrix for note making. The SDT is able to guide the student to a greater understanding of the nuances of language while at the same time providing a safety net for the organisation of information. Carefully constructed grids mean that the dyslexic student simply deals with the immediate information and makes a single decision as to its location in the grid. That is, in which box would this piece of information be best located? Once all the information has been gathered, further decisions about priority and relationships can be made so that the final product has a better structure and is more coherent and cohesive.

As the student brings further essay titles, the SDT is able to gradually hand over the decision-making about how to design a working grid according to the task in hand and the dyslexic student begins to take control of the process.

Having made up a comprehensive matrix of evidence for the essay the student is now ready to manage the drafting and editing stages. However, a note of caution for the inexperienced SDT: many students are unaware of the differences between these two processes. Some try to cut corners and combine the two activities, thinking that they will save time. However, combining the processes successfully requires good working memory capacity and language processing skills.

3.7 Support for the drafting process

Drafting is often referred to as the composing part of the writing process. It is at this stage that ideas are ordered and structured. It should be considered as the first stage of the finished product. During the drafting phase the student has the chance to get initial thoughts into sentences and paragraphs, in order to communicate knowledge to the reader (i.e. the academic tutor or examiner).

Sequencing difficulties in the drafting process will have been more or less eliminated by the use of grids so that the student starts the drafting process with a clearer conception of what she wants to communicate. Therefore, she reduces the memory overload by concentrating upon sentence-level operational planning, in the knowledge that the more global paragraph-planning has been sorted out by prioritising information within the grid or matrix.

Most dyslexic writers lack confidence in their compositional skills so are unsure of the efficacy of what they have written. For example, many students think that their sentences are adequate and that the message is clear. Expert writers are able to view their writing objectively to polish or edit it.

3.8 Support for the editing process

Many students confuse editing and proof-reading. Editing is the act of revising and amending the language to produce prose which is not only coherent and cohesive but which accurately reflects the writer's thoughts and ideas. It is, therefore, a difficult activity for those with language retrieval difficulties. However, often students can improve upon their prose because they can hear that what is written does not make sense or is not exactly what they wished to say. The auditory solution should be encouraged. Students may use a tutorial session to help them to hear what they have written. Nevertheless, the aim is to hand over control to the student, so other solutions need to be discussed. Basic, written construction is at the heart of effective communication. Before the SDT explores ways of editing it may be necessary to go back to basics for some students whose prose does not rely upon the rules of written English. External editing solutions frequently offered are:

- Asking the SDT to read the text aloud
- Asking a friend or partner to read the text aloud
- Using voice recognition software to read the text aloud

If this is to be an educational opportunity for gaining skills, it is vital that the student rectifies the problem and modifies the language herself. It is tempting to 'do it for them' but this must be resisted if the student is to take control eventually. Indeed, at the early stages the SDT might model the thinking skills which she would use to alter language so that the dyslexic student is aware of those hidden cognitive skills which work below the surface with expert writers.

3.9 How to avoid plagiarism

> I didn't know that I'd plagiarised things. I took words and phrases on the internet and re-arranged them into my own sentence. I was shocked and humiliated when I was told to go to my tutor about cheating. (Chris, 1st Year Geography student)

These sentiments reflect the dilemma many dyslexic students face. However, they are more vulnerable to plagiarism because of their inherent language difficulties, lack of summary skills and memory problems. Firstly, they may be unable to manipulate language effectively and so rely over-heavily upon the prose of others to save time. Secondly, by the time they have gone through note-making, drafting and editing, they may not always remember which are their words and which are the phrases of others. Nevertheless, plagiarism is grounds for failure and is taken seriously. All universities and colleges have regulations which are announced on the main institutional website or translated in course handbooks and departmental guidelines.

Chris, the Geography student above, writes by Patchwriting, a term penned by Howard (1995), which aptly conjures up what the student may be doing when writing. During the drafting process, students look at information from a variety of sources: books, articles and departmental information. They may alter the odd word from lots of sources, paraphrasing information. Whilst patching together other people's ideas may be the technique which the dyslexic student has always used, it can result in disjointed and fragmented prose which is too close to the original text.

This can be overcome if the student has used a grid or matrix to gather information. Such grids are purposely small so that the student is discouraged from copying word for word from text and has to learn to write in bullet points, thus summarising the information in her own words. This should be made explicit to the student so that she is aware that in using grids she is not only organising her thoughts but also avoiding plagiarism.

One of the main culprits for engendering plagiarism is the internet. Students are now proficient at cutting and pasting information from quick searches and lose track of the origins. Having to squeeze this information into small boxes makes the student get the gist of the message to summarise. Teaching students to summarise is described in Chapter 8, where support for research reading is explored in detail.

4. Proof-reading

Proof-reading is more to do with the mechanics of writing. It is, therefore, vital that the SDT makes the dyslexic writer aware of the different skills which are needed for the different activities. Being able to spot your own errors relies upon good visual discrimination and visual sequencing skills, which the dyslexic, cognitive profile often lacks.

Many students are so pleased to have finished an essay (or they have left it to the last minute and have run out of time!) that they do not want or do not have time to do this essential aspect of writing. Proof-reading involves looking out for errors which can be classified into various categories:

- typographical errors (the type of errors made when trying to type too fast)

- irritating spelling errors

- poor sentence constructions.

Some Higher Education Institutions (HEIs) provide proof-reading facilities for students. The purpose of such services has derived from knee-jerk reactions to SENDA (HMSO, 2001) and as a result of increased numbers of students for whom English is an additional language. Some SDTs use tutorial sessions to proof-read students' work. Whilst this may be understandable, it is not serving an educational purpose. Certainly the student's work is checked. Passive students who simply want this part of the writing process done for them are happy. Yet, it is a missed opportunity to increase the individual's skills and to hand over control to the student. It adopts a short-term, first-aid approach rather than the long-term, strategy-building system which is advocated throughout this book.

Students need to be encouraged to be on the look out for patterns of errors. The SDT can go through the student's written work and identify these for the student and then systematically use them as the basis for future teaching and individual target-setting. This could be part of any pre-session planning. These targets should be negotiated with the student so that she is involved in the whole process and makes decisions about which errors to concentrate upon over a period of a term or semester, and the number of error types with which she feels she is able to cope. This provides opportunities for the SDT to teach specific language and spelling rules which are relevant to course needs and the individual's developmental progress. Another solution is to encourage the dyslexic student to set up her own proof-reading buddies. In this way she is taking control of her learning and compensating for her intractable difficulties in a pragmatic manner. A word of caution is needed, however, when suggesting this system to students because they could fall into the same trap as that engendered by institutional systems. Students should ensure that their 'buddies' simply highlight errors but do not change them. Doing the work for them is not part of the dynamics of long-term progression!

Becoming aware of one's own errors can be a cathartic experience which needs to be sensitively handled by the SDT. It will inevitably bring underlying spelling difficulties to the surface. However, this will give the SDT ample opportunities to encourage the student to choose which spellings might need to be worked upon. Many dyslexic students have an aversion to spelling and are not keen to spend the valuable time needed to overcome the problems. This means that it is even more important for them to recognise errors which are irritating to others, which can result in lower grades. They should also be encouraged to look for patterns of spelling errors and the mis-spelling of high frequency technical terminology.

5. Supporting coursework: laboratory reports

In some subject areas such as engineering, psychology, chemistry and medicine, students have to manage a weekly workload of written reports. Often these reports form part of the final grade. Such written work is routine and is driven, in the main, by a practical activity. The kind of writing required for this type of activity is factual and does not have a layer of criticality which is inherent in other writing tasks. It should be more manageable but for the dyslexic student it can become a problem because of weak organisation, both in personal and in written spheres, and faulty time management. The latter has been dealt with in the previous chapter.

Laboratory reports are spontaneous by nature, and this can be challenging for some dyslexic students, who often need time to consider what to say and how best to express the information. To help ensure that the student's efficiency is maintained, it is worth discussing the expected format with the student at the outset of the course. Bullet point writing and brief notes will be less of a drain on time and organisation for the dyslexic writer but the SDT may need to act as advocate for the student with the academic tutors to obtain permission for slight changes in format.

A practical solution to support can be provided by the SDT in a support session. Report writing is an ideal candidate for templates which will not only save the student time but also help to prompt what needs to be written, and in this way support weak memory and sequencing skills. Templates are frameworks which provide the writer with headings to prompt writing. Because of the nature of the diversity of the subjects which the SDT is supporting, it is inappropriate to provide frameworks in this book. It is much more educationally supportive to work alongside a student to provide a customised template to meet current academic needs. Such practice involves the student, and the end-product will be a valuable resource which the student has had to think about. Consequently, the rationale or thinking behind the formulation of the headings will, by expert SDT prompting, have been thought through by the student, and she will remember how to use it when the support is not available to help her remember what information was supposed to go where on the template. Such templates can be designed in a session on a computer. The student then has the option of printing out a number of blank templates to keep in the laboratory file or which can be used directly on screen with a laptop. In this way the student not only takes control of the formulation of the template but also makes decisions about the practical issues of use and any personal preferences.

Another aspect of practical support for report writing is to work on the subject-specific vocabulary needed for this activity in the early stages of teaching support. Again, it is vital that the student takes an active part in the compilation of this vocabulary: it is, after all, part of the content knowledge which she brings along to the sessions. Students should be encouraged to bring along these resources when working on this aspect of report writing and coursework support. Once the terminology needed for the report writing has been identified it is easy to slot it into the most appropriate sections of the electronic template so that the language sits there as a prompt.

6. Supporting dissertation work

Most students are required to present a large written project, usually during the final year of study. The writing techniques and strategies which have been taught and developed for coursework assignments and essays will be needed for dissertation writing. However, dissertations are more an organisational and time management problem.

7. Supporting doctoral students

Although SDTs are often wary of taking on students at PhD level because it may be beyond their own learning experience, the SDT does indeed have the expertise to deal with the difficulties encountered by dyslexic doctoral students. In one sense these students are no different from other dyslexic writers in terms of their cognitive profile and its impact upon their writing. However, in another sense, there are other important issues which need to be taken into account when supporting such students. Before an intervention programme is devised, an assessment of the doctoral student's needs must take into account:

- the learning experiences the student has undergone in her undergraduate and possibly post-graduate studies (master's level study)

- previous specialist support (if any) received in HE

- previous writing experiences

- individual strengths, weaknesses and learned writing strategies

- use of technology

- type of doctoral studies chosen

- stage reached in the doctoral cycle

- the challenges of working in a research community.

Doctoral students will have already gone through undergraduate studies, and some may have gone on to post-graduate studies before being accepted onto a doctoral programme. In order to gain one of these treasured places, the dyslexic student will have had to demonstrate academic success at a high level. It is likely that such students will have developed some entrenched ways of working which may need to be adapted and changed to meet the demands of a higher level of study. This, added to the fact that all doctoral students are at the limit of their understanding of the subject, results in the need to deal with emotional as well as academic matters.

However, by far the most sensitive issue for the SDT to resolve is the final challenge in the list above: working in a research community. Concerns about the erosion of standards in the research community can sometimes cause unease. In many departments the staff who supervise doctoral students are, necessarily, more senior and often nationally and internationally renowned in their field. Many regard themselves as the gate-keepers of standards within their research community. Accepting a student with a history of learning difficulties at this level of study can be anathema to some academic tutors. The fierce competition within this community often results in the need to be resilient and confident academically in order to be able to defend one's ideas. Thus, dyslexic doctoral students have to be prepared for some prejudice. They will need to develop academic confidence so they can stand in front of a group of international peers and explain their new innovations and ideas. It is vital that the SDT is aware of the climate in which the dyslexic student has to operate so that she can negotiate her position appropriately to collaborate most effectively with both student and supervisor.

7.1 Funding pathways

There are three recognised funding pathways:

- self funding
- HE departmental scholarship
- Research Council Grant

The first two pathways would enable the student to apply for DSA funding whereas the Research Councils have their own mechanisms for supporting disabled students. Currently, the amount provided by these two sources may differ. However, this may soon change. SDTs need to find out about Research Council funding to ensure that they help the student to obtain appropriate financial support.

7.2 Types of doctoral study

An understanding of the type of doctoral programme in conjunction with its academic cycle and demands is necessary to ensure that the SDT provision is personalised. Doctoral programmes fall into three main categories:

- PhD programme (PhD). It is often chosen by those who wish to remain in the academic sphere, continuing research in a chosen field. The research can be esoteric or philosophical and does not have to be related to practice. The first year may consist of taught units which are all related to research methods and an exploration of the uses of different methodological approaches to specific types of research questions. The principles of statistical analysis and the presentation of data forms a part of this research programme. Each of the taught units is assessed by written assignments usually of 6,000 words in length. The driving force behind this type of programme is the need to design innovative research which will inform the research community. The thesis is usually 75,000 – 85,000 words in length.

- Taught programmes such as Eng.D (Doctor of Engineering) or Ed.D (Doctor of Education). This type of programme has a two year taught element, consisting of core and elective units. Each unit has a written component which is assessed and is generally up to 10,000 words in length. The thesis is usually about 20,000 words. Practitioners tend to choose this type of doctoral programme because it is closely allied to work. The thesis is related to action research in the field and does not rely so heavily upon innovative research design.

- The new doctoral programmes, termed Integrated PhD, are hybrids, taking some elements from each of the previous types and analogous to sandwich degrees. They are closely associated with practical application. The first year is spent in the university studying research methods alongside the PhD students. Each of the research methods units is assessed by written assignments, usually of 6,000 words in length. This is followed by one or two years in the field conducting a research project with a practical application. During this time, the student is paid by a sponsor, usually an employer, to carry out research which will be beneficial to the company or sponsor. The thesis is developed from this work and usually consists of 50,000 words.

Whatever the doctoral programme the demands of time management and writing are similar to other levels of study but they are more intensive and require a greater degree of expertise. The student is expected to be a critical writer, which is very different from the demands of most undergraduate courses. The crucial skills required for criticality in thought which is translated into critical reading and critical writing hinge upon strong summary skills, manipulation of language and interactivity in learning. If the student has not developed a metacognitive, reflective approach to her own learning she will find adopting a critical approach difficult. The majority of the background reading is to be found in peer-reviewed journal articles which are frequently complex to read and stretch a student's understanding and language skills to the full.

Managing the writing of a large thesis will be one of the student's most difficult and challenging tasks. If the SDT is to provide appropriate support, she must be aware of the writing regulations, referencing rules and the need to encourage doctoral students to begin writing as soon as possible. There will be a considerable number of drafts for each chapter and many editing stages to be organised with the student. Collaborative dialogues at the planning stages have proved to be the most effective for dyslexic doctoral students. These are entirely student-driven because the content and subject matter will be innovative. Nevertheless, the use of explicit questioning techniques to develop and hone the students' self-questioning skills will be a valuable source of support.

Each doctoral student will have at least one supervisor. Many departments have a group of supervisors with carefully defined roles. Thus, a student who wishes to conduct a microbiological research study, e.g. the failure to adapt to virus growth in human tissue, will have a specialist micro-virologist supervisor who will guide her in the fieldwork and specific research methods. She may also have a general research supervisor who will stimulate thought about research methodology and guide the thesis production. It is advisable to liaise with the student's supervisor(s) at the outset so that each of the parties are aware of the boundaries. This tripartite method of support gives a strengthened scaffold to the dyslexic student.

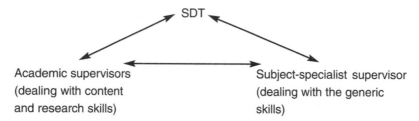

7.3 Support issues

The PhD context places different demands on the dyslexic doctoral student. In addition to the usual support issues for dyslexic students, the following checklist should be taken into account by the SDT:

- What are the barriers to data collection – who will be responsible for transcription etc.?

- Many doctoral students are used as teachers or lecturers for undergraduate programmes – how will the individual cope? (See the section on trainee teachers in Chapter 12, *Supporting Students in Placement*)

- How can SDTs help these students prepare for conference presentations and poster creation?

- How confident is the dyslexic student when using very specific research terminology?

- How can dyslexic students be helped to prepare for the viva – the oral examination? The SDT will need to explore this phenomenon with academic tutors so that she can analyse the needs of this unique situation and discuss the individual solutions with the dyslexic student.

8. Technology

The use of assistive technology as a scaffold to learning is a topic which has captured the interest of researchers in recent years, although the number of studies remains low (Yelland and Masters, 2005). Much of this research explores the interaction between tutors, students and software within a social-constructivist paradigm. Many dyslexic students use technology as a compensatory tool to support their studies. However, not all use it efficiently. Some use it as a glorified typewriter and miss out on the sophisticated facilities which would enhance the quality of time available for learning. Some are disappointed when the technology does not write their essays. These students are often under the misapprehension that technology will provide a magic wand, transforming their dyslexic writing into that of an expert at the touch of a key. Increasingly, students arrive at university with some experience of computers and word processors. Nevertheless, the SDT must be prepared for mature returners who may not have had sufficient exposure to appropriate technology and are frightened to use it. They will need to be persuaded to consider how technology might buy them time and improve their quality of studies. The most useful programs for supporting writing are:

- concept-mapping tools
- word processors
- voice-activated software
- voice recognition software

The range of specialist software grows by the year but the vital question is not what is available but whether it is relevant to the individual's needs. Assistive technology must do what it says: assist. It should not be a further barrier to writing! Technology can support three components of the writing process:

- planning
- gathering information
- drafting

8.1 Planning

Concept mapping tools can provide appropriate support. There are a variety of programs on the market and students need to try out different ones to find out which one they prefer. Each program has its advantages and disadvantages. Typical software which is available is:

- Mind Manager
- Mind Genius
- Inspiration

The latter is most widely used and is often found on workstations around the university. A word of caution is needed: it does not suit all students because, contrary to popular belief, not all dyslexic students are visual learners. Mapping tools can be used as an initial brainstorm facility. They are ideally suited to the recursivity of the planning process in writing in that, as the writing process proceeds, the map can be adjusted quickly to provide a clear picture of the most current planning. Because many dyslexic students become bogged down with the fine detail of planning at different levels, they appreciate being able to 'see' the big planning picture set out on one page. The mapping tools can also help the student to monitor time management.

8.2 Gathering information

Technology can be of great use when the student is at the chaotic stage of gathering information which might be of use for a written assignment. Concept mapping software can be a hook used for management and organisation of working. An example of how one student used Inspiration creatively will provide the SDT with insights into its use. The software became a technological scaffold which operated on various levels to provide support for weaknesses in her cognitive profile. The combination of traditional and creative modes of using the software demonstrates its duality of use. Firstly, she worked on screen using the software as a prompt for the generation of initial ideas. At the next stage she re-arranged the ideas bubbles into a numbered flow chart with bullet-point reminders. This enabled her to physically work on the sequencing of her planning. Once this was completed she printed out a hard copy of the flow chart, which provided her with the basis for planning operations. The chart opposite was kindly provided by this student, using Inspiration©.

As the student conducted her search for information from books, articles and printouts of electronic information she was able to sort out each and put them in piles (on the floor!) behind each A4 idea bubble planning sheet. In this way she was able to pick up one section at a time and work on all the data. This minimised pressure on her weak working memory and enabled her to concentrate more fully on the draft of each section.

Some students prefer to use the word processor to make notes while they gather information. To some extent this helps the insecure student who is not confident about selecting the most relevant information. All notes can be accumulated and it is then a quicker task to cut and paste. Making electronic notes, however, does rely upon good summary skills if the student is to use her time efficiently. The SDT may need to model how to summarise notes into bullet points on screen.

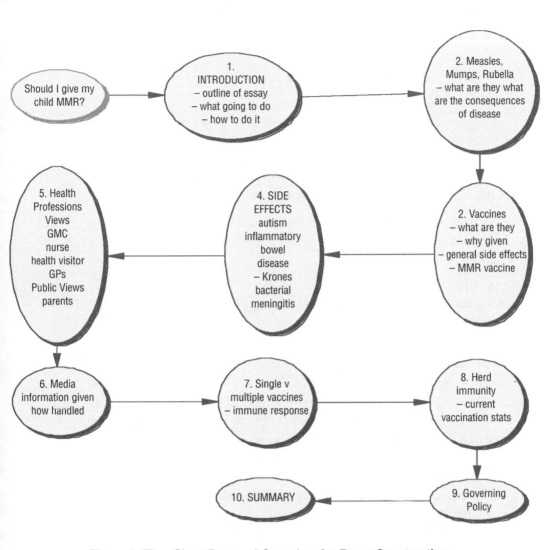

Figure 1: Flow Chart Personal Organiser for Essay Construction

8.3 Drafting

The most frequently used programs for drafting are:

- word processor
- voice-activated software
- voice recognition software

The SDT needs to discuss how the student uses a word processor to assess whether current working strategies are the most effective for the work environment. The simple functions of word processing should be taught in an hierarchical manner to ensure greatest success (See Appendix 2)

One student found that she could avoid plagiarism by using colour-coding facilities in her notes on the word processor. She used colour to differentiate the source of her text, e.g.

Green = own words notes
Black = text lifted from other sources
Red = things to check before putting in the essay
Blue = essay text.

There is a relatively small percentage of the dyslexic HE population who regularly use voice-activated software to draft written work. It requires sophisticated summary skills and a good working memory capacity to hold many chunks of language information in the head while dictating to the screen. For these reasons it is not an ideal technological tool for all dyslexic students. Despite what the manufacturers say, it requires patience and time to customise the system to individual use. If dyslexic students are introduced to the software later rather than earlier in their writing careers, it may present barriers to learning and may not be the scaffold hoped for. Students need to have the time to customise the system. Technical vocabulary is best introduced during the Summer vacation in preparation for the coming academic year. The SDT should provide sessions during this time to enhance the coming learning experience and to hand over control to the student.

Voice recognition software can be used more widely. When drafting it is useful to play the ideas back. Most expert writers participate in this rehearsal silently but the dyslexic learner often needs her work read aloud to make decisions about its coherence and cohesion.

In conclusion...

This chapter has highlighted the underlying skills which are needed for writing. The developmental, scaffolded, interactive model of teaching is applied to the support of writing. This chapter examines the underlying cognitive difficulties which can affect the writing process for dyslexic students.

Further reading

Couzijn, M (1999) Learning to write by observation of writing and reading processes: effects on learning and transfer. *Learning and Instruction*, 9(2), 109-142

de Bono, E (1991) *CoRT Thinking* (2nd ed. Vol. 1). Oxford: Pergamon Press. A good resource which can be adapted to many HE writing tasks is Edward de Bono's CoRT system which is a cognitive reasoning and thinking approach. The use of the grids can be adapted and modelled by the SDT

Galbraith, D, and Rijlaarsdam, G (1999) Effective strategies for the teaching and learning of writing. *Learning and Instruction*, 9(2), 93-108

Graal, M and Clark, R. (eds) (1999) *Partnerships across the curriculum*. Leicester: University of Leicester

Rugg, G. and Petre, M. (2004). *The unwritten rules of PhD research*. Buckingham: Open University Press.

Pears, R and Shields, G (2005) *Cite them right: referencing made easy.* (2nd ed) Newcastle, Pear Tree Books. This booklet is worth purchasing because it outlines key features of ways of referencing a wide variety of different sources.

Useful web resources:

Research Council contact details:

Arts and Humanities: 10, Carlton House Terrace, London. www.ahrb.ac.uk

Biotechnology and Biological Sciences: Polaris House, North Star Avenue, Swindon. www.bbsrc.ac.uk

Economic and Research Council (ESRC): Polaris House, North Star Avenue, Swindon. www.esrc.ac.uk

Engineering and Physical Sciences Research Council: Polaris House, North Star Avenue, Swindon. www.eosrc.ac.uk/student/default.asp

Medical Research Council: 20, Park Crescent, London. www.mrc.ac.uk

Main research councils: www.research-councils.ac.uk

Useful research project about dyslexic doctoral students can be found on: www.premia.ac.uk

Appendix 1: Common Instruction Terminology

Account for	Give the reason for. Not to be confused with 'Give an account of' which is only asking for description
Analyse	Describe the main ideas in depth, showing why they are important and how they are connected
Assess	Discuss the strong and weak points of the subject. Put your own judgement clearly in the conclusion
Comment	State your views on the subject clearly. Back up your points with sufficient evidence and examples
Compare	Look for similarities and differences
Contrast	Show how the subjects are different.
Criticise	Give your opinion/judgement about the merit of theories/facts; back this up by discussing the evidence or reasoning involved
Define	Give clear, concise meanings. State limitations of the definition
Describe	Give a detailed or graphic account of
Discuss	Give reasons for and against; examine implications
Evaluate	Weigh things up; look at the strengths and weaknesses and assess
Examine	Look closely at all aspects
Explain	Give reasons for something
Illustrate	Make clear by the use of examples/diagrams; clarify points
Interpret	Express in simple terms. You are usually expected to include your own judgements.
Justify	Show adequate grounds for decisions/conclusions/ ideas/theories;
Prove	Establish that something is true by presenting factual evidence or giving clear, logical reasons.
Outline	Give the main features or general principles of a subject – should not include all the details
Relate	Show how things are connected to each other; how they affect each other;

Review	Make a survey of something
State	Present brief, clear information
Summarise	Give a concise account for the main points – should not include details
Trace	Follow the development of a topic
To what extent...	Another way of saying evaluate but suggests that you bring out how much (or how little)

Appendix 2: Hierarchy of Word Processing Skills

- Open a document
- Cutting and pasting
- Save a document – 'save as' and 'save' should be taught separately
- Setting up a filing system
- Simple formatting: Font selection, underlining, bold and italics
- Ensuring that the default language is English (UK) and not English (USA)
- How to use the spelling checker
- Printing

Once these basics have been mastered the SDT is advised to model more sophisticated uses of the word processor which will assist language processing difficulties and enhance the student experience. The following facilities are most commonly regarded as the most effective:

- Autocorrect: only really effective if the dyslexic student is monitoring her common typographical and spelling errors

- Find: this facility can speed up both scanning for information and changing errors in a document

- Track changes: this is a facility which is not for the faint-hearted. It is excellent for monitoring different draft versions but may be confusing to some dyslexic readers because of the additional information on screen

- Inserting – diagrams, tables etc.

- Inserting footnotes if they are part of the departmental writing regulations.

11

Supporting subject-specific work

This chapter looks briefly at specific challenges for dyslexic learners studying different courses.

Using this chapter

This chapter will enable you to:

1. Common challenges

SDTs working on an individual basis with students will be looking at generic skills, taking into account individual needs. Many dyslexic students will struggle with:

- note-taking and note-making
- planning and writing essays

A tutorial on note-taking might well be similar whether the student is studying a Science or an Arts subject. Specific examples will be different and students might well be approaching the tutorial from a different perspective but the underlying teaching will be similar. Often subject choices are made on the basis of the amount of prose writing which is *perceived by the student* to be required. Hence, some students studying Science, Engineering, Archaeology or Fine Art, for example, are surprised when they come to university and are presented with assessments which rely upon sound writing expertise. A student struggling with writing will require help with planning or drafting, whatever the subject. The SDT will need to be aware of varying expectations from subject disciplines and the variations in genre. Although work is individualised, and it is impossible to make generalisations, different subjects present specific challenges for dyslexic students.

2. Supporting students on Mathematics courses

Students with short-term working memory difficulties, sequencing difficulties and/or left-right confusion can find some aspects of mathematics quite difficult even when they are mathematically very able.

2.1 Potential challenges

- Remembering mathematical terminology and formulae
- Difficulty remembering mathematical symbols and signs
- Confusing visually similar words
- Remembering mathematical procedures and sequences
- Losing their place when completing calculations that have different stages
- Following the logical sequence of steps in calculations
- Reversing numbers or writing down numbers incorrectly, particularly when copying from overheads or boards.
- Misreading the question
- Inability to remember multiplication tables

2.2 Possible solutions

- Use colour to differentiate different sections of calculations and formulae
- Use cards and mind maps to remember formulae
- Present symbols and word definitions together in teaching sessions

- Checklist of key terms and symbols with clear definitions

- Use a calculator rather than try to remember multiplication tables etc

- Break down tasks into smaller components

- Use space in text containing graphs and mathematical equations

- Solution sheets for students to check their calculations and methods.

3. Supporting students on Music courses
'Melody begins when words are no longer accurate'. (Claude Debussy)

Music can offer particular challenges for dyslexic students because of co-ordination difficulties, visual stress, short term memory, sequencing and carrying out complicated sequences at speed. Some students will find it easier to read music than words whereas others will struggle continually. Some students have difficulty sight reading and recalling notes in the right order. Others will struggle to acquire rhythmic accuracy and perception, especially related to notation. Some dyslexic musicians struggle with timing and rhythm skills (Thomson, 2006).

Delay in acquiring automaticity means that practice is more difficult for dyslexic students and constant repetition is required. Sometimes, when a piece is played again it feels as if it is a completely new piece. Watching a conductor in an orchestra and switching attention from the conductor to the lines of music to the instrument while maintaining rhythm and co-ordination and keeping in time with others can be very challenging indeed for some dyslexics (Miles and Westcombe, 2001).

Contributors to *Music and Dyslexia* (Miles and Westcombe, 2001) point to the need for dyslexic music students to be aware of their individual learning style and to use their strengths even if they do not learn in the traditional way expected by many music teachers. Multi-sensory methods are suggested to be as useful to the learning of music as to literacy. Dyslexic musicians are often good at seeing the big picture and need to experience the music as a whole to begin with rather than breaking it down in the traditional hierarchical way non dyslexics do. This ability can be an advantage, increasing their musical sensitivity and appreciation and can produce expressive playing.

As can be seen, the underlying, cognitive needs of music students are similar to those of any dyslexic student. Consequently, the strategies used to guide students in coping with alphabetic demands can be transferred to musical notation. For example, some students find that they do not automatically discriminate between the different shapes of notes, and a system of colour-coding the value of the notes is a method of imprinting this into long term memory. This will enhance sight reading and performance fluency. Many non-dyslexic musicians write the fingering on manuscripts while they are developing the kinaesthetic imprint for performing specific sections of music. Mnemonic strategies are also useful to enable the dyslexic student to recall musical rests so that she can read these at speed when sight reading or performing.

4. Supporting students on modern language courses

The difficulties many dyslexic students experience in learning a second language are similar to the difficulties they experience in acquiring skill in their native language. Difficulties in reaching proficiency in a second language may only become apparent under pressure, when the dyslexic student makes 'careless' mistakes with grammar and spelling. The difficulty for dyslexic students varies with different languages. Languages with perfect orthography (one letter for each sound) are easiest for dyslexic learners as they do not make such heavy demands on memory.

4.1 Potential challenges

Dyslexic students may have weak phonological skills or weak sequencing ability which can affect language learning, particularly of grammatical sequences. Weak working memory can make it difficult to retain vocabulary.

4.2 Possible solutions

- Multi-sensory presentation of vocabulary and grammatical sequences

- Use of rhythm to aid memory

- Overlearning

- Use of colour-coding to distinguish between different grammatical structures for example masculine/feminine, verb endings

- Use of a dictaphone or recorder for grammar and vocabulary. The use of the student's own voice is helpful in retaining information

- Extra time allowance for timed assessments, including class dictations and translation modules

- Some oral translation exercises might pose extra load on memory and it is important that students are given the option to take time to process and understand what they are translating and the option to go back and listen again. It should be recognised that in some cases memory skills are being tested as much as language skills and this should be minimised as far as possible

■ Reading techniques which the dyslexic student often uses with English text can work equally well with modern foreign languages but in the majority of cases the SDT will be unable to support the student unless she is a competent linguist. The SDT's role is often, therefore, to offer advice to the student and the department

Software options

■ Talking dictionaries

■ TextHelp Read & Write screen reader with foreign language capabilities

■ Dragon Naturally Speaking with foreign language voice recognition

■ Microsoft proofing tool

■ Scanner – scan text and listen via screen reader

■ Recording lectures and essays

5. Supporting students on Art and Design courses

Students studying on art and design courses very often think in terms of pictures rather than words, and this can cause some difficulty. Students may be required to:

■ write essays and dissertations on art history

■ undertake project work, often in the form of an ongoing visual, annotated reflective diary that discusses their own work in relation to the contemporary context

■ annotate their sketchbooks by handwriting directly on the pages

5.1 Potential challenges

■ Written assignments may be difficult for all visual thinkers, but particularly for dyslexic students. Some students express surprise, even irritation that they have to complete written assignments as part of an art course. By comparison with their artwork, their writing can appear messy, simplistic, even appearing to miss the point because it does not capture the organic, holistic experience of both creating and viewing the artwork.

■ Students might also struggle with organisation, as they are required to apportion their time between studio work and traditional university activities: lectures and independent study as well as providing ongoing, structured documentation on the creative process. Dyslexic art students sometimes feel torn between studio work and researching and documenting activities. Writing about and creating art appear as very different activities and take place in very different environments. Studio practice is inevitably seen as the main element of their course but other work, although often carrying a relatively small percentage of the marks for each unit, seems to take up an inordinate amount of time because of their dyslexia. The introduction of project rather than essay-based assignments helps but does not automatically remove the difficulty. It often requires the assembling of visuals and information from a variety of sources over a longer period of time to produce a linear record of work in progress and therefore still makes demands on students' organisational skills. As a result of spending long hours in the studio, dyslexic art students especially may miss vital information disseminated via email, virtual learning environments, course handbooks and notices.

- Students may be required to talk about their work in a formal group session and take comments from tutors and peers. This may involve revealing sources of inspiration which can be very personal and showing experimental stages of their work. Dyslexic students may find addressing a group stressful and feel they cannot describe their work in sufficient depth to meet assessment criteria. They may take the brief of 'personal' inspiration rather literally and feel they have to reveal all their hidden secrets or whole life story. They may feel they lack the subtleties of language needed to adopt an artist's persona and a certain amount of distance from their own work while talking.

5.2 Possible solutions

- Use of 'visual' note-taking in lectures – using symbols, images and diagrams to note concepts rather than individual words. Lectures could be recorded and the key points noted in this way after the lecture

- Planning written assignments using visual means with PowerPoint, flow charts, time lines or picture story boards

- Use of imagination: for example incorporating narratives and corresponding film frames as structural devices as if making a film, rather than completing a piece of written work. When note-taking, paraphrasing or trying to follow instructions, identify trigger-words, usually concrete imagery or a visual analogy that make the link between word and image, e.g. instructions for loading a camera: 'insert a tongue of film'. This makes the word more three-dimensional and therefore easier to cope with

■ Compile lists of appropriate academic words used to describe creative objects and processes to refer to. Develop these lists by making word webs of synonyms and antonyms to describe objects. See example below.

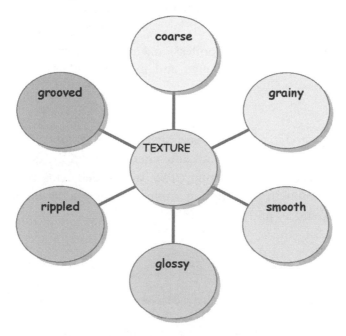

Organisational strategies

■ SDTs can help students to get an overview of the course structure and highlight key themes, technical terms and learning outcomes in different colours for each unit . At the start of each course unit students should record studio time, plus the dates when written work is set and when it should be handed in, on a large wall calendar or in a spacious diary. The student should decide on the best time for non-studio work: either first thing or at the end of the day.

■ Students should be encouraged to aim to do something, however small, towards a written assignment within the first 48 hours, such as obtain library books, list key terms, search the Internet, mind map the question.

■ Recording thoughts on work in progress can be helpful. Students should be encouraged to listen to them frequently so that they can identify major influences, breakthroughs and key changes of direction. Although students may feel that work develops organically, if thoughts are recorded on a regular basis, the reflective diary will be structured and accumulative.

Managing group critiques
- When talking and writing about work, it may be a good idea to mentally separate the *person* from the *artist*. To make it easier, when planning a talk in rough, students could write, 'The artist' or 'she experimented with ...' rather than 'I experimented with ...' to help achieve a sense of distance.

- Students can look at how professional artists describe their work on their websites, in newspapers and journals and exhibition catalogues.

In conclusion ...

SDTs are not expected to provide subject-specific support for courses but an understanding of the similarities and differences between the different disciplines can be helpful to the support that is provided. This chapter has offered a few pointers to help support students undertaking mathematics, language, music and art and design courses.

Further Reading

Corrigan, C (ed) (2001) *Dyslexia A Guide for Staff.* London: Centre for Learning and Teaching in Art and Design

Miles, TR and Westcombe, J (eds) (2001) *Music and Dyslexia, opening new doors*, London: Whurr Publishers

Peer, L and Reid, G (eds) (2000) *Multilingualism, Literacy and Dyslexia, a Challenge for Educators*, Chichester, David Fulton Publishers

Price, G A and Maier, P (2007) *Effective Study Skills.* London, Pearson. This book is aimed at students and academic tutors with the intention that the latter can use the information to embed skills teaching into the discipline teaching.

12

Supporting students on placements and fieldwork

This chapter will look at the challenges facing student health professionals, teachers, social work students and students undertaking other placements as part of their academic course and suggest some possible strategies.

Using this chapter

This chapter will enable you to:

1. Support students on clinical placement

    1.1 Challenges and strengths

    1.2 Memory

    1.3 Personal organisation and time management

    1.4 Reading

    1.5 Writing and spelling

    1.6 Motor skills

2. Support students on fieldwork trips

    2.1 Potential challenges

    2.2 Possible strategies

3. Support students on placements abroad

4. Support students on social work placements

5. Support trainee teachers

    5.1 Classroom challenges

    5.2 Government skills tests in numeracy, literacy and ICT

There are many different courses which involve a work placement or fieldwork trip: health professions; teaching; social work studies; geography; archaeology; language; teaching; business courses. Students might spend a considerable time away from the university campus. Students who are used to receiving academic support will sometimes find such trips and placements challenging. It is important that the SDT discusses students' concerns with them before placement and provides support in advance if at all possible or arranges support for the students while they are away from the institution if that is feasible.

Students are unlikely to experience more than a couple of the challenges discussed, and, whilst it is important for the SDT not to be negative or suggest problems where none exist, it can be helpful to discuss areas where the student feels she might struggle and to talk through possible strategies, prior to the start of the placement. Many of the ideas presented here are part of good practice anyway and are useful for all students, not just those with dyslexia.

1. Supporting students on clinical placement

Students taking nursing diplomas or degrees in medicine, occupational therapy, physiotherapy and podiatry spend up to fifty per cent of their time on clinical placement. In most cases they need to pass the placement in order to gain a professional qualification in addition to the degree. Students are often expected to work shifts and might well be located some distance from the university. It becomes more difficult for them to access dyslexia support during this time. Yet they are still involved with academic work and possibly revising for examinations or continuing to study for assignments at the same time as working in their placement.

There is sometimes little shared understanding of what support is actually required for dyslexic students on clinical placements. The full assessment procedure, whether carried out by an Educational Psychologist or an SDT, often does not address students' needs on clinical placement. Similarly, assessments of study needs carried out by Access Centres do not always make allowances for placements.

The academic parts of the courses are supervised by academic tutors who sometimes act as link tutors for the people supervising the students on placement. Staff supervising nurses are usually referred to as mentors whereas staff supervising student physiotherapists and occupational therapists are referred to as clinical supervisors, clinicians or placement educators. The terms vary according to the particular institution and Health Authority. Link tutors often act as a bridge between the learning on the academic courses and the learning in the clinical placements. Sometimes additional staff are involved in students' learning, such as student placement learning advisors. The SDT's role in the process is not clearly defined; it has been suggested that it might be necessary to re-think dyslexia support to take into account the type of support needed in the clinical setting (Price and Skinner, 2005).

A front-loaded model of support is suggested, where academic and workplace skills are addressed while the students are still on campus in preparation for off-campus placement. This will need collaboration between academic schools and dyslexia departments as well as placement providers. A detailed analysis of the skills needed for clinical placement will enable specialist dyslexia tutors to match need and workplace demands more effectively. However, it will still be necessary for students to receive support and adjustments whilst on placement, particularly at the beginning of each placement. When considering any reasonable adjustments for dyslexic students in the clinical setting there should be a balance between meeting the requirements of the Disability Discrimination Act (DDA) (1995) with meeting the need to ensure patient safety. Any adjustments should take these two needs into account in order to be fair to the student but also to ensure that professional standards are maintained and fitness to practise issues are addressed. For example, while it is quite reasonable to allow a scribe or note taker in the academic setting it is not reasonable in the clinical setting as all health professionals have to demonstrate adequate literacy skills to produce clear patient records and reports. Allowing extra time to process information might not be appropriate in a busy clinical environment where acting quickly is often vital for patient safety. Students with weak short-term working memory might be able to use mini disc recorders to record information but this might similarly be unethical in a clinical setting.

Price (2005) has pointed to public concern over the potential difficulties relating to the safety of nurses which has led to some concern about employing dyslexic nurses at all. Headlines such as 'Dyslexic nurses give pills by colour' and 'Council to probe threat to public from nurses' do much to heighten this (Price, 2005). Other student health professionals do not appear to give such cause for concern. Thankfully, these highly publicised cases are very rare and one wonders, if all the facts were available, quite what part dyslexia plays in the mistakes that have been made and how much is due to lack of professional skills. Dyslexic students should be expected to reach the same competences and achieve the same professional standards by the end of their courses as any other students. 'Reasonable adjustments' are a way to help them, as long as the adjustments are fair and reasonable and do not offer artificial compensation.

In her research, Price (2005) found that dyslexic nurses had a high level of self-awareness and showed great concern for safety. Whereas the non-dyslexic control group did not mention safety as an issue, the dyslexic group put in place many excellent coping strategies to ensure safety because they were aware of the potential for error.

SDTs are usually well prepared to help students with their academic work and help them develop strategies to minimise the effects of dyslexia and build on strengths. They might, however, have little knowledge of the structure of different clinical settings and what is expected of students on clinical placement or how this varies with each individual placement. They might also have little knowledge of the type of competences and skills students are expected to demonstrate. SDTs see only a small selection of students at different stages in their training and each student's needs are individual and not representative of the full range of placement experiences.

In most cases it is the mentors or supervisors who are best placed to suggest 'reasonable adjustments' and support for individual students in the clinical setting. SDTs should expect to play an advisory role; they should be prepared to offer advice about students' individual profiles to academic departments and placement providers so that individual students obtain the reasonable adjustments they need in the clinical setting.

1.1 Challenges and strengths

Clinical placement can be stressful for students, and their dyslexia can affect their clinical skills if no support mechanisms are put in place. Some dyslexic student health professionals are under emotional stress as they are struggling to conceal their difficulties because of fear of discrimination. Some dyslexic students may feel overwhelmed by their inability to keep up with their peers. They may feel isolated in the clinical situation and feel that other students are learning the procedures and tasks far more quickly than they are. Student health professionals might experience some difficulty on the ward because of weaknesses with short term working memory or weak organisational or literacy skills (Price and Skinner, 2005). This can affect all aspects of clinical practice, at least initially. Student health professionals might find the change from academic study to full time work in a clinical placement quite exhausting, and the effects of dyslexia can exacerbate this. Wards are often busy and noisy, which can be difficult for many dyslexic students. Students are placed in a variety of different clinical settings, which means their learning environment is constantly changing. Every clinical placement will have a slightly different set up and routine as well as specialist terminology and medical abbreviations which the students have to learn in order to function efficiently. Additionally, they might struggle to balance course work and placement commitments.

Even though dyslexic students find some tasks particularly difficult, it is usually possible to overcome these difficulties by taking a slightly different approach to tasks (Price and Gale, 2004). Most dyslexic students are well aware of their strengths and the potential challenges and are able to outline their needs to staff working with them. Dyslexia brings strengths as well as challenges, although some institutions and health care settings have a negative attitude towards dyslexic students (Sanderson-Mann and McCandless, 2005). Dyslexic people often have a different way of thinking and learning: they may have an ability to think holistically and to see the big picture. Many are very creative and imaginative, have good visual and problem-solving skills and can bring these strengths to the workplace. Strategies can be developed in many cases which can go a long way towards helping them cope with any difficulties that arise.

1.2 Memory
Some dyslexic students have difficulty following instructions, remembering drug names and medical conditions as well as colleagues' names and job titles. They might struggle to remember all the information at handover sessions or details of specific procedures, instructions or observations. They might misread dates or confuse times, which could affect the administration of medication. They might have an apparent short attention span and find it hard to concentrate in meetings or supervisory sessions.

1.3 Personal organisation and time management
Some dyslexic students will need support with planning their work and estimating how much time is needed for a specific task. Initially, it might take them longer than their contemporaries to learn routines and procedures and to complete tasks on time. It might also take them longer at the beginning of a placement to learn to cope with the multi-tasking so often expected in the clinical setting, for example, listening to a patient, making an initial assessment or taking notes and coming to a conclusion about diagnosis whilst the patient is talking. A typical placement for student nurses will entail working shifts on a busy, noisy ward with many potential distractions. Challenges for

students working in clinics or in the community will be similar. The learning environment is constantly changing as students are placed in a variety of different settings. Students will need to learn a different management structure and different routines for everyday procedures. Daily care schedules for patients require careful planning and the student will need to be constantly changing focus to take account of new patients or clients arriving as well as departing. Ensuring each patient or client receives timely, individual care puts pressure on fragile working memory and sequencing skills (Price and Skinner, 2005).

Possible strategies

■ Pre-placement visits are helpful in providing students with information about what to expect from the placement. Such visits can also give the students an opportunity to discuss any concerns they might have and to talk about possible support.

■ Students and mentors or supervisors could work together to draw up detailed plans for the placement, highlighting meetings, supervision, feedback, visits etc. This might include setting target dates for fulfilling placement competences. Realistic daily targets could be agreed, breaking tasks down into manageable chunks. Electronic diaries might be more helpful to some students than hard copies. They can also be used to record common spellings and specific medical abbreviations. A small A-Z notebook is a good alternative.

■ Students might need more time to gain the skill of multi-tasking. It is helpful if they feel they can ask their mentors to explain tasks more than once and to request additional time for supervisory sessions if they need it.

■ Students will benefit from being able to spend some time observing mentors or supervisors working with patients in the first few days and demonstrating different procedures.

■ It is helpful if students are not given too many instructions at once, particularly if the instructions are only given verbally. Instructions in written form as well can be useful.

■ When a job or task involves following a sequence of steps, these could be set out clearly on a wall chart, manual or instruction sheet. A simple flow chart on a small card could act as a memory aid. An SDT could assist the student with this, if appropriate. Prompt sheets to help with the sequencing of tasks could be useful.

▓ The SDT could help the student devise some appropriate proforma telephone pads for taking down messages, with as much information as possible filled out beforehand (e.g. date/ref/from).

▓ Placement packs with useful information and standard procedures can sometimes be provided. Maps of the building will help students with orientation difficulties.

1.4 Reading

Some dyslexic students might struggle to understand medical and pharmacological language and abbreviations and to differentiate between drug names, especially at the beginning of each new placement. CABG (pronounced cabbage) for example is not a reference to a vegetable but a medical abbreviation for 'coronary artery bypass' (Price and Skinner, 2005).

Figure one shows examples of similar-sounding words which might pose a challenge for some students. *Gastrectomy* refers to removal of the stomach; *gastrostomy* refers to a surgical opening into the stomach for feeding; *gastrotomy* refers to a surgical incision into the stomach for examination or to remove a foreign object, whereas a *gastroscopy* is a surgical procedure involving an instrument passed into the mouth to examine the stomach to see if ulcers are present!

gastrectomy	gastrostomy	gastrotomy	gastroscopy
prednisone	prednisolone	prednesol	phentermine
phentolamine	phenylephrine	phenothrin	
hypercalcaemia	hypercalciuria	hypercapnia	hypercarbia

Figure 1: Reading and Language Challenges

Some students might have difficulty reading information on whiteboards. Where different information is presented about patients on a whiteboard, it is often hand-written closely together. Apart from difficulty with reading the handwriting, lack of spacing can make it difficult for students to access the information accurately. This could lead to possible mis-reading of information. Reading information on charts can also be challenging for students with spatial difficulties, if several different layers of information are presented on one chart, as the small boxes are so close together. It is particularly difficult if information is presented on different levels – reading both across and down.

Possible strategies

■ Students might find it helpful to ask for essential reading well in advance of meetings, with important parts highlighted

■ They might need a little extra time for reading

■ Use of colour on whiteboards to differentiate sections, for example red for physiotherapy, can make text easier to read

■ An alphabetical note-book can be useful to record the meaning of abbreviations and common medical terminology

■ Flow charts or mind maps could be used as an alternative to text, where appropriate

■ Written information would benefit from being dyslexia friendly: well spaced, clear font; written in a logical sequence; avoiding small print and little jargon or abbreviations

■ Coloured overlays might aid the reading process for some students. It is thought that, for some students, a pastel-coloured plastic overlay will reduce the glare from the page and make reading more comfortable.

1.6 Writing and spelling

Some students might have difficulty keeping accurate, legible, succinct patient notes and filling out forms appropriately under time pressure. They might well struggle with the spelling of drug names and medical terms, especially those which look or sound similar, for example, **hypertension** and **hypotension**. The dyslexic student health professional might also struggle with the dual-naming of drugs – the chemical or generic label and the manufacturer's brand name, such as diazepam and valium (Price and Skinner, 2005).

Possible strategies

■ Students might need a little extra time to write reports and to develop good checking procedures. It might be helpful to write notes on rough paper, which could be checked by the mentor or supervisor before they are written up, particularly at the beginning of a placement. An SDT could help the student with proof reading skills.

■ A small personal dictionary or electronic speller that can be carried in the uniform pocket is a good idea for recording spellings and essential technical vocabulary particular to the placement setting. Students might consider asking mentors or supervisors to help them with a checklist of vocabulary typical of the placement, such as drug names, common medical terms and conditions.

- Specialised reference books such as Mosby's *Medical Drug List* (2006) give the pronunciation of words which can aid spelling.

- If one is available, students could write notes on computer.

- Alternatively, students could summarise the main points that should be covered using a visual map, spider diagram or flow chart and then transfer the notes into the required format.

- A recording device to record ideas could be useful – as long as this does not breach patient confidentiality.

- It is helpful if students can familiarise themselves with a sample or model report, so that they have a clear idea about the level and content required and the expected format. If none are available, templates for letters, memos and other paperwork could be devised.

- Where possible, reports should be submitted on cream or pastel paper with a dyslexia-friendly font such as Arial or Comic Sans, and the right margin left unjustified.

1.7 Motor skills

Some dyslexic students have difficulties with right and left co-ordination. The ability to follow a sequence, e.g. wound dressing, takes these students much longer to learn.

Possible strategies

- Demonstration of skills

- Students could ask their mentors or supervisors to supervise their practice until the sequence is secure.

- Diagrams and flow charts can help.

2. Supporting students on fieldwork trips

Fieldwork trips are a routine part of many degree courses such as geography, geology, oceanography and archaeology. Field trips vary in length from a day to lengthier stays abroad for subjects such as archaeology, geography and geology. Many students with dyslexia welcome fieldwork trips as a break from the emphasis on written work and see the trip as an opportunity to demonstrate other more practical skills. However, some dyslexic students find that their dyslexia causes them difficulties in the fieldwork setting.

It is seldom possible for an SDT to provide any dyslexia support for students during fieldtrips, although preparatory support sessions can be offered in advance. However, SDTs might be able to offer advice to any departments who are concerned about how their dyslexic students will cope with this aspect of the course. Good communication between academic departments, the SDT and the student can be helpful when considering any potential difficulties caused by fieldwork. When thinking about any adjustments that need to be put in place, the learning outcomes expected will need to be taken into consideration, along with the exact nature of the fieldtrip and the students' particular dyslexic profiles. Support sessions to help with potential challenges can be arranged well in advance.

Many of the technological aids such as Personal Digital Assistants (PDAs) and recording devices which could be useful on placement could be paid for through the students' Disabled Students' Allowances (DSA). PDAs are hand-held computers, sometimes called palmtop computers, which can be used as personal organisers as well as for note-taking and video recording.

2.1 Potential challenges

- **Working under time pressure**: In the academic setting dyslexic students quite often spend considerably more time on their studies than other students. On a fieldwork trip this is not possible and the standard of students' work might not be as high as usual because they have not had the opportunity to work on a draft of the written assignment. Similarly, slow reading speeds might affect the dyslexic students' ability to complete all the reading and this could prevent their not having all the information they need to complete the task.

- **Taking accurate notes** in the field and daily notes of the activities carried out can be stressful. Slow writing speeds can make note-taking even more difficult.

- **Recording accurate data** and making calculations under timed pressure can be difficult.

- **Multi-tasking**: Students are expected to listen to orally presented information and take notes at the same time. This is particularly difficult for dyslexic students. Usual strategies adopted in the academic setting might not be possible on a fieldwork trip.

- **Poor concentration levels** or distraction due to background noise might affect dyslexic students' ability to complete tasks on the trip.

2.2 Possible strategies

- Pre-reading material and fieldwork information given to the students well in advance of the trip

- The SDT could meet with the student to talk through any potential challenges and discuss appropriate strategies. For example, a session on note-taking might be helpful

- If a student is unable to take notes, a note-taker might be arranged, possibly another student on the trip. Alternatively, a student might record notes on a mini-disc recorder or use a lap-top computer or digital note book or palm-top

- In group work sessions, dyslexic students should not be expected to take notes or read aloud

- Handouts in accessible formats will aid reading: sans serif font; cream paper; avoidance of too much underlining, capitals and italics; bullet points rather than continuous text; wide spacing and left-hand justified margin only

- Five minute sessions with a tutor at the end of the day could be useful to make sure students have not missed any essential information.

3. Supporting students on placements abroad

Students taking modern language degrees often spend a year abroad in their third year. They either work in the country or attend universities abroad. Whilst this immersion in the culture of a different country will aid their language skills immensely it can bring with it some challenges for dyslexic students. Dyslexic support might occasionally be available, but in most cases the student has to manage alone. There is a limit to the level of support that can be provided in these circumstances by the student's own institution. Occasionally institutions are able to offer email communication and support, but this is often impractical and of limited value. It is usually expected that support will be provided by the host institution or placement provider.

The SDT can help students with DSA applications well in advance so that they have any equipment they need to take with them. Students who are to spend some time abroad might well find a lap-top computer essential, and this should be flagged up at the Assessment of Needs. Similarly, a mini-disc recorder and proof reading software will be of great benefit when no human support is available.

The SDT can act as an advocate for students and communicate with departments as necessary and with DSA providers if the technological support breaks down while the student is abroad.

4. Supporting students on social work placements

Students taking the Diploma in Social Work have placements of varying length with a local authority or with other agencies. They are supervised by practice teachers who meet regularly with the students to discuss their client cases. Campbell and Cowe (1998) have produced a very informative guide which sets out the potential challenges a dyslexic student might face in the placement setting and offers possible solutions. Such a guide would be a useful reference tool for the SDT. Campbell and Cowe (1998) point to the emphasis on the written word and record keeping that exists in Social Work both in the educational setting and in the placement setting. Students are expected to keep written records of clients and produce reports as well as a learning log or reflective diary. Campbell and Cowe believe that dyslexic strengths of creativity and lateral thinking are of particular benefit to social work because of the focus on problem solving.

The SDT's role would again mainly be advisory: she might be asked to discuss individual students' needs with the practice teacher and provide advice to students about to begin a placement. As with all types of placement, a pre-placement planning meeting to discuss the students' potential needs and to focus their learning is essential in ensuring that learning needs are met.

Students often have short reports on individual case work and diaries and logs to be filled in regularly. Sometimes sessions can be arranged with the SDT around the placement commitments where the SDT can help with planning and writing skills for this work.

5. Supporting trainee teachers

Dyslexia can pose a challenge for students undertaking teacher training courses, but in most cases dyslexia should not be a barrier for students considering entering the profession. At times dyslexia can be considered enabling for the teacher as she shows greater awareness of the difficulties pupils experience. The dyslexic teacher, arguably, is in a better position to understand the emotional difficulties and frustration experienced by dyslexic pupils. It can mean that dyslexic teachers' practice is more inclusive and dyslexia friendly. However, trainee teachers need to recognise that strategies which work for them might be very different from the strategies that work for their pupils.

An SDT might needs to support trainee teachers with:

- writing skills – blackboard/whiteboard/pupil reports
- memory skills

- organisational skills: Electronic organisers/planners

- use of lap-top with prepared notes

- checklist or flashcards of spellings

- spelling sessions for primary teachers to supplement the Literacy Strategy

- review of multi-sensory learning techniques

- use of proformas or templates

5.1 Classroom challenges

Dyslexic trainee teachers find the spontaneity of performance in front of a class of children a challenge. This is partly because of lack of automaticity of language processing but it is also connected with weak language retrieval skills. All classroom teachers have to have good and quick auditory processing skills to be able to respond to the quick-fire questions the pupils put to them. Teaching is all about explaining difficult concepts in appropriate language to differentiate the learning experience to respond to pupils' diverse needs. This relies upon good vocabulary and speed of retrieval and access to language resources – skills which will put pressure upon a dyslexic, cognitive profile.

Writing on the board is another stumbling block for these trainees. Some information can be put up in advance so that spelling and inaccuracies can be checked while there is less pressure. However, there are times when this is impossible, either because of room availability or because of the structure of the lesson. In these cases, the dyslexic trainee teacher should have worked on her common spelling errors and learned the subject-specific vocabulary required on a weekly basis. However, more and more often, interactive white boards and PowerPoint presentations are used in classrooms so that much preparation can be done in advance to avoid errors. Some dyslexic trainees teachers tend to adopt the approach of: 'let's get the pupils to spell for me'. The SDT is advised to warn them of the dangers of doing this.

Fitness for Purpose is a crucial factor in this sphere and dyslexic students need to consider the severity of their dyslexia in relation to the job specification. They should be aware that, if they choose to become primary school teachers, the Literacy Strategy is stringent and depends upon a sound knowledge of the structure of the language. Students have to be confident that they can explain complex syntactical and grammatical structures to pupils.

Not only do trainee teachers have to plan weekly lesson structures with learning outcomes and targets; write reports for pupils; articulate self-reflection and monitoring but they will also play a crucial part in the assessment process of pupils. Thus they will be expected to give positive feedback on work. At times they will have to identify spelling and grammatical errors and provide accurate replacements.

5.2 Government skills tests in numeracy, literacy and ICT

In order to achieve qualified teacher status (QTS), trainee teachers have to complete the QTS skills in numeracy, literacy and information and communication technology (ICT). The SDT should advise students that they can apply for 25 per cent extra time and may be able to take their test on paper rather than on a computer. If a student requires 25 per cent extra time she just needs to book a test with the extra time and does not need to contact the Teacher Training Agency in advance to request permission. The Teacher Training Agency carries out spot checks to verify whether the student is entitled to the extra time, so it is advisable for the student to take a copy of an assessment report or alternative evidence with her to the test.

If a student requires further arrangements in addition to extra time, a form needs to be completed on her behalf by the training providers. This needs to be sent to the Teacher Training Agency, together with the relevant documentation providing evidence.

In conclusion ...

This chapter has looked at the potential challenges students face when part of the learning takes place off campus in the workplace setting. It has shown how dyslexic students can be supported in order to achieve professional competence and go on to be successful practitioners in areas such as health professions, teaching and social work. Dyslexia is not a barrier for students taking courses which lead to a professional qualification. Dyslexic students might need some extra support, particularly at the beginning of placements, to demonstrate that they have achieved the skills and competences required for them to be successful practitioners, but in many cases the strengths they bring to the workplace, such as empathy and creativity, are extremely beneficial for patients, clients and pupils. Some people still query the safety issues in the clinical setting but most dyslexic health professionals are safer than many non-dyslexic professionals because they are so conscious of possible pitfalls and work hard to develop checking procedures which become second nature.

Further reading

Association of Dyslexia Specialists in Higher Education (ADSHE) (2006) *Guidelines for Good Practice: Supporting Learners on Placement.* www.adshe.org.uk

Chartered Society of Physiotherapy. (2002) *Supporting disabled physiotherapy students on clinical placement.* The Chartered Society of Physiotherapy, 14 Bedford Row, London, WC1R, 4ED

Dale, C and Aiken, F (2007) *A Review of the Literature in to Dyslexia in Nursing Practice: Final Report.* Royal College of Nursing, Practice Education Forum. A Project which looks at nursing students in clinical practice and makes some recommendations.

Department for Education and Skills (2002) *Providing work placements for disabled Students: A good practice guide for further and higher education institutions*

The Geography Discipline Network: *Providing Learning Support for Students with Dyslexia and Hidden Disabilities Undertaking Fieldwork and Related Activities.* (2003) GEMRU, University of Gloucestershire

University of Southampton (2006) *Supporting dyslexic students on practice placements.* This booklet is for supervisors and mentors working with students on health and social care courses

13

Setting up a support service

This chapter looks at the role of the SDT in the Higher Education institution and suggests ways to organise a support service for students with specific learning difficulties.

Using this chapter

This chapter will enable you to:

1. Look at models of dyslexia support

2. Consider the role of the SDT within the university dyslexia support service

3. Consider the administrative procedures associated with running a support service

    3.1 Student Agreements

    3.2 Student Registration

4. Consider record keeping and evaluation

1. Models of dyslexia support

Institutions adopt various methods of organising dyslexia support. In some institutions it is part of the university disability service. The logic of this is understandable, as dyslexic students are entitled to DSA, reasonable adjustments and special examination considerations in a similar way to students with disabilities. However, their needs are very different, and in larger institutions it is often more manageable to run two services in parallel. Dyslexic students rarely see themselves as 'disabled' and might prefer an alternative model. Other institutions see the dyslexia service as part of counselling or welfare. Some students might be uncomfortable with this as they consider their needs to be primarily educational rather than a welfare issue.

Other institutions embed the dyslexia service within the generic learning and academic skills department or within the library services.

There is a great variety too in the way each dyslexia service is run. It is generally accepted that dyslexia services should be run by trained dyslexia personnel, usually those with a practising certificate. Ideally, the service should be managed by a dyslexia specialist who is also a practitioner. Some institutions separate the varied roles played by the SDT and employ dyslexia advisors, dyslexia tutors and assessors. The dyslexia advisors meet students to discuss their needs, sometimes carry out initial screening assessments and offer guidance about application for the Disabled Students' Allowance (DSA); dyslexia tutors offer individual or group tutorials; assessors carry out the full assessments. Assessors are more often than not even now educational psychologists rather than SDTs. It is interesting to speculate about why this is so, but the DfES guidelines of 2005 will go a long way to encourage more institutions to employ SDTs as well as psychologists to assess their students. Feedback sessions with students following on from the full assessments are usually carried out by dyslexia advisors. For SDTs, a far more satisfying model is one where they are involved in the whole process i.e. they are responsible for screening and assessment as well as setting up support needs, advising the students and providing tutorial support. See Figure 1 on page 233.

Whatever model is adopted the dyslexia support service will need to agree procedures so that the institution as a whole is aware of how support for dyslexic students is accessed. Singleton (1999) stresses the importance of an institutional policy to ensure equal provision for all students and to develop awareness among the academic staff.

> All HEIs require policy and procedural guidelines to embed dyslexia support. The maintenance of professional and academic standards must underpin this process... Each institution should have a clear general policy setting out regulations, procedures and guidelines, as appropriate, for the identification and support of students with dyslexia. Within the policy, dyslexia should be explicitly recognised both as a disability and as a special educational need. (Singleton, 1999:66)

Although most dyslexic students do not see dyslexia as a disability, it is important that the institution recognises its obligation to provide reasonable adjustments under the law and this should be implicit in any policy that is agreed. The institutional policy should be widely publicised, as should the availability and location of the support. The SDT might find that she is expected to provide information about the service in the form of publicity leaflets or on a website. She might also be expected to produce some form of guidelines to aid academic tutors. Appendix 2 provides an example of a guidelines document.

Dyslexia support services should promote understanding of dyslexia and dyslexia friendly practices which are beneficial for all students. Dyslexia-friendly practices and inclusive learning throughout the institution are an ideal which SDTs can help to promote throughout their institutions.

2. The role of the SDT within the Dyslexia Support Service

> The role of learning support personnel will therefore depend very much on the teaching/assessment culture and methodologies of the institution, on the way which 'support' is viewed by the institution, and on the philosophy and organisation of the support service itself and its personnel. (Herrington, 2001:173)

The role of the SDT is a complex one and will vary from institution to institution. The SDT, however, should have a clear and focused view of how she sees her role and what approach she wishes to take with the students (see Chapter 3 for further discussion). There should be room for individual variation but most successful dyslexia departments will share a common aim and approach and the support provided will reflect this. Do they see dyslexia and other specific learning difficulties as a difference or a disability? Very often the SDT will see herself first and foremost as an educator and the other parts of the role will flow from this. The majority of her time will be taken up with providing an educational service. At times she will be called on to be a counsellor, providing a degree of emotional support for the student. The SDT should be empathetic and a good listener and know when it is important to let a student offload something that is worrying her in order to free her mind to get on with the tutorial but equally the SDT should recognise when other issues are becoming paramount and should then suggest professional counselling.

The SDT will also be expected to play an advisory role. She might need to liaise with other departments and offer advice and guidance to both students and staff. She might be called on to be an advocate for the student in requesting non standard reasonable adjustments such as extensions for essays in exceptional circumstances or might support the student in an appeals process.

To ensure uniformity of practice and to protect staff and students, it is usual for dyslexia departments to draw up a Code of Practice which deals with many of the ethical issues which are related to the role (see Appendix 1).

Dyslexia Support services are responsible for driving forward policy relating to dyslexia and making institutional recommendations for special examination arrangements and support needs. So they will be involved in surveying current practices and policies in other institutions to help inform future developments. Figure 1 opposite outlines the varied responsibilities which could be taken by specialist dyslexia tutors.

3. Administration

It is advisable to draw up a dyslexia service Code of Practice so that all students and staff are aware of what is offered and what is not. These services and procedural information can be made transparent to staff and students electronically and also as services guidance booklets and handbooks. An example of the type of information appreciated by staff and students is given in Appendix 2.

3.1 Student Agreements

In the current climate it is necessary for both staff and students to draw up a working, operational agreement which sets out terms of support to meet the individual's needs. Such agreements are jointly drawn up so that the student is involved right from the beginning in the whole process. Appendix 3 gives an example of an agreement form. The student will also need to sign a confidentiality form to enable information about her dyslexia to be shared with the academic department as well as administrative personnel such as examination officers. (See Appendix 4 for an example of a confidentiality form.)

3.2 Student Registration

It is useful to ask students to fill in a Registration form. This is vital not only for student information but also for the provision of statistical information which is sometimes required as part of institutional quality assurance procedures. Appendix 5 gives an example of a registration form. Examples of disclosure forms can be seen on the ADSHE website. http://www.adshe.org.uk/docs/currentactivities/htm

The dyslexia support service will need to set up systems to pass on the necessary information to academic departments. These will include the recommendations made in the Student Agreement, together with suggestions as to how the department can help and what the dyslexia service can offer. An example of this can be found in Appendix 6.

4. Record keeping and evaluation

The dyslexia service should set up a procedure to monitor individual student progress through a form of regular reviews where student and SDT discuss support provided and plan for future sessions. Similarly, the dyslexia support service should evaluate the service as a whole in order to understand stu-

Educator/ Assessor

Individual and group tutorials
Evaluating and monitoring support
Peer mentoring
Training
Initial interviews/screening assessments
Full assessments
Feedback sessions
Recommendations for special examination arrangements and other reasonable adjustments

Advisor

Staff

    Queries about dyslexia
    Queries about individual students
    Staff awareness training
    Liaison with other departments: admissions, library, marketing, other support services

Students

    DSA applications
    Acting as advocate for extensions/adjustments/appeals

External agencies

    Liaison with other educational providers such as previous schools
    Liaison with Access Centres carrying out Assessment of Needs

Administrator

Publicity of service
Information for prospective students
Ensuring all new students contacted prior to entry
    + following up those who 'declare' but do not come forward
Funding for assessments/tutorials
Record keeping
Statistics of support provided

Figure 1: The roles of a Specialist Dyslexia Tutor (SDT)

dents' perceptions of the support provided and to improve the support in the future.

Individual SDTs should also regularly monitor their own teaching and assessment. This can be partly achieved through keeping up the practising certificate portfolio and through regular CPD sessions. The dyslexia service can also operate a system of peer mentoring where individual SDTs share ideas through discussion or observation of individual sessions.

Record keeping is essential. The SDT will need not only to record what has taken place in a support session but should also make brief notes on any communication with the student or others by telephone or emails. Copies of important emails should be retained in the student file together with copies of the student's assessment report, registration and confidentiality form, written communication to academic departments etc. If students are in receipt of the Disabled Students' Allowance it will also be necessary to devise a sheet they sign each time they have a tutorial, as Local Authorities and other funding bodies often require this as evidence.

In conclusion ...

This chapter has made suggestions about how to organise the educational support necessary for students with specific learning difficulties and has given examples of how to devise relevant paperwork and documentation.

Further reading

Association of Dyslexia Specialists in Higher Education (ADSHE) *Establishing systems for Specialist Dyslexia Teaching*. http://www.adshe.org.uk/docs/currentactivities.htm

Singleton, C. (ed) (1999) *Dyslexia in Higher Education: policy, provision and practice*. Chris Singleton and the National Working Party on Dyslexia in Higher Education. University of Hull

Appendix 1: Example of Dyslexia Service Code of Practice

Introduction

Mission statement

Services provided

Confidentiality

Evidence of specific learning difficulty

Special examination arrangements

Making contact

Making appointments

Missed appointments

The library

Feedback

Complaints

University policies (for example, Equal Opportunities Policy; Harassment Policy; Student Complaints; Discipline regulations for students; Examination Policy; Disability/Dyslexia Policy

Contact details

Appendix 2: Example of a Guidelines booklet for Academic Tutors

Contents

Services for students

Services for staff

Recognising students with dyslexia or other specific learning difficulties

Difficulties specific to Higher Education

Reasonable adjustments

Examination policy and procedures for students with specific learning difficulties

Guidelines for marking the work of students with dyslexia/dyspraxia

Useful strategies for helping SpLD students

       Assignments
       Lectures
       Reading
       Targeted tutorial time
       Dyslexia-friendly handouts
       Use of coloured overlays in reading

Disabled Students' Allowance (DSA)

Further information

Contact details

Appendix 3: Example of Support Agreement

Student name: Number:

Course: Year of entry:

Department: Faculty:

Recommendations for Special Examination Arrangements
The Dyslexia Service will inform your department and the examinations office of these recommendations.

Recommendations for Academic Study Skills Tutorials
Tutorial support can be arranged through *the Dyslexia Service*, subject to availability of appointments. Notice should be given if an appointment has to be cancelled.

It has been agreed that the following would be useful:

Reading/research skills   Organisation/time management
Note-taking   Essay planning/organisation
Revision/examination techniques   Learning styles/memory techniques
Punctuation/sentence structure   Proofreading skills
Other

Initial recommendation for number of sessions: ....

Applying DSA: Yes / No   **Full assessment in file**: Yes/ No

I agree to the above recommendations. I agree that my department should be informed of my specific learning difficulty in order that appropriate recommendations and support can be arranged.

Signed: ....

Student   Dyslexia tutor on behalf the *Dyslexia Service*

Date:

Appendix 4: Example of Confidentiality Form

A copy of your assessment report and a copy of the Student Agreement, together with this form, will be kept confidentially within *the Dyslexia Service*. However, in order to facilitate support during your studies at the University it will be necessary to pass information about your specific learning difficulty to other members of staff. Your explicit consent is needed in order for any information to be disclosed.

Consent to process sensitive personal data

In order to facilitate the requisite support for my studies, I understand that information relating to my specific learning difficulty will be recorded and processed by *the Dyslexia Service* and may be disclosed by it to the individuals/organisations listed below. I hereby give my explicit consent to such disclosure:

(Please tick)

☐ Tutors and administrative staff in my department

☐ Administrative staff within University

☐ Examinations officers in my department

☐ Specialist dyslexia tutor who will provide tutorials

☐ Educational Psychologist/Specialist dyslexia tutor who will carry out an assessment

☐ Local Authority/NHS Student Grants Unit/other funding body

☐ Placement provider (e.g. mentor/clinician)

☐ Parent/Guardian/Partner

I confirm that this consent shall remain valid until such time as I notify *the Dyslexia Service* otherwise. I understand that this information may be discussed by those within *the Dyslexia Service* and that edited information, which would not identify me, may be included in reports and presentations made by *the Dyslexia Service*. I further understand that I am entitled to see the information on request.

Signature...   Date:........................

Appendix 5: Example of Registration Form

Name: Student Number:

Date:

Gender: Female ☐ Male ☐   Campus:

Date of Birth: University email:

Contact details
Term-time address: Home address:
(Please include postcode)   (Please include postcode)

Telephone: Telephone:
Mobile:

Course details
Department of: Degree:
Tutor:
Year of entry: Length of course:
Full/Part time   Foundation/Undergraduate/Postgraduate
UK/EU Student/International Student   NHS/LA

Nursing students only:
Degree/Diploma/Advanced Diploma/Other   Branch:
Award leader: Bursary/Seconded

Ethnicity:

White   **Mixed**
British ☐   White and Black Caribbean ☐
Irish ☐   White and Black African ☐
Any other white background (Please describe)   White and Asian ☐
                                         Any other mixed background
                                         (Please describe)

Asian or Asian British   **Black or Black British**
Indian ☐   Caribbean ☐
Bangladeshi ☐   African ☐
Pakistani ☐   Any other black background
Any other Asian background (Please describe)   (Please describe)

Chinese or other ethnic group
Chinese ☐
Any other ethnic group (Please describe)

Appendix 6: Example of Department Memo

Confidential

Name: **Number:**

Course: **Date:**

X registered with the Dyslexia Service on   . An initial screening assessment was carried out on and X was then referred for a full assessment. The full assessment report has now been received and concludes that X has a specific learning difficulty (dyslexia).

Insert summary of main findings

Suggested strategies for the department
Example
- Guided reading list with texts listed in order of priority.
- Handouts from lectures provided in advance would be very useful.
- All tutors to be informed about X's dyslexia as far as possible. (Extra copies of this memo can be provided on request.)

Dyslexia Service Support
Example
- Individual tutorial sessions with dyslexia tutor to cover: reading and research skills; proof reading skills; examination and revision techniques.
- Application for the Disabled Students' Allowance (DSA) to provide technological equipment and dyslexia tutorial support. The Dyslexia Service can help with this application.

Recommendations for Special Examination Arrangements
Example
- 25% extra time in all timed assessments, including practical examinations when appropriate.
- Examination scripts to be flagged with a coloured sticker to indicate dyslexia. This is in order to ensure that in anonymous marking a dyslexic student is not penalised for typical dyslexic spelling and syntax errors.
- Separate room with other students receiving additional time in order that X is not disturbed when other students leave the room.
- The Dyslexia Service will inform the Examinations Office and the department of these requirements.

Suggested strategies for placement
If you would like to discuss the contents of this memo or would like to receive further details, please contact ....

Copies to: Personal tutor:
Student:
File:

References

ADSHE (2002) The dyslexia screening process in HE. Unpublished survey: Association of Dyslexia Specialists in Higher Education (ADSHE)

ADSHE (2006) *Guidelines for good practice: supporting learners on placement.* Association of Dyslexia Specialists in Higher Education (ADSHE)

Anastasi, A (1982) *Psychological Testing (5th Edition).* New York: Macmillan

Avramidis, E, and Skidmore, D (2004) Reappraising Learning Support in Higher Education. *Research in Post-Compulsory Education,* 5(1), 63-82

Backhouse, G and Morris, K (eds) (2005) *Dyslexia Assessing and reporting – the PATOSS Guide.* London: Hodder-Murray

Baddeley, A D (1990) *Human Memory.* Hove: Lawrence Erlbaum Associates

Barnett, R (1997) *Higher Education: A Critical Business.* Buckinghamshire: Open University Press

BDA (2006) *The British Dyslexia Association Dyslexia Handbook.* Somerset: REM

Beard, R (1993) *Teaching Literacy: Balancing Perspectives.* London: Hodder and Stoughton

Bereiter, C and Scardamalia, M (1987) *The Psychology of Written Composition.* New Jersey: Lawrence Erlbaum Associates

Bereiter, C and Scardamalia, M (1992) Cognition in the curriculum. In P. W. Jackson (ed) *Handbook of research on curriculum* (pp.517-542). New York: American Educational Research Association

Berninger, V W and Richards, T L (2002) *Brain literacy for educators and psychologists.* London: Academic Press

Blakemore, S and Frith, U (2000) *The implications of recent developments in neuroscience for research on teaching and learning: Discussion document.* London: Institute of Cognitive Neuroscience, University College London

Blakemore, S, Winston, J and Frith, U (2004) Social cognitive neuroscience: where are we heading? *Trends in Cognitive Science,* 8(5), 216-222

Brooks, P, Everatt, J and Fidler, R (2004) *Adult Reading Test (ART).* Oxford: Harcourt Assessment

Brown, A (1992) Reciprocal Teaching: An Approach to Improving Reading Comprehension by Training Metacognitive Strategies. In F. Satow and B. Gatherer (eds) *Literacy without Frontiers*. Widnes: United Kingdom Reading Association

Brown, G T, Rodger, S and Davis, A (2003) Test of Visual Perceptual Skills-Revised: An Overview and Critique. *Scandinavian Journal of Occupational Therapy,* 10, 3-15

Bruner, J (1990) *Acts of Meaning.* Cambridge, MA: Harvard University Press

Brunswick, N, McCrory, E, Price, C, Frith, D and Frith, U (1999) Explicit and implicit processing of words and pseudowords by adult developmental dyslexics. A search for Wernicke's wortschatz. *Brain,* 122, 1901-1917

Butterworth, B (1999) *The Mathematical Brain.* London: Macmillan

Byrnes, J P (2001) *Minds, brains and learning: understanding the psychological and educational relevance of neuroscientific research.* New York: Guildford Press

Campbell, J, and Cowe, T (1998) *Working with DipSW Students with Dyslexia: A Guide for Practice Teachers.* Strathclyde: University of Strathclyde, Faculty of Education

Cardon, L R, Smith, S D, Fulker, D W, Kimberling, W J, Pennington, B F and DeFries, J C (1994) Quantitative trait locus for reading disability on chromosome 6. *Science* 266, 276-279

Cavalier, A R, Ferretti, R P, and Okolo, C M (1994) Technology and individual differences. *Journal of Special Education Technology,* 12, 175-181

Chartered Society of Physiotherapy (2004) *Supporting disabled physiotherapy students on clinical placement.* London: The Chartered Society of Physiotherapy

Cline, T, Ganschow, L and Reason, R (2000) Multilingualism and Dyslexia: Special Issue, Part 1. *Dyslexia: An International Journal of Research and Practice,* 6(1), 3-82

Cline, T, Ganschow, L and Reason, R (2000) Multilingualism and Dyslexia: Special Issue, Part 2. *Dyslexia: An International Journal of Research and Practice,* 6(2), 87-163

Coffield, F J, Moseley, D V, Hall, E and Ecclestone, K (2004) *Should we be using learning styles? What research has to say to practice.* London: Learning and Skills Research Centre

Colley, M (2000) *Living with Dyspraxia.* Chippenham: Dyspraxia Foundation Adult Support Group

Colley, M (2006) *Living with Dyspraxia: A Guide for Adults with Developmental Dyspraxia,* (revised edition). London: Jessica Kingsley

Cornelissen, P, Hansen, P, Hutton, J, Evangelinou, V and Stein, J (1998) Magnocellular visual function and children's single word reading. *Vision Research,* 38, 471-482

Corrigan, C (ed) (2001) *Dyslexia: A Guide for Staff.* London: Centre for learning and Teaching in Art and Design

Cottrell, S (2001) *Teaching Study Skills and Supporting Learning.* Basingstoke: Palgrave

Couzijn, M (1999) Learning to write by observation of writing and reading processes: effects on learning and transfer. *Learning and Instruction,* 9(2), 109-142

Critchley, M (1970) *The Dyslexic Child.* London: Heinemann Medical Books

Critchley, M and Critchley, ER (1978) *Dyslexia defined.* London: Heinemann.

REFERENCES

Cronbach, L J (1990) *Essentials of Psychological testing* (5th Edition). New York: Harper Collins

Dale, C and Aiken, F (2007) *A Review of the Literature into Dyslexia in Nursing Practice: Final Report.* London: Royal College of Nursing, Practice Education Forum

de Bono, E (1991) *CoRT Thinking* (2nd ed. Vol. 1). Oxford: Pergamon Press

Deary, I J (2001) *Intelligence: A very short introduction.* Oxford: Oxford University Press

deFries, J C and Alarcon, M (1996) Genetics of specific reading disability. *Mental Retardation and Developmental Disabilities Research Reviews,* 2, 39-47

Deponio, P (2004) The co-occurrence of specific learning difficulties: implications for identification and assessment. In G. Reid and A. Fawcett (eds) *Dyslexia in Context: Research, Policy and Practice.* London: Whurr Publishers

DfEE (2001) *Special Educational Needs and Disability Act* (SENDA). London: HMSO

DfES (2002) *Access for All: Guidance on Making the Adult Literacy and Numeracy Core Curricula Accessible.* London: Learning and Skills Development Agency (LSDA) and the Basic Skills Agency (BSA)

DfES (2002) *Providing work placements for disabled students: A good practice guide for further and higher education institutions.* London: DfES publications

DfES (2005) *Assessment of Dyslexia, Dyspraxia, Dyscalculia and Attention Deficit Disorder (ADD) in Higher Education.* London: Department for Education and Skills

DRC (2003) *Examinations: The Disability Discrimination Act Part 4 (EDU9).* London: Disability Rights Commission

Drew, S (2005) *Developmental Co-ordination Disorder in Adults.* London: Wiley and Sons

Eden, G, Van Meter, J, Rumsey, J, Maisog, J, Woods, R and Zeffiro, T (1996) Abnormal processing of visual motion in dyslexia revealed by functional brain imaging. *Nature,* 382, 66-69

Elliott, J (2003) Dynamic Assessment in Educational Settings: realising potential. *Educational Review,* 55(1), 15-32

Ellsworth, A, Witt, D, Dugdale, D and Oliver, L (2006) *Mosby's Medical Drug Reference.* Missouri: Mosby Inc, Harcourt Health Sciences

Evans, B (2001) *Dyslexia and Vision.* London: Whurr Publishers

Eysenck, H J (ed) (1982) *A model for intelligence.* New York: Springer-Verlag

Farmer, M, Riddick, B and Sterling, C (2002) *Dyslexia and Inclusion: Assessment and Support in Higher Education.* London: Whurr Publishers

Farmer, M, Riddick, B, Sterling, C and Simpson, B (2001) *Assessment of the functional needs of dyslexic students in higher education.* Paper presented at the 5th British Dyslexia Association International Conference, University of York

Fawcett, A (ed) (2001) *Dyslexia: Theory and Good Practice.* London: Whurr

Fawcett, A and Nicolson, R (1998) *The Dyslexia Adult Screening Test (DAST).* London: Psychological Corporation

Fawcett, A and Nicolson, R (1999) Performance of dyslexic children on cognitive and cerebellar tests. *Annals of Dyslexia*, 46, 259-283

Feuerstein, R, Feuerstein, R S, Fakik, L and Rand, Y (2002) *The Dynamic Assessment of Cognitive Modifiability.* Jerusalem: The ICELP Press

Flower, L S and Hayes, J R (1981) A cognitive process theory of writing. *College Composition and Communication*, 32(4), 365-387

Flower, L S, Schriver, K A, Carey, L, Haas, C and Hayes, J R (1992) Planning in writing: the cognition of a constructive process. In S. Witte, N. Nakadate and R. Cherry (eds) *A rhetoric of doing.* Carbondale, South Illin: University Press

Freewood, M, Cunliffe-Charlesworth, H and Hewson, J (eds) (2003) *Accessible arrangements: staff guide to inclusive practice.* Sheffield: Sheffield Hallam University.

Frith, U (1985) Beneath the surface of developmental dyslexia. In M. Coltheart, K. Patterson and J. Marshall (eds) *Surface Dyslexia* (pp.301-330). London: Lawrence Erlbaum

Frith, U (1995) Dyslexia: Can we have a shared theoretical framework? *Journal of Educational Psychology,* 12, 6-17

Frith, U (1997) Brain, mind and behaviour in dyslexia. *Dyslexia: An International Journal of Research and Practice*, 5(4), 192-214

Frith, U (1999) Paradoxes in the definition of dyslexia. *Dyslexia: An International Journal of Research and Practice*, 5, 192-214

Frith, U (2001) What framework should we use for understanding developmental disorders? *Developmental Neuropsychology*, 20(2), 555-583

Gains, C and Wray, D (1995) *Reading.* Nasen Enterprises

Galaburda, A M (1989) Ordinary and extraordinary brain development: Anatomical variation in developmental dyslexia. *Annals of Dyslexia,* 39, 67-80

Galaburda, A M, Sherman, G F, Rosen, G D, Aboitiz, F and Geschwind, N (1985) Developmental dyslexia: Four consecutive patients with cortical anomalies. *Annals of Neurology*, 18, 222-233

Galbraith, D and Rijlaarsdam, G (1999) Effective strategies for the teaching and learning of writing. *Learning and Instruction*, 9(2), 93-108

Gale, A and Price, G A (2004) *Automaticity, dysfunctional organisation and the dyslexic profile: issues connected with nursing practice and the professional's dilemma.* Paper presented at the 6th British Dyslexia Association International Conference

Gardner, H (1993) *Multiple Intelligences.* New York: Basic Books

Gardner, H (1999) *Intelligence Reframed. Multiple intelligences for the 21st century.* New York: Basic Books

Gathercole, S. E. and Baddeley, A. D. (1993) *Working Memory and Language.* Hove: Lawrence Erlbaum Associates.

GEMRU (2003) *Providing Learning Support for Students with Dyslexia and Hidden Disabilities Undertaking Fieldwork and Related Activities.* Gloucester: The Geography Discipline Network:University of Gloucestershire

Gilroy, D E and Miles, T R (1995) *Dyslexia at College*. London: Routledge

Glutting,J, Adams, W and Sheslow, D (2000) *Wide Range Intelligence Test (WRIT)*. Wilmington: Wide Range

Glynn, T, Wearmouth, J and Berryman, M (2006) *Supporting students with literacy difficulties*. Maidenhead: Open University Press

Goodwin, V and Thompson, B (2004) *Making dyslexia work for you: a self-help guide*. London: David Fulton

Goswami, U (2004) Neuroscience, education and special education. *British Journal of Special Education*, 31(4), 175-183

Goulandris, N (ed) (2003) *Dyslexia in Different Languages: Cross-Linguistic Comparisons*. London: Whurr Publishers

Graal, M and Clark, R (eds) (1999) *Partnerships across the curriculum*. Leicester: University of Leicester

Grabe, W and Kaplan, R B (1996) *Theory and Practice of Writing*. London: Longman

Grant, D (2001) *That's the way I think – Dyslexia and creativity*. Proceedings of 5th BDA International Conference, University of York

Grant, D (2005) *Formal identification of a range of specific learning differences in Neuro-diversity in FE and HE*. Conference proceedings., De Montforte University

Gregg, N (2003) Diagnostic issues surrounding students with learning disabilities. In Vogel, G, Vogel, V, Sharoni and O. Dahan (eds) *Learning Disabilities in Higher Education and Beyond: An International Perspective* (pp. 93-106). Baltimore: York Press

Hacker, D J, Dunlosky, J and Graesser, A (eds) (1998) *Metacognition in educational theory and practice*. Mahwah, NJ: Lawrence Erlbaum Associates

Hales, G (1994) *Dyslexia Matters*. London: Whurr

Haller, E P, Child, D A and Walberg, H J (1988) Can comprehension be taught? A quantitative synthesis of metacognitive studies. *Educational Researcher,* 17, 5-8

Halpern, D F (1997) *Critical thinking across the curriculum: A brief edition of thought and knowledge*. Mahwah, NJ: Lawrence Erlbaum Associates

Harpur, J, Lawlor, M and Fitzgerald, M (2004) *Succeeding in College with Asperger Syndrome*. London and New York: Jessica Kingsley Publishing

Harrison, R (2000) Learner managed learning: managing to learn or learning to manage? *International Journal of Lifelong Learning,* 19(4), 312-321

Hatcher, J (2001) *An evaluation of the types of provision for dyslexic students*. Paper presented at the 5th British Dyslexia Association International Conference., University of York

Haywood, H C (2004) Thinking In, Around and About The Curriculum: the role of cognitive education. *International Journal of Disability, Development and Education*, 51(3), 231-252

Healy Eames, F (2002) Changing Definitions and Concepts of Literacy: Implications for Pedagogy and Research. In G. Reid and J. Wearmouth (eds) *Dyslexia and Literacy*. Chichester: John Wiley and Sons

Heaton, P and Mitchell, G (2001) *Dyslexia: students in need.* London: Whurr Publishers

HEFCE (1998) *Widening Participation in Higher Education.* London: HEFCE

Helland, T (2007) Dyslexia at a Behavioural and a Cognitive Level. *Dyslexia: An International Journal of Research and Practice,* 13(1), 25-41

Henry, M, Ganschow, L and Miles, T R (2000) The issue of definition: some problems. *Perspectives: International Dyslexia Association,* Winter, 38-43

Herrington, M (2001) An approach to specialist learning support in higher education. In M Hunter-Carsch and M Herrington (eds) *Dyslexia and effective learning in secondary and tertiary education.* London: Whurr Publishers

Herrington, M and Simpson, D (eds) (2002) *Making reasonable adjustments with disabled student in HE: staff development materials, case studies and exercises.* Nottingham: University of Nottingham

Herrnstein, R J and Murray, C (1994) *The bell curve: Intelligence and class structure in American life.* New York: Free Press

HESA (2004) *Analysis of degree classes of students with disabilities in Higher Education Institutions.* Cheltenham: HESA

Hinshelwood, J (1917) *Congenital word blindness.* London: H.K. Lewis

HMSO (1995) Disability Discrimination Act. London: HMSO

HMSO (2001) *The Special Educational Needs and Disability Act (SENDA).* London: HMSO

Howard, R M (1995) Plagiarism, authors and the academic death penalty. *College English,* 57, 788-806

Hulme, C and Snowling, M (1997) *Dyslexia: Biology, Cognition and Intervention.* London: Whurr Publishers

Hunter-Carsch, M (ed) (2001a) *Dyslexia: a psychosocial perspective.* London: Whurr Publishers

Hunter-Carsch, M and Herrington, M (eds) (2001) *Dyslexia and effective learning in secondary and tertiary education.* London: Whurr Publishers

IDA (2000) *Dyslexia: Definition by the Committee of the IDA*

Irlen, H (1991) *Reading by the colors.* New York: Avery Publishing Group

James, G (ed) (1984) *The ESP Classroom.* Exeter: University of Exeter

Jones, A (2004) Teaching critical thinking: an investigation of a task in introductory macroeconomics. *Higher Education Research and Development,* 23(2), 167-181

Kaufman, A S (1994) *Intelligent Testing with the WISC-III.* New York: John Wiley and Sons

Kiziewicz, M (2000) *Ourselves in Place.* Paper presented at the Dyslexia in Higher Education Art and Design: a creative opportunity, Surrey Institute of Art and Design

Klein, C (1993) *Diagnosing Dyslexia – A Guide to the Assessment of Adults with Specific Learning Difficulties.* London: Adult Literacy and Skills Unit

LDC (2006) *Guide for Tutors: Learning Differences Centre Guidance.* Southampton: University of Southampton

Lee, J (2000) The challenge of dyslexia in adults. In J. Towend and M. Turner (eds) *Dyslexia in practice: a guide for teachers*. New York: Klumer Academic

Levine, M (1997) *Educational Care*. Cambridge, MA: Educators Publishing Service, Inc

Lofting, C (2003) *Thinking Through Ellipses*. Paper presented at the Arts and Visual Thinking, Falmouth College

Martin, N (2007) *Test of Visual Perceptual Skills 3*. Austin, Texas: Pro-ed Inc

Martin, N and Brownell, R (2006) *Test of Auditory-Processing Skills – 3rd Edition*. Austin, Texas: Pro-ed Inc

McLoughlin, D and Beard, J (2000) Dyslexic support in a multilingual university environment. In L. Peer and G. Reid (eds) *Multilingualism, dyslexia and literacy*. London: David Fulton

McLoughlin, D, Fitzgibbon, G and Young, V (1994) *Adult Dyslexia: Assessment, Counselling and Training*. London: Whurr Publishers

McLoughlin, D, Leather, C and Stringer, P (2002) *The Adult Dyslexic: Interventions and Outcomes*. London: Whurr Publishers

McNaughton, D, Hughes, C and Clark, K (1997) The effects of five proof-reading conditions on the spelling performance of college students with learning disabilities. *Journal of Learning Disabilities*, 30(6), 643-651

Miles, T R and Westcombe, J (eds) (2001) *Music and Dyslexia, opening new doors*. London: Whurr Publishers

Moody, S (2006) *How to survive and succeed at work*. London: Random House

Moody, S (2007) *Dyslexia: Surviving and succeeding at college*. London: Routledge

Morgan, E (2001) Staff development in Higher Education: a student-centred approach. In M. Hunter-Carsch and M. Herrington (eds) *Dyslexia and effective learning in secondary and tertiary education*. London: Whurr Publishers

Morgan, E and Klein, C (2000) *The dyslexic adult in a non-dyslexic world*. London: Whurr Publishers

Morris, D and Turnball, P (2005) Clinical experiences of students with dyslexia. *Journal of Advanced Nursing*

Neisser, U, Boodoo, G, Bouchard, T, Boykin, A, Brody, N and Ceci, S (1996) Intelligence: Knowns and unknowns. *American Psychologist*, 51, 77-101

Newell, A (1990) *United theories of cognition*. Cambridge, MA: Harvard University Press

Nicolson, R and Fawcett, A (1999) Developmental Dyslexia: The role of the Cerebellum. *Dyslexia: An International Journal of Research and Practice*, 5, 155-177

Nicolson, R and Fawcett, A (2001) Developmental Dyslexia: The cerebellar deficit hypothesis. *Trends in Neurosciences*, 24(9), 508-516

Olson, R (2002) Dyslexia: nature and nurture. *Dyslexia: An International Journal of Research and Practice*, 8(3), 143-159

Palincsar, A and Brown, A L (1984) Reciprocal teaching of comprehension-fostering and comprehension-monitoring activities. *Cognition and Instruction*, 1, 117-175

Palincsar, A S (1998) Social Constructivist Perspectives on Teaching and Learning. *Annual Review of Psychology*, 49, 345-375

Palincsar, A , Anderson, C. and David, Y M (1993) Pursuing Scientific Literacy in the Middle Grades Through Collaborative Problem Solving. *The Elementary School Journal*, 93(5), 643-658

Palincsar, A S and Brown, A L (1989) Classroom dialogues to promote self-regulated comprehension. In J. Brophy (ed) *Advances in Research in Teaching*. Greenwich: JAI

Pavlides, G T (1981) Do eye movements hold the key to dyslexia? *Neuropsychologia*, 19, 57-64

Pears, R and Shields, G (2005) *Cite them right: referencing made easy.* (2nd ed). Newcastle: Pear Tree Books

Peer, L and Reid, G (eds) (2000) *Multilingualism, Literacy and Dyslexia.* London: David Fulton Publishers

Perin, D (1983) Perin Spoonerism Task. *British Journal of Psychology*, 74, 129-144

Peterson, P and Walberg, H J (es) (1979) *Research in Teaching.* CA: McCutchan

Pickering, S J and Gathercole, S E (2004) Working memory deficits in dyslexia: Are they located in the phonological loop, visuo-spatial sketchpad or central executive?

Pillai, M (2003) *Developing positive learning environments and facilitating help-seeking. Paper presented at the Supporting the dyslexic student in HE and FE: strategies for success.* De Montfort University

Pollak, D (2005) *Specific learning differences in HE and FE: dealing with neurodiversity.* Leicester: Student Services: SLAS, De Montfort University

Pollack, D (2005) *Dyslexia, the Self and Higher Education.* Stoke on Trent: Trentham Books

Price, G A (2001) *Report of the Survey of Academic Study Skills at Southampton University.* Southampton: University of Southampton

Price, G A (2003) *Cognitive Load and the Writing Process:The Paradox of the Dyslexic Writer In Higher Education.* Southampton, Southampton

Price, G A (2006) Creative solutions to making technology work: three case studies of dyslexic writers in Higher Education. *ALT-J Research in Learning Technology,* 14(1), 21-38

Price, G A and Gale, A (2006) How do dyslexic nursing students cope with clinical practice placements? The impact of the dyslexic profile on the clinical practice of dyslexic nursing students: Pedagogical issues and considerations. *Learning Disabilities: A contemporary journal,* 4(1), 19-36

Price, G. A and Maier, P. (2007) *Effective Study Skills.* Harlow: Pearson Educational

Price, G and Skinner, J P (2005) Dyslexic Students and Clinical Practice: Reflections, paradoxes and challenges. *Journal of PATOSS, Professional Association of Teachers of Students with Specific Learning Difficulties,* 18(2)

Prior, S M and Welling, K A (2001) 'Read in your head': A Vygotskian analysis of the transition from oral to silent reading. *Reading Psychology,* 22(1), 1-15

QAA (2000) *Code of Practice for the Assurance of Academic Quality and Standards in Higher Education: Guidelines for HE Progress Files.* London: Quality Assurance Agency

Rack, J (1997) Issues in the assessment of developmental dyslexia in adults. *Journal of Research in Reading*, 20(1), 66-76

Radloff, P (1998) *Do we treat time and space seriously enough in teaching and learning?* Paper presented at the Teaching and Learning in Changing Times, Perth, University of Western Australia

Reid, A A, Szczerbinski, M, Iskierka-Kasperek, E and Hansen, P (2007) Cognitive profiles of adult developmental dyslexics: theoretical implications. *Dyslexia: An International Journal of Research and Practice,* 13(1), 1-24

Reid, G (2003) *Dyslexia: A practitioner's handbook. (3rd Edition)* London: John Wiley and Sons

Reid, G and Fawcett, A (eds) (2004) *Dyslexia in context: research, policy and practice.* London: Whurr Publishers

Reid, G and Kirk, J (2001) *Dyslexia in Adults, Education and Employment.* West Sussex: John Wiley

Reid Lyon, G (1995) Towards a definition of Dyslexia. *Annals of Dyslexia*

Reynold, C R, Pearson, N A and Voress, J K (2002) *Developmental Test of Visual Perception – Adolescent and Adult (DTVP-A).* Austin, Texas: Pro-ed Inc

Riddick, B, Sterling, C, Farmer, M and Morgan, S (1999) Self-esteem and anxiety in the educational histories of adult dyslexic students. *Dyslexia: An International Journal of Research and Practice*, 5(4), 227-248

Robertson, J (2005) *Does Dyscalculia affect the Learning in Mathematical Concepts (The 'Twoness' of Two)* Paper presented at the Brain He. Neurodiversity in FE and HE: positive initiatives for specific learning differences

Robertson, J (2005) Maths and Dyslexia in Further and Higher Education. In D. Pollack (ed) *Proceedings of a joint conference: Supporting the dyslexic student in HE and FE: strategies for success.* Leicester: De Montfort University

Rugg, G and Petre, M (2004) *The unwritten rules of PhD research.* Buckingham: Open University Press

Sanderson, A and Pillai, M (2001) *The Lottery of Support in Higher Education.* Paper presented at the Dyslexia at the Dawn of the new century: BDA 5th International Conference, University of York

Sanderson-Mann, J and McCandless, F (2005) Understanding dyslexia and nurse education in the clinical setting. *Nurse Education in Practice*, 6, 127-133

SCIPS (2004) *Academic Standards and Benchmark Descriptors: Developing Strategies for Inclusivity: Strategy for Creating Inclusive Programmes of Study (SCIPS).* Worcester: University College Worcester

Scott, R (2004) *Dyslexia and Counselling.* London: Whurr Publishers

Shaywitz, S E (1996) Dyslexia. *Scientific American,* 94, 98-104

Sheslow, D and Adams, W (2001) *Wide Range Assessment of Memory and Learning (WRAML2)*. Wilmington: Wide Range

Shulman, D (2002) Diagnosing learning disabilities in community college culturally and linguistically diverse students. *Journal of Post-secondary Education and Disability*

Singleton, C (1999) *Dyslexia in Higher Education: Policy, provision and practice Report of the National Working Party on Dyslexia in Higher Education*. Hull: Department of Psychology, University of Hull

Singleton, C, Horne, J and Thomas, K (2002) *Lucid Adult Dyslexia Screening Plus (LADS)*. Beverley, East Yorkshire: Lucid Innovations Ltd

Singleton, C H and Aisbitt, J (2001) *A follow-up of the National Working Party survey of dyslexia provision in UK universities*. Paper presented at the 5th British Dyslexia Association International Conference, University of York

Smith, A (1973) *Symbol Digit Modalities Test*. Los Angeles: Western Psychological Services

Smith, V and Armstrong, A (2005) *Beyond Prejudice: Inclusive Learning in Practice*. Learning and Skills Development Agency

Snowling, M (2000) *Dyslexia (2nd Edition) (2nd Edition ed)*. Oxford: Blackwell

Snowling, M, Nation, K, Moxhan, P, Gallagher, A and Frith, U (1997) Phonological processing skills of dyslexic students in higher education: a preliminary report. *Journal of Research in Reading*, 20(1), 31-41

SPACE (2007) *Inclusive Assessment in Higher Education: A Resource for Change*. Staff-Student Partnership for Assessment, Change and Evaluation Project (SPACE). Plymouth: Disability Assist Services, University of Plymouth

Spearman, C (1973) *The nature of 'intelligence' and the principles of cognition*. New York: Arno Press

Stanovich, K E (1991) Discrepancy definitions of reading disability: Has intelligence led us astray? *Reading Research Quarterly*, 26, 7-29

Stanovich, K E (1994) Annotation: does dyslexia exist? *Journal of Child Psychology and Psychiatry*, 35, 579-595

Stanovich, K E and Stanovich, P J (1997) Further thoughts on aptitude/achievement discrepancy. *Educational Psychology in Practice*, 1313-8

Stein, J (1991) Vision and language In M. Snowling and M. Thomson (eds.) *Dyslexia: Integrating Theory and Practice*. London: Whurr Publishers

Stein, J (2004) Dyslexia genetics In G. Reid and A. Fawcett (eds) *Dyslexia in Context: Research, Policy and Practice*. London: Whurr Publishers

Stein, J, Talcott, J and Witton, C (2001) The sensorimotor basis of developmental dyslexia. In A. Fawcett (ed), *Dyslexia: Theory and Good Practice*. London: Whurr Publishers

Stein, J and Walsh, V (1997) To see but not to read: the magnocellular theory of dyslexia. *Trends in Neurological Science,* 20(4147-152)

Stein, J F and Fowler, S (1982) Visual Dyslexia. *British Journal of Optholmology,* 37(11)

Sterling, C. Farmer, M, Riddick, B, Morgan, S and Matthews, C (1998) Adult dyslexic writing. *Dyslexia: An International Journal of Research and Practice*, 4, 1-15

Sternberg, R (1985) *Beyond IQ: a triarchic theory of human intelligence.* New York: Cambridge University Press

Sternberg, R J. and Grigorenko, E L (2002) *Dynamic Testing.* New York: Cambridge University Press

Sunderland, H, Klein, C, Savinson, R and Partridge, T (1997) *Dyslexia and the bilingual learner: assessing and teaching adults and young people who speak English as an additional language.* London: London Language and Literacy Unit

Tallal, P (1984) Temporal or phonetical processing deficit in dyslexia? *Applied Psycholinguistics*, 5, 167-169

Tallal, P (1997) The role of temporal processing in developmental language-bases disorders: Research and clinical implications. In B. A. Blachman (Ed.), *Foundations of Reading Acquisition and Dyslexia: Implications for early intervention.* Mahwah, NJ: Lawrence Erlbaum Associates

Taylor, B and Carter, C (2003) *A Rationale for Making Reasonable Adjustments for Students with Dyslexia.* Nottingham: University of Nottingham

Thomas, M E (1990) *Developmental dyslexia.* London: Whurr Publishers

Thomson, J and Bishop-Leibler, P (2006) Dyslexia and Music: Current Directions in Research and Student Support. *Patoss Bulletin*, 19(2)

Thomson, M (2001) *The Psychology of Dyslexia: A Handbook for Teachers.* London: Whurr Publishers

Tonnessen, E (1997) How can we best define 'Dyslexia'? *Dyslexia*, 3(2), 78-92

Torgesen, J (1999) *Test of Word Reading Efficiency (TOWRE).* Texas: Pro-Ed Inc

Torrance, M and Jeffery, G C (1999) Writing Processes and cognitive demands. In M. Torrance and G. C. Jeffery (Eds.), *The cognitive demands of writing: Processing capacity and working memory effects in text production.* Amsterdam: Amsterdam University Press

Towend, J and Turner, M (2000) *Dyslexia in practice: a guide for teachers.* New York: Kluwer Academic

Turner, M (1996) *The Psychological Assessment of Reading.* London: Whurr Publishers

Turner, M (1997) *Psychological Assessment of Dyslexia.* London: Whurr Publishers

Turner, M and Rack, J (eds) (2004) *The study of dyslexia.* London: Kluwer Academic

Turner, M and Risdale, J (2002) *Digit Memory Test.* London: Dyslexia Institute

Vogel, S, Vogel, G, Sharoni, V and Dahan, O (eds) (2003) *Learning Disabilities in Higher Education and Beyond: An International Perspective.* Baltimore: York Press

Vygotsky, L (1978) *Mind in Society.* MA: Harvard University Press

Vygotsky, L S (1962) *Thought and Language.* Cambridge, MA: MIT Press

Wagner, R, Torgesen, J and Rashotte, C (1999) *Comprehensive Test of Phonological Processing (CTOPP).* Texas: Pro-Ed. Inc

Wechsler, D (1998) *Wechsler Adult Intelligence Scale 3rd Edition (WAIS III)*. New York: Harcourt Brace Psychological Corporation

Wiederholt, J L (2001) *Gray Silent Reading Test (GSRT)*. Texas: Pro-Ed. Inc

Wilkins, A J (1995) Helping reading with colour. *Dyslexia Review*, 7(3), 4-7

Wilkins, A J (1996) *Wilkin's Rate of Reading Test*. London: i.o.o. Sales Ltd

Wilkins, A J (2003) *Reading through colour*. Chichester: Wiley

Wilkinson, G S (1993) *Wide Range Achievement Test (WRAT3)*. Wilmington: Wide Range

Wilkinson, G S (2006) *Wide Range Achievement Test (WRAT4)*. Wilmington: Wide Range

Wolf, M and O'Brien, B (2001) On issues of time, fluency and intervention. In A. Fawcett (ed) *Dyslexia: Theory and Good Practice*. London: Whurr Publishers

Woodcock, R W (1998) *Woodcock Reading Mastery Tests (Revised) (WRMT-R)*. Minnesota: American Guidance Service, Inc

Yelland, N and Masters, J (2005) Rethinking scaffolding in the information age. *Computers and Education*, In press

Young, P and Tyre, C (1983) *Dyslexia or Illiteracy? Realising the Right to Read*. Milton Keynes: Open University Press

Zdzienski, D (1997) *Quick Scan in Study Scan*. London: Pico Educational Systems Ltd

Web addresses

www.adshe.org.uk Association of Dyslexia Specialists in Higher Education

www.ahrb.ac.uk Arts and Humanities Research Council Funding: 10, Carlton House Terrace, London.

www.bdadyslexia.org.uk British Dyslexia Association

www.bbsrc.ac.uk Biotechnology and Biological Sciences Research Council Funding: Polaris House, North Star Avenue, Swindon.

www.brainhe.com Best resources for achievement and intervention re neurodiversity in HE

www.ceriumvistech.co.uk Information about coloured overlays and visual stress

http:ddig.lboro.ac.uk *The Dyscalculia and Dyslexia Interest Group* (DDIG) provides a forum for SDTs to discuss support as sell as some tips about supporting students.

www.duncanwil.co.uk/norm.html The Bell Curve

www.dyspraxiafoundation.org.uk/services/ad_symptoms The Dyspraxia Foundation

www.eosrc.ac.uk/student/default.asp Engineering and Physical Sciences Research Council: Polaris House, North Star Avenue, Swindon.

www.esrc.ac.uk Economic and Research Council (ESRC): Polaris House, North Star Avenue, Swindon.

www.futurenet.co.uk/charity/ado/adomenu The Adult Dyslexia Organisation

www.ioosales.co.uk Information about visual stress and coloured overlays.

www.makingthemodernworld.org.uk/.../?section=3 Normal Curve of Distribution

http://www.mathcentre.ac.uk *The MathCentre* website is useful as a resource although it is not intended for dyslexic students.

www.mrc.ac.uk Medical Research Council: 20, Park Crescent, London.

www.patoss-dyslexia.org.uk Patoss Guidance on Practising Certificates

www.premia.ac.uk Useful research project about dyslexic doctoral students

www.research-councils.ac.uk Main research councils:

www.tda.gov.uk/skillstests.aspx Information and practice QTS tests

Index